All Year Round

All Year Round

Christian Calendar of Celebrations

Ann Druitt
Christine Fynes-Clinton
Marije Rowling

Hawthorn Press

Published by Hawthorn Press, Hawthorn House, 1 Lansdown Lane, Stroud, Gloucestershire, GL5 1BJ. UK
Tel: (01453) 757040 Fax: (01453) 751138
E-mail: info@hawthornpress.com
www.hawthornpress.com

Acknowledgements
Sue Patience for her prompt and efficient typing
Anne Cook, our caring American proof-reader
Anke Albertine Cram for her contribution to The Christmas Play

Typeset in Optima by Southgate Solutions, Gloucestershire
Cover illustration by Marije Rowling
Printed in Great Britain
First edition 1995
Reprinted 1997
Reprinted 1999
Reprinted in 2001 by The Bath Press, Bath
Reprinted 2003
Reprinted 2006
Printed on environmentally-friendly paper

British Library data available on request.

ISBN 1 869 890 47 7
 978-1-869890-47-6

Contents

Authors' preface

We came together to write this book from very different landscapes: Christine from the mountains of Switzerland, Marije from the lowlands of Holland, and Ann from the gently rolling hills of rural England. The culture of these different geographies shaped the perspectives of our early lives and fashioned, in part, the way we connected with the seasons and their festivals.

The real work of the book began in England, where all our ten children were born. During these family years we felt the need to learn and practise the steps of the year's dance, and we set about it with great enthusiasm. Family celebrations dappled the course of the year with a complex composition of light and shade, of merriment and tears, of high drama and evanescent joy. We took advice and inspiration from others gladly, but everyday life insisted that we each interpret the style of the dance for our own family, while remaining true to the choreography. Trials and errors came to us too. These were added to the melting pot of family and community festival events from which we were learning our practical skills.

Marije began teaching Art, Christine developed her music, but we always found others who shared our interest in the festivals. For several years Christine and Ann held Festival Workshops, and it was out of this fertile ground of discussion, experiment and interchange, that the idea of a book was born. The book is now published, but not finished. It rests with you, the reader, to find space between the words in which to evolve your own ideas, compare your own traditions, allow the spirit of the book to meet and mingle with your own individual lifestyle. The words are ours, the festivals are yours.

Ann Druitt
Christine Fynes-Clinton
Marije Rowling

3

For your information

Oven temperature conversions:

Gas Mark	Fahrenheit (°F)	Centigrade (°C)	
1	275	140	slow
2	300	150	
3	325	160	moderate
4	350	180	
5	375	190	
6	400	200	hot
7	425	220	
8	450	230	

Some weight conversions:

Recipes throughout this book give measurements in metric weight. Here are some equivalent measures for American cups.

Butter, margarine	250 g	1 cup
Flour	125 g	1 cup
Granulated sugar	125 g	1 cup
Icing sugar	150 g	1 cup
Honey, syrup	300 g	1 cup
Ground nuts	250 g	1.33 cup
Grated carrots	250 g	1.5 cup

Fluid volume conversion:

250 ml	1 cup

Knitting abbreviations:

st(s).	stitch(es)
k.	knit
p.	purl
g.st.	garter stitch
st.st.	stocking stitch
alt.	alternate

Glossary:

Icing	frosting
Icing sugar	confectioner's sugar or powdered sugar
Biscuits	cookies
Sweets	candies
Greaseproof paper	wax paper
Conkers	horse chestnuts

For American readers:

Wherever possible we have attempted to use terms that are understandable both in Britain and the United States. Nevertheless, there are some for which we have not been able to discover the American equivalent:

Blu-tack	pliable adhesive, similar to used chewing gum
Nightlight candle	short fat candle in a metal container which will burn for about eight hours
Florist's foam	water-retentive synthetic foam block used for flower arranging

Why festivals?

Ann: Christine, you and I have been holding workshops on the Festivals for a number of years now. Looking back over that time — and also, of course, over your experiences within your own family — is it easy for you to pick out aspects of the celebration of festivals that are of particular benefit to family life?

Christine: Oh yes, indeed, quite a number actually. But if I'm going to answer the question properly, can I first take a look at just how most of us are living nowadays? One knows that life is always changing but the speed of change seems to be increasing. We are quickly moving away from a society which was very supportive of what we are as human beings, in terms of our basic make-up. For example, we are actually very 'rhythmical' creatures. We depend a great deal on rhythm in a physical sense — our breathing and heart beat are both rhythmical; all our main organs have their own rhythm and we live in a rhythm of sleeping and waking. If these basic needs of ours are seriously interfered with, life becomes impossible.

On the other hand, there are rhythms which are simply 'given' to us from outside. We don't have to do anything to achieve them — day and night, the seasons, the year and so on — they provide a structure to our lives, to which we respond in many subtle ways. In so-called Western societies the world over, this structure is crumbling. We have now largely freed ourselves from these mighty rhythms of nature, which, of course, has made life a lot easier and much more comfortable for us, hasn't it? We don't have to stop working when it gets dark; when we're cold we don't have to chop wood and make a fire — we just press a button. We can eat more or less anything all the year round — it's summer fruits at Christmas, and spring flowers in November. In many almost unnoticeable ways, we dismantle this framework of rhythm which has supported us for centuries, which has been mirroring to us aspects of our breathing, our sleeping and waking, and so on, and so reinforcing one of our basic requirements for a healthy life.

Ann: What do you mean when you say 'mirroring' our rhythms? And can buying a bunch of daffs in November really be a health hazard?

Christine: That's putting it rather dramatically! But all the same I hold there's some truth in it. When I say 'mirroring' I mean that a world which 'goes to sleep' at night and 'wakes up' at dawn reflects and reinforces our own need for a sleeping and waking rhythm. When the fruiting plants and trees 'hold their breath' in autumn and winter, and 'breathe out' in spring and summer as they blossom and fruit, this also carries us as part of the creation which lives in a breathing rhythm. People are beginning to accept now that to live as though we were not intimately bound up with the whole of the natural world has its negative repercussions (quite often in terms of health) and I would include the rhythms of nature as part of this, too. I think you'd agree that in this sense modern life has become quite arhythmical, and our children don't experience these world rhythms reflected in life around them half as strongly as we did at their age.

6

Ann: Yes, many of my special childhood memories were of the rhythmical kind — the scrubbing of the kitchen table, and the particular way my mother had of slicing thin bread for tea — and then there were all the routines of the day and the week. I imagine that this element was even stronger for you as a child in Switzerland?

Christine: It certainly was, and I regret the fact that our children live their lives without all the rhythmic activities going on around them that were once commonplace: spinning, wood-chopping, milking — even sweeping and polishing by hand are becoming rare. Most of these simple manual tasks have been taken over by machine, and mechanical rhythms unfortunately, are too enervating to be helpful to us. All the same, I want to say that I appreciate my household gadgets and I'm glad to have them. I don't wish to put the clock back eighty years. What's important for me is to be aware that what is a gain in time and strength on the one hand, is also a significant loss on the other. Harmony and beauty are implicit in natural rhythms, and these are the precious qualities we are losing from our lives. Observing a seasonal round of festivals is one very enjoyable way in which we can restore something of the healthy gift of rhythm to our children's lives — and to our own, of course, as adults in a highly mechanised world.

Ann: Our society has a very greedy attitude to time, doesn't it? All our machines, especially the car and the microwave, are wonderful at gobbling up time! We seem always to want to pull the future towards us — to have everything happen more quickly. And then we complain because we never have *enough* time!

Christine: Well, precisely — but then see how the seasons out-smart us! No amount of 'planes or word processors will make Christmas come any sooner. It is because we have no option but to immerse ourselves in the process of time unfolding that we are able really to savour the bitter-sweet, tummy-tickling, taste of anticipation, which, you know, can be a very strong bonding force between people. You're English so you'll understand what I mean if you think of the solidarity and warm fellow-feeling generated among a few strangers waiting for a late bus on a cold afternoon. You'll be able to sense what could live in a family waiting for the first cherries to ripen on the garden tree, or the first roasted chestnut heralding the winter season. When so much else aspires to instant gratification today, it can be a healing experience simply to wait, and wonder... and hope.

Ann: They say that to travel hopefully is better than to arrive, and having arrived at a Festival moment one hopes this won't be an anti-climax, but in reality I've heard many adults admit to feeling let down when they recall childhood birthdays or Christmases, a feeling of "is this all?"

Christine: There may be many reasons for this which perhaps we could go into later, but my guess is that this happens chiefly when too much attention is paid to physical nourishment. By this I mean not only the special meal, or special sweets, but also many of the gifts received on these occasions — and not enough thought is given to what I call 'soul nourishment.' We are all acutely aware of the suffering caused by bodily hunger in the world, but a 'hunger of the soul,' in a broad and general sense, is perhaps even more widespread and the cause of a different, but equally significant, degree of suffering. Read a little further than the newspaper headlines, and you will see that people everywhere are searching for meaning in their lives, for an enrichment which they can't fulfil by means of material goods. I'll give you an example: we may strive for happiness, but how often do we experience real *joy* — not an ephemeral 'high,' but deep, comforting, slow burning joy?

So I would see the actual Festival Day as an opportunity to celebrate also some of these forgotten corners, the sort of things that don't appear on a certificate of education, but without which we shall always remain lesser men and women. The talent for reverence I would include here: the ability to be able to acknowledge something greater than ourselves. Each time we plant a small sunflower seed at a spring festival, and gather the huge ripe head of the fruited sunflower at harvest time, we allow this mood its place in our lives. It sounds a big word — 'reverence' — but it can be experienced in very ordinary ways.

Ann: I once overheard two small boys who were watching bricklayers at work on a new house: the one said, "Gosh!" as he watched the hod-carrier with his load, "He must be awfully strong to lift all that!" The other replied, "So what? Superman can lift a house!"

Christine: Well that's a very good example of how, little by little, qualities which can fill out, round off — ennoble, if you like — our development as people, can be eroded. That which lies just beyond our reach exists as a very healthy source of motivation for our personal growth. Do you recall that deeply satisfying childhood moment when, on tiptoe you reached at last the rim of the kitchen sink, or the top shelf of the bookcase? In just the same way we monitor our own inner growth when we find ourselves equal to some of the tasks in life previously carried by our elders and betters. Superman can't build our confidence — he makes us feel helpless and weak — but ordinary men and women whom we look up to, can. They help us to grow.

To be present as one of life's mysteries unfolds before us — to see a duckling's beak pushing through the egg shell, or frost patterns growing on a window pane — the very untouchableness (if that is a word!) of this experience is a call to us to grow in feeling, in understanding, in wisdom, towards something more encompassing than ourselves. This is what I mean by reverence — it is always a religious experience, but doesn't necessarily need a church building in which to grow.

Ann: Mystery is a spice to life, isn't it? I am reminded of how we say "I wonder..." when we ponder on something which we still have to learn. 'Wonder' leads us to learning, and I would say it's definitely a partner to 'reverence.'

Christine: I'd almost put wonder at the top of the list when it comes to deciding what should be the real keynote to each festival that we prepare. Anticipation — Reverence — Wonder —

just watch them live in the eyes of a small child waiting for the annual visit of Father Christmas or Santa Claus, and ask yourself if these experiences are not diluted somewhat if the child also visits a few 'Santa's Grottoes' in the days before Christmas. At some point we have to decide whether we consider such intangible gifts as 'wonder,' etc., worthy and desirable for our children, and then be prepared to tackle the practical difficulties. We don't think twice about making financial sacrifices to give our children something that they really need, and it may be that we have to make other kinds of sacrifices to be able to give them such qualitative gifts that are possible in the way that festivals are celebrated within the family.

Ann: What kind of sacrifices are you talking about?

Christine: I'm thinking more of social aspects, I suppose. Maybe the sidestepping of some of the commercial pressures that compromise us — especially at big seasonal festivals such as Christmas — when it would be so much easier just to swim along with the tide; maybe being prepared to sacrifice some of our inherited familial/cultural traditions where these are no longer working in a helpful way; maybe even being able to sacrifice the convenience of spending money to acquire something in favour of spending time to make it at home. This would allow the rest of the family to share in the excitement of preparation and the pleasure of watching a creative process unfold.

If we ourselves have made something, or perhaps just watched it being made, we care for that thing in a different way. Many things today are being made in such a way that we don't have to care for them, from window frames to furniture, to textiles, to the whole range of 'disposables,' and the question may well be asked if there is any virtue at all in developing an ability to care for things. Well, we relate to such a question in individual ways, I'm sure. For me it has a lot to do with whether we want to give beauty a place in our lives. For the most part the 'easi-care' treatment of artifacts diminishes their aesthetic quality. Compare a french polish or beeswax finish on wood to the modern wood sealants; compare the feel of pure cotton or wool to a synthetic fibre; compare a polished brass with a lacquered variety — and it speaks for itself.

We often have to weigh beauty with convenience, and I certainly opt for convenience at times, but I also need beauty around me, and am prepared to put in some work to maintain it. Beauty is more than a juggling of aesthetic considerations, it keeps me in touch with the fundamentals of life — with the "lovely freshness deep down things" which Manley Hopkins speaks of — it connects me with moral and spiritual qualities which are otherwise easily overlooked in the daily round.

Have you ever noticed what a place of honour beauty holds in our memories — how it can generate a glowing inner happiness? I have a conviction that the experiences of beauty cultivated during our life are harvested eventually in old age as a rich and gladdening content to our memories. (That's my conviction, you understand — talk to me again in fifty years!) But that's one reason why I feel it's very, very important that our children make friends with beauty in an age when monsters and beasts are constantly offered to them as companions.

Especially at festival times, beauty can find a place in family life — not as a remote quality to be wondered at, but as a friend that needs caring for in order to give its best. Even the youngest child can enter into this reciprocal relationship — not in any precious way, but as a simple practical adjunct to daily life: polishing the candlestick, replacing faded flowers in the vase, watering the Nature Garden.

Ann: It would be nice to think that if children have become accustomed to caring for the mini-environment of the home, they won't need to be taught how to care for the greater environment. We could hope for that, anyway. But are there any more immediate benefits from the festivals in family life that come to mind?

Christine: There are so many that it's not easy to pick examples — but take a little one: how much easier it is to help a very small child to orientate itself in time if one celebrates the festivals at home! To say that the family will go on holiday at the end of June is fairly meaningless to a little one, but they can grasp that when the Midsummer candle has been lit then the packing of suitcases will begin. Children love things to be orderly and predictable, and the rhythm of the festivals gives them this security within the endless passage of time.

More examples will show themselves in the course of the book, but for me, I can only reiterate the points I made earlier, and express my especial gratitude that the festivals remind us again and again that Beauty, Wonder, Anticipation and Reverence are worth making space for in our lives.

The ring of changes

Ann: I know you love the theme of rhythm, Christine, so I'd like you to talk a bit about the rhythms of nature and what the changing seasons mean to you.

Christine: Yes, I do think a lot about rhythm, and as my family and I get older I appreciate it more and more as a real cornerstone to family life. For me it's almost a case of "life equals rhythm" and vice versa. I made the point earlier that we are born rhythmical creatures, and this I'd like you to understand not only in the sense of body, i.e. bodily functions and so on, but also as regards the soul.

We take for granted the rhythm of breathing: filling our lungs with air and emptying them again, drawing something from outside into us and then releasing something of ourselves (for *we* make the CO_2!) back out into the world. But how aware are we of the way the soul breathes also — taking in the content of the world through our eyes, ears, etc., transforming it and releasing it again, maybe as a poem, a piece of knitting, or a nice clean kitchen? This 'soul breathing' goes on all the time and one can see different rhythmic patterns in it. For example, some people observe that experiences of the daytime are often 'breathed out' at night in dreams; and I know many women who find it difficult to ignore their monthly 'mood rhythm.' Now, you asked me about the changing of the season, so I'll try to describe this and show how very much of a breathing rhythm it is.

Let's start with winter, a time of shrinking days and bitter cold. Human life withdraws into the warmth of the house, and most of the natural world has also withdrawn — the seeds into the earth, plants into their roots or bulbs, the small creatures into hibernation and, well... you tell me, where *do* flies go in the wintertime?!

In a country such as Finland, where for months of the year there is little or no daylight and everything is covered with snow, they have a tradition of storytelling around the hearth. The history and the folklore of the people wakes up, and, in an inner world of pictures and memories, it lives and works strongly during just this time when outer activity is inhibited. Things are different in our part of Europe of course. Nevertheless, wherever in the world there is a winter season, family life becomes more concentrated, whether this is around a TV set, or a board game, or roasting chestnuts at the fire. Beneath the earth in winter, preparations are being made for seeds to germinate, the root systems of other plants are developing and establishing unseen. Above the earth, things are not so very different: gardeners sit with their catalogues, and dreamers with their travel brochures — both are germinating new ideas for the summertime — while others scheme and plan to extend their roots into a new garage or converted attic.

Ann: So the picture of winter is of a time when we are being 'breathed in'?

Christine: That's it. And not only 'breathed in' to our house to be busy at the fireside, but drawn even further into the 'house' of our body where we are active inwardly playing with ideas, planning new beginnings, being creative...

11

Ann: And in summer we have an opposite picture.

Christine: Well, one can never generalize, of course, about an English summer... (See how English I've become — I can now make jokes about the weather!)... but in a good year our lives are lived much more out of doors in the open air. We like to eat outside, work, read or play outside, even sleep outside. Like flowers, we put on our brightest colours and lift our faces to the sun. We pack our suitcases and leave our house altogether; we are 'breathed out' into the world as we travel off on holiday.

Ann: Look at the wonderful, rounded, puffed-up shapes of English woods in full summer leaf, and then think back to winter and recall the figures of your breath in the frosty air. Might we imagine — in a poetic way — the summer trees to be the breath forms of the earth as she exhales?

Christine: Nature really does breathe out all her creativity at this time — all the different leaf forms and flowers; the air is filled with insects and many of the bugs which have spent the winter under the earth emerge and are active on the surface. As the activity within the earth subsides while the plant energies go into flowering and fruiting, so also do we human beings experience a subtle 'falling asleep' inwardly in the summer. Although most of us become more active and revel in the freedom the good weather brings, we also find it more difficult to concentrate; we become a little less centred in our daily life, more relaxed in our attitudes and routines. Sometimes we find the children 'scatty,' forgetful about things, a bit 'out of themselves.' This dreamy state is only resolved as high summer moves into autumn and Nature begins to draw in her breath again. The weight of fruit on the trees bends the twigs away from the sun towards the ground. Petals fall, seeds fall, the upward thrust of growth is scarcely seen, and finally the leaves drop from the trees to become part of the body of the earth once more. The activity of the summer is absorbed, and earth-life becomes more inward. You and I share in this; very often we remain unaware, actually, of our dreamy summer state, until the autumn restores to us a clarity of mind that brings its own vigour and freshness. Then we begin to feel awake and renewed.

Ann: There are moments, both at Midsummer and Midwinter when nothing much seems to happen in nature. There seems to be a kind of hiatus, a moment of rest before the mood changes. In contrast to this, there is an awful lot going on in autumn.

Christine: And in spring too — both the Spring Equinox in March and the Autumn Equinox in September mark the points in the calendar when the length of day and night are equal, when the balance is just tipping as the breathing of the earth gains momentum in a new direction. Therefore they are both transitional times.

Ann: You haven't said much about spring so far. Could you say a few words now?

Christine: Well, let's look at the theme of transition. One only has to consider the teenage years as an example, to realise that transitional times are particularly challenging — they can be both painful and disorientating — and spring is no exception. Although our associations with spring are mostly joyful — new life, warmth, colour — it can also be a testing time. We are often dismayed at how easily a late frost can shrivel leaves and flower buds, tarnish the beauty of growing things, and even destroy growth completely. Many people are especially vulnerable to setbacks in their personal growth at this time. It can be a time of coughs and colds, of illness and emotional disturbance — almost as if Nature's insistence upon growing, blossoming and being fruitful is simply too demanding to cope with straight away — and a period is first needed to build up strength to meet the challenge.

In autumn, also, we find that we need to prepare to meet the demands of the coming months, and we do this best by managing to come to terms with the passing of summer. Often we experience a sense of loss — not only of the warmth and long days, but also of the wishes and dreams invested in the summer. It's in the nature of dreams to be a little beyond the attainable, and with the falling leaves we also begin to 'come down to earth' and face the realities of life. This can be an uncomfortable, though strengthening and maturing, process.

Ann: So it's not only the autumn leaves, with their burning colours, that are undergoing a trial by fire?

Christine: It does seem that we tend to seek out challenges at this time of the year — we may enrol at college, or take up a new hobby. Just as we light bonfires to clear our garden at the end of summer, so we welcome opportunities to sort out our lives, to burn up the overgrowth of the past year, clearing the way for the new.

Ash has always been a traditional fertiliser — so we could take the fire picture further, and ask if perhaps we sense the need for this kind of ash to feed our germinal endeavours. Do we hope, maybe, that the flames of our 'inner fire' will give light and warmth through the wintry darkness ahead?

The inner circle

Christine: Although I've made the general comment that people are getting out of touch with the seasons, it's actually not so very difficult to maintain a connection if we really want to, even in a city. Nature paints her pictures everywhere, and we only have to take a little trouble to observe them, not just with our eyes, but with our other senses as well. If we make that effort, we can begin to follow her rhythms and know something of our own place in them. But that's still only part of the story, isn't it?

Ann: The question that arises now is: To what extent are we a part of the natural world? On one hand, we certainly are bound up with Nature — the minerals of the earth build our body; we live, and experience our life in processes as plants do; like the animals, we are able to express ourselves and be receptive to the expressions of others, and so on. In these ways we are borne by Nature, and share with her, sympathetically, the path of the year. On the other hand, it is also true that to develop the nobility and inner strength of the human being, we have to be able to free ourselves from the demands of our natural inclinations. In the language of fairy tale — it is the one who can stay awake through the night who succeeds in the quest!

Civilisation has brought us both the good and the bad, but nevertheless it demonstrates how much we move apart from Nature whenever we exercise our human creativity, our moral codes, and our capacity for self-sacrifice. Even to be a devoted and sensitive observer of the natural world, we need first to 'stand back.' It's just such a shame that today this 'standing back' has so often become estrangement: a major concern for the conservationists. That's an issue which we can't go into now... the point I need to make here is that we have a potent inner life which is not bound by the outer world. Even the wettest rain cannot quench the fire in a true lover's heart!

But how to keep in touch with this inner life — the hidden workings of your soul? You pointed out that Nature shows us her moods each day, but do I observe a seasonal path unfolding within my own soul? And if I do, how far can I judge this to be a generally human experience rather than merely an expression of my personal idiosyncracies?

Christine: You mean, is my present inner mood really a reflection of the season, or is it more influenced by the fact that I shall turn forty next week?

Ann: Yes, that sort of thing. These are all questions we have to ask because we can't so easily peep into the souls of our friends for comparison. We have to find a framework somewhere else within which to place our inner experiences during the course of the year.

Christine: Now, for yourself, you have found such a framework in the Festivals of the Christian year, so tell me more about that — and is it of any use to the non-Christians who will be reading this book?

Ann: The seasons of nature play themselves out in a colourful and detailed setting, and in a similar way the seasonal moods of our soul have also a colourful, imaginative, and very profound backdrop. This backdrop is the multitude of pictures that have arisen from the various cultures over centuries. Pictures which have been able to distil into simple imaginations the complex reflections of countless souls within a common culture and geography, and, for the most part, have been given outer form in the holy books and religious practices established by that culture.

Christine: So you think that among the many pictures of the culture within which I live, I shall find the images which make clear to me the movements of my inner life throughout the year?

Ann: I'm saying that this is a source that I have found to be very helpful and accessible. They may be Biblical pictures or icons, well-loved stories or folk customs, and the culture may be the one you were brought up in, or one you have chosen for yourself; nevertheless it is this picture world that is so fruitful when we are looking for a harmony of experience between our inner life and the seasons. I have chosen to explore Western Christianity in this way, but I would encourage everyone to investigate the culture in which they feel most at home, and discover for themselves the common threads that connect their personal experience with the insights of the unnumbered fellow creatures who gave life to that particular culture. The different cultures of the world are a rich catalogue of human soul life, and all can teach us so much about ourselves.

Christine: Can you give me an impression, briefly, of what you have found in this respect out of the Christian year?

Ann: Well, the first thing that strikes me when I look at the cycle of Christian Festivals and compare them with the seasons in this part of the world, is that the two seem to pull in opposite directions. For example, in the depths of winter, when the life of Nature shelters drably beneath the earth, we look upwards for the life of our Festivals. The first Christmas was proclaimed from above, and we have continued, in our own way, to try to bring something of heavenly glory to earth at this time. We hang twinkling lights in the streets and stars at our windows... we even make room for angels to alight on the mantelpiece! What a blossoming of rich colours there is within our houses — what a host of novelties! Yet outside the world is stark and subdued. Nature reins in her gift-giving, but we allow ourselves to be extravagant and indulgent.

Christine: It's very understandable, isn't it, that in the cold and dark of December we are grateful for the Christmas message of inner warmth and light.

Ann: Of course it is. But look, for a moment, at the opposite end of the year — at the Festival of St John, at Midsummer. Amid the abundance of growth and fruiting, what picture does this Saint's Day give us to contemplate? If you read the third chapter of the gospel of St

Matthew, the pictures you are given are those of John the Baptist, meanly clad, fasting in the wilderness. In the heat and brilliance of Midsummer, you may find that John's message of repentance strikes a little stern and chill. Nature expands in her celebration of life and increase, but we are urged to look deep within ourselves and deal with the dead wood we find there.

Can you see from this example that the traditions of our Festivals have developed, not so much out of a need to escape from the realities of the season — the tedium of winter, etcetera — but out of a genuine need of the human soul for balance? To be able to be awake to the mysteries of the universe while the beetle sleeps under her stone; to be, on the other hand, introspective while Nature is at her most extrovert, these are precious human faculties.

Christine: So you actually discover your humanity through the effort to create a balance between...

Ann: ...between that part of me which belongs to, and is supported and nourished by the natural world and its material needs and demands, and that part which has its allegiance elsewhere.

Christine: A spiritual allegiance, do you mean?

Ann: Spirit, Mind, Immortal Soul — the terms are not so important. What is real is that, from time to time, I feel I have the choice of whether my actions are guided by natural laws and instincts, or can be free of these. These days the world is becoming a shade more ecology minded, thankfully, but if we identify too closely with Nature we risk losing sight of the deep, rich and resourceful landscape of our own inner world. We could so easily overlook this uniquely human contribution to life if it weren't for help and encouragement of the kind given us by the Festivals. They are like signposts on an inner map, guiding us to areas of human resource which, if only they were developed, could make all the difference to our quality of life. Our traditional Christmas celebrations, for example, make space for us to cultivate *gratitude:* just think how an extra little drop or two of *gratitude* could transform the office or staff room!

Christine: Going back to the difference you described between the inner experience of the Festival, and the outer world at midwinter and midsummer, do you find this polarity so strong at other times of the year?

Ann: Oh, it's there wherever you look. Sometimes it's almost shockingly obvious. In spring, for instance, at a time when each new sign of life in the garden and field is eagerly looked for, the Festival of Lent preoccupies us with thoughts of death. When Easter comes, it is celebrated as a perfect completion — the "first fruit" of the life of Jesus Christ. The Easter experience is of fulfilment — whereas Nature's festival of spring speaks to us of beginnings.

Again, in the autumn when all around we see Nature's cycle coming to an end, the polarity strikes us once more. In the Festival of St Michael and All Angels, or Michaelmas, we are presented with a very dramatic picture from the Book of Revelation: Michael and his Angels warring against the Dragon. The result of this great war in Heaven was that the Dragon was thrown down to earth — the implication being that we on earth now have the task to continue the battle. So, as the outer season reminds us that a growth cycle has been completed, the inner circle of our Festival experience arrives at the point where we may renew our commitment to a task — a task which could mark a new chapter in our biography of inner growth.

Christine: Your observations here all arise out of the culture of the northern hemisphere. Do they have any relevance to other parts of the world — Australia for example?

Ann: That's a very good question — I've heard from a number of visitors to Australia and New Zealand who felt it quite bizarre to celebrate Christmas in a European way at Midsummer!

I think we tend to forget that Christianity and a land such as Australia have been introduced to one another only comparatively recently. The Christian Festivals must have the time to evolve a tradition of their own there — one that feels right in that land, and is not just an unthinking importation from the 'old country' culture. However long this may take, my conviction is that new Festival traditions will arise that have formed themselves out of this human inclination to balance the inner world against the outer world. Maybe the Australian Christmas will grow to be more inward and thoughtful in character, while the parties and present-giving gravitate towards St John's... who knows?

A colourful conversation

Ann: Marije, you've done these beautiful illustrations for us, but they're all in black and white — are we to think that you prefer not to use colour?

Marije: Good Heavens, no! — quite the opposite, in fact. If I had my way, every page would be awash with colour! But even I have to come down to earth sometimes and respect the finances of a project — which means in this case sticking to black and white. Don't forget, though, it's a marvellous challenge to an artist to work in a restricted medium — and I've loved doing it.

Ann: It's true, isn't it, that different colours evoke different moods in us? Is this why we associate certain colours with particular Festivals?

Marije: We are certainly affected by colour, often in quite subtle ways. It has an immediate impact — which could even mean that we respond differently to a person if they are wearing purple or bright orange. Young children are especially sensitive — my small son actually burst into tears when the decorator joked with him that his room was to be painted black! But even crusty old ladies like us can develop more sensitivity to the mood of a colour if we sharpen our observation. Next time you feel really ill, for example, use your misery to do some research: ask yourself which colours make you feel more uncomfortable, and which bring some rest and healing... This could lead us into all sorts of issues now about hospital décor and so on, but I must come back to your question about the Festivals.

First, let me show you something interesting. If the sequence of rainbow colours — red, orange, yellow, green, blue, indigo, violet — are placed in a circle, each one blending a little at the edges with its neighbours, we find that those colours associated more with the warm, active, vital seasons of spring, summer and early autumn, all stand together on one side of the circle. The more sombre, cooler colours in the moribund mood of late autumn and winter, stand on the other side! We find we have a ring of colours to accompany us through the year, following the natural cycle of growth and decay. The fresh yellow-green of early leaves and shoots moves into the vibrant colours of summer flowers and the warm purples of fruits and berries. Then comes the ash colour of the ripened seed and the deep indigo of rotting leaves. Finally, we arrive at the darkest blue where I feel myself to be in the depths of all existence. Please don't ask me where that is, because I don't know! But this is another important aspect of colour, of course, that you don't need to have it in front of you to experience it.

Ann: What do you mean exactly?

Marije: Well, I mean that I can 'feel blue' from time to time, or even 'see red!' These are inner experiences. Now, on a less personal level, look and see how the ring of colours comes alive in a different way as the inner mood of the year develops with the progression of the Festivals.

Ann: By 'inner mood,' do you mean how we relate to colour — how we feel about certain colours at the different Festival times?

Marije: Precisely so. Evergreen trees, for example, are with us all year round, aren't they? But it's in the depths of winter, when we celebrate the Mystery of Creation, that we most appreciate their thoughtful, dark blue-green tones around us!

And then, wherever in the world we happen to live, the peace and freedom of the colour of fresh green, and the radiance and purity of pale yellow will echo Easter themes in our heart. The power of gold, orange and yellow-red, on the other hand, meet us in the same challenging mood as the message of John the Baptist at Midsummer, the next cardinal point of the year.

Then comes crimson, as we move a little further round the circle. This is a blue red which no longer has the youthful enthusiasm of vermilion, but instead a serious dignity that speaks of maturity and the shouldering of earthly responsibilities — the tasks which are brought to mind each autumn at the Festival of Michaelmas. Finally, we pass through violet and indigo, developing the sober inward mood of the days of All Saints and All Souls and other Festivals of Remembrance at this time of the year, until we are led back to the womb-like, creative world of blue at Advent, and so complete the circle at Christmas.

Ann: The year caught up in a rainbow! That's a really colourful picture, Marije, and it certainly helps us to follow the progression of the Festivals round the year.

Around the seasonal table

Christine: Does the word 'festival' sound rather grand to you?

Ann: I suppose it can sometimes sound weighty, but it needn't be so at all. There may be very grand festivals, but there are others we hardly notice. If I pick a few flowers from the garden to bring indoors to enjoy, I am, without thinking much about it, celebrating the season. Little festivals like this are important…

Christine: …and much appreciated by little people. Most children enjoy having a corner of their own in which they can set out their collection of seasonal fragments and celebrate them in a child's way.

Ann: Are we now talking about a Seasonal Table?

Christine: Yes, a place where the treasures of the day are gathered in an imaginative setting. A special place where they can not only be displayed but also woven together with other elements of the season's mood: light, colour, gesture… Such a nature table could accompany a family (or playgroup or classroom, for that matter) throughout the year. It could develop, on occasion, into a Festival Garden or Birthday Table. A small reminder like this, of the progress of the year, is of even more value in a city environment where one can so easily overlook all but the broadest indication of the seasons.

Ann: Would you like to describe how such a corner could be set up?

Christine: To start with one has to be very practical, especially when considering the location. A place in the living room or the child's bedroom is very suitable, but a large landing or hallway could also be used. A small space in the centre of the dining table will do if there is nowhere else. Then one has to ask — is it low enough for the child to see? Is it high enough to avoid the toddler's inquisitive fingers? Is it on a chest that needs to be opened often? Should it be in a cosy niche, or in a sunny window space? It is always best to choose the most convenient option, so that the Seasonal Table can remain a pleasure to live with. A cosy corner might be just the thing in winter, but a window area is often preferred in summer.

From time to time it may be necessary to give the Table a rest, leaving behind only a plant, a picture , or a candle. Bearing in mind that children usually like things to stay the same, it is perhaps advisable not to chop and change too much.

Ann: You spoke earlier of "other elements of the seasonal mood." Could you say more on that? How do you define, for example, the 'gesture' of a season?

Christine: It's not easy to give a ready answer there, but I can indicate some areas to be explored. We could start with colour. If some thought has been given to the particular colours which enhance the mood of a season, this will be of immeasurable help when it comes to choosing cloths or dyed muslin veils to cover, or hang behind, the Table.

May I just say a word about these cloths first? I recommend them for a number of reasons, apart from the fact that they protect the surface that lies beneath. If the cloth is loosely arranged and not laid flat on the Table, it makes a comfortable setting for a variety of objects which might otherwise wobble or roll. Muslin veils are light enough to hang from a wall fixed only with pins or a pliant adhesive such as Blu-tack, and yet they are strong enough to bear light objects pinned to them. They camouflage unsightly vases, and their folds create a useful wealth of caves and valleys. Most important of all, however, is that the colour of the veil immediately establishes the mood of a season.

Ann: It's not so easy to pinpoint a mood, is it? Does it live out there in Nature, or inside me? I think perhaps both are true. There are many oaks in this part of Sussex, and their spring leaves are a soft brown, yet when my heart begins to yearn for spring I find myself seeking out the shining yellow-green of the hawthorn and beech.

Christine: Yes, I really love to see the slant of sunlight on new grass, and the yellow primrose against green moss — delicate yellow and green, radiant in the light. These seem to be the colours that define the mood of spring for us. No doubt other parts of the world experience a different mood, but it will still arise at the point where an inner delight meets Nature's gifts. I think this meeting invariably comes about through the seasonal character of the light.

Ann: It is certainly the quality of colour in the light which carries the mood in summer. We may be surrounded at this time by trees in heavy growth, but my memory pictures of summer are not painted in shades of dark green. It is much more the pervading gold of the high sun, or the ethereal rose-pink, apricot, pale blue and mauve of a summer sunset, that conveys the essence of the season.

Christine: Just the sort of colours I would choose for the Seasonal Table — they complement the brilliance of summer flowers. In autumn one would need something completely different again, for the light is so changed. Think of the warm honey and russet tones of autumn — the buttery glow of sunlight through drying leaves!

Ann: And do you think that it is because the absence of light is so conspicuous in this part of the world when December comes round, that the deep blue of the night sky makes a perfect background colour for the Winter Table?

Christine: Well, this whole realm gives us food for thought, and so does the next area that I should like to look at.

As I observe a season and try to characterize its gesture, I find it helpful to bear in mind the four elements of Earth, Water, Air and Fire. The Ancient Greeks considered the whole of creation to be made up of combinations of these basic elements, with their different qualities of coldness, wetness, dryness and warmth. These are qualities that are with us throughout the year, of course, but at each season it seems to me that one of the elements occupies centre-stage. For example, in spring the Water element is strong in the soft growth of new vegetation, damp with April showers. In summer we experience the freedom that comes with the warm Air, as it brings us its light burden of summer scents and busy pollinating insects. Later in the year Fire works strongly, 'cooking' the autumn harvest to the right point of sweetness and digestibility, and dehydrating all the lush growth of spring. By the time we reach the depths of winter, the bony contours of the earth stand out in near-nakedness, and the hardness and coldness of the Earth element grips the flowing stream and turns it to ice.

So it should not surprise us that the clear, sharp forms of the crystals, especially the ice-like quartz crystals that look so appropriate on the Winter Table, do not appear so comfortable in an Easter Garden. Here, the rounded shapes of water-worn pebbles and moss-softened rocks are more at home, whereas on a Summer Table one might prefer polished, translucent stones of delicate hue, ones with a shimmering, sparkling quality that reflects the light.

Ann: How far can we go towards creating the 'total' mood of a season, do you think? It's not a question of bringing as many objects as possible together on the Table, is it?

Christine: No it's not. But we can ensure that all four elements are represented in some way. The Autumn Garden will have a different 'feel' if, among the nuts and dried seed pods, the brittle leaves and hard grain, some juicy berries or fat plums appear. We appreciate even such a slight presence of Water — it always refreshes us! Later on in the year we may find that it is more through the still, reflective quality of the crystal that we remember Water, which is hardened now by winter.

The Air element is everywhere, of course, but there are many different ways of experiencing it. We 'hear' the breeze when the wind chimes sound, we 'see' the air as the mobile turns above the Summer Table, we 'feel' the free space around the carrot tops growing in an Easter Garden, as they unfold their ferny leaves. All our five senses (and perhaps even a few more!) can be active in appreciating the Seasonal Table.

Ann: This is something else to keep in mind, surely, as we try to sum up a mood, that the mood is enhanced through our own participation. If I see a chestnut gleaming in the grass, pick it up and run its smooth skin against my cheek, smell it… I learn a lot about that chestnut. But if I gather enough chestnuts to fill a large basket, plunge my hand in and rumble them round and round, that's when I begin to feel the infinite bounty of autumn.

Christine: There are so many ways in which we can increase our sensitivity to the seasons and their shifting moods and gestures. As we grow more observant we are able to follow creatively the way in which the hopeful, rising expectation of spring fulfils itself in the joyous, expansive gesture of summer. We see how all the transient show of nature falls outside the comfortable gesture of autumn, as she gathers and consolidates her harvest. Finally, we may even penetrate the bleak outer mood of midwinter to approach the inward, protective, gentle gesture of a cradle.

Ann: I think we've both enjoyed talking about all these things, Christine, but I know that you will agree with me when I say that, in the end, it is in the 'doing' that one comes by all the impressions, the insights, and the *fun* that will keep one's enthusiasm alive year after year.

The calendar of festivals

For each season we shall list the festivals which we mark on our calendar. These will be *very personal* lists — which may include secular festivals and even some dates which we hope to get around to celebrating at home one day! We have noted the solstices and equinoxes as significant landmarks in the year. We have omitted most of the Saints' Days, and maybe even some Festivals that are considered very important to other Christians. The scope of this book was never intended to cover the celebration of festivals in a church context; we wish only to share with you the store of experiences gathered within the circle of our own domestic lives, and make no apologies for its idiosyncracies!

SPRING

"I knew when Spring was come —
Not by the murmurous hum
   Of bees in the willow-trees,
      Or frills
      Of daffodils,
   Or the scent of the breeze;
But because there were whips and tops
By the jars of lollipops
In the two little village shops..."

From "The Calendar"
by Barbara Euphan Todd.

25

Spring

Spring, the most welcome of seasons, comes yet very slowly. The spell of winter is hard to shake off. Catkins seem in no hurry to lengthen, a new shoot pushes through a clod of earth but lingers, reluctant to rise in the cold air. As the days grow longer and the breeze softens, we patiently wait and hope. The stony ground relaxes, the ditches gurgle with the spring rains, and juicy buds swell on the twig. Suddenly comes the surprise of a warm day, and with it the urgent activity of growth. Beneath our feet the ground turns lush, the hedges fatten in a haze of green, and a hungry bee flies past. Nature springs effortlessly into creative action; the birds sing praise in concert.

By the end of January we have done with the winter festivals. The snowdrops are emerging and we turn expectantly to look for a new beginning, to see Persephone emerge from Hades. Our hopes have an almost childish fervour. A hiatus at this time can throw me back on myself — to ask "Where is *my* new growth?" On the other hand, I may be overwhelmed by a sudden hustle of seasonal development and wonder "Am I ready for this?" I realise I am no longer carried by Nature as I was when a child; I have to find my *own* way back to life. For the adult, transitions can be lonely times, and to find our way from the dead of winter to new life in the year ahead we may need to tap much deeper sources of hope and inner confidence. In this, the sequence of the Festivals can be a support.

The festivals in spring

See page 24.

February 2	Candlemas
February 14	Valentine's Day
	Shrove Tuesday (Pancake Day)
	Lent
	Ash Wednesday
	Mothering Sunday
March 21	Spring Equinox
April 1	April Fool's Day
Holy Week:	Palm Sunday
	Maundy Thursday
	Good Friday
	Holy Saturday
	Easter Sunday

The seasonal table in spring

An old English tradition dictated that every scrap of winter greenery and Christmas decoration had to be removed from the house by February 1st. This may go back to the time when Christmas was celebrated on January 6th, but nevertheless, the day before Candlemas is still a good moment to have a completely fresh start to the Seasonal Table. A pale coloured cloth and one special candle establishes a mood of expectancy — of hopeful waiting.

Although each new messenger of spring that finds its way to the Table — the first little flowers, the yellow catkins, the fat buds — may not completely satisfy our expectancy, no matter, for we are 'travelling hopefully' and have no need to arrive just yet. The journey of springtime with its familiar landmarks takes us into Lent. Now the pretty gifts of February begin to move aside to make space on the Table for the prophetic simplicity of bare twigs, a shallow tray of earth and an unlit candle. In the silence of their austerity is heard the urgent call to life, to light, to fruitfulness.

In response to this call, the Table could become a Lenten Garden during Holy Week (see p46) where, in quiet stillness, preparations are made to receive the resurrecting power of Easter.

When the sun rises on the Easter Garden (see p56) our waiting is over, our hopes are fulfilled. Spring has come and will lead us all into the joy of summer.

Candlemas

The saying "Candlemas — Candle-less" indicates that the days are noticeably lengthening at this time of the year, and there is less need to work by artificial light. The day was marked in pre-Christian times by an important Festival of Lights (Imbolg) held on February 1st in honour of the Celtic goddess Brigit. This was a purification Festival to celebrate the Virgin Earth of Spring. In Britain, at Candlemas, the first snowdrops are already standing like little lamps, their colours of green and shining white heralding the vitality and purity of the emerging life of the earth.

In the early centuries A.D., February 1st was dedicated to St Brigid, (or St Bride), and in 542 A.D. the celebration of the Purification of the Blessed Virgin was moved from February 15th to February 2nd, which is forty days after the Nativity. This Feast recalls the occasion when the Holy Child was presented in the Temple, according to custom, and was venerated by the aged Anna, and by old Simeon who proclaimed Him to be "a light" (Luke 2: 22 - 39). Eastern churches have used February 2nd to commemorate this in the Festival of 'The Meeting' of the very old with the very new. In many other parts of the world, the custom has grown of bringing new candles into the church to be blessed.

At the beginning of February, when the infant light of spring is greeted thankfully by the hoary winter earth, it seems fitting that we should celebrate a candle Festival to remember that moment when the Light of the World was received into the Temple, when the old yielded to the new.

Candlemas candle fun

At the threshold of a new season, what better way to celebrate than to surrender the old and prepare for the new! Your hoard of old candle stubs could now be melted down to make new candles, for use as gifts or for the other festivals of the year ahead. First read about candlemaking (p246) then try your hand at some of the techniques below.

Floating candles

Candles floating on water are magical! The flames sparkle twice — each light reflected from below. A delightful centre-piece for the party table — star shapes at Christmas, hearts on Valentine's Day, and flower forms for summer evenings.

You will need:
Small biscuit cutters as moulds
Candlewax
Narrow wick, 4cm length per candle
Sheet of aluminium foil, greased
Wax container and pan

Melt the wax in a container that stands in simmering water. Add dye if you wish to colour the wax. Dip each 4cm length of wick in the wax to stiffen and straighten it. Brush the biscuit cutters with oil and stand them

on the aluminium foil. Pour some wax, not too hot, into each cutter, about 5mm deep. While pouring the wax, press each cutter firmly down on the foil and hold it for a few seconds to prevent the wax leaking. When a skin has formed on the surface of the wax, stick a wick into the centre. Hold the wick in place and fill the cutter shape with wax to the brim. Hold the wick upright with the help of two matches.

Leave to set. Remove the candle from the mould and leave it overnight to harden.

Floating candles can also be made by filling half a walnut shell with wax. Follow wick instructions for the floating candles above. There is no need to oil the walnut shells, as the candles stay in them and float as little boats.

Walnut candle boats

This is a more elaborate version of the floating walnut shell candle mentioned above.

You will need:
Walnut halves
Melted candlewax
Birthday cake candles (one per boat)
Goldfoil cut in star shapes (see p254 for star pattern and use a radius of 1.25cm)
Paper punch

Fill the walnut halves with wax. Push a cake candle into the wax while it is still soft. Make sure the candle is upright. At this point test the candle boat for stability: holding it by the 'mast,' set it down carefully in a bowl of water. Punch a hole in the centre of a goldfoil star, and slip the star over the candle 'mast.'

Sand candle

A simple candle can be made using damp sand as a mould.

You will need:
Flower pot (approx. 12cm diam.) almost
    filled with damp sand
Tennis ball
Wooden cooking spoon
Wick
Melted candlewax

Press the tennis ball exactly half way into the sand. Remove tennis ball. With the end of the spoon handle, poke three holes approx. 2.5cm deep into the base of the mould as shown:

These will form 'legs' on which the candle can stand. Prepare wick as for Floating Candles above. Push it into place and steady it between two sticks resting on the rim of the flower pot. Pour in melted wax. The hotter the wax, the more it will penetrate into the sand, so do some experimenting!

As the candle cools, top up the centre with wax if necessary. Leave candle to set overnight. Lift it out of the mould and brush off excess sand. Trim the top and bottom of wick if necessary.

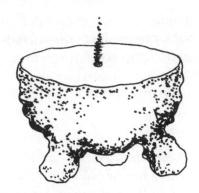

Now light your earth candle: if the candle is large and the weather is kind, it could burn on into the early hours...

Sand candles are appropriately 'earthy' for the Autumn Garden (see p126). Always make sure that they stand on a dish when alight.

Earth candle

You will need:
Plot of earth or lawn in a sheltered place (tub or flower pot filled with earth could also be used)
Twig approx. 30cm long
Length of wick suitable for a thick candle
Small metal weight (a nut or washer)
Quantity of melted wax, not too hot (see p246)

Dig a hole in the lawn or earth. (Judge the size as best you can — the available wax must easily fill it.)

Tie the weight to one end of the wick. Tie other end of the wick tightly to the middle of the twig. Lay the twig across the hole with the weight sitting centrally at the bottom of the hole. Take up any slack in the wick by rolling the twig.

Pour wax directly into the hole. In cold weather the top layer of wax will set quickly. The wick may then be cut to within 1cm of the candle surface, and the twig removed.

Water-dip candles

These candles are great fun to make but are too fragile to wrap, or transport other than by hand.

You will need:
Dipped candle or ordinary household candle
Greased ladle
Sink or bucket nearly full of cold water
Small quantity of melted wax in a pouring container
Another pair of hands

Hold the candle upright in the ladle, above the cold water. Ask someone to half-fill the ladle very carefully with melted wax.

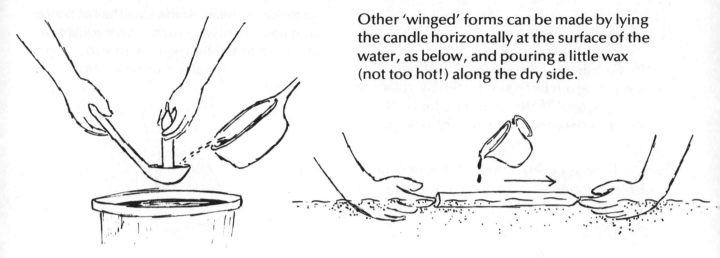

Other 'winged' forms can be made by lying the candle horizontally at the surface of the water, as below, and pouring a little wax (not too hot!) along the dry side.

As soon as this is done, plunge candle and ladle smoothly down into cold water until they are totally immersed, keeping the candle upright and pressed to the ladle all the time. The wax will swirl around the candle like frozen flames. Hold candle and ladle under water for a minute or two to harden the wax, then carefully lift out and drain. Release the transformed candle by twisting it in the ladle. If this is not successful, heat ladle from below, just enough to unstick the wax. Trim base if necessary so that the candle is upright and stable. These delicate forms look best in white wax or pastel shades.

Plunge candle into the water as before, but horizontally. Repeat two or three times, turning the candle to a fresh side (dried with kitchen paper) each time. If you are doing this with children, pour the wax for them using a spoon or very small jug, taking care that the wax is not too hot for little fingers. Different temperatures of wax will give different effects.

31

Flower fairies

By Candlemas, the spring flowers are capturing our hearts and claiming a place on the Seasonal Table. Small children will be delighted to find a flower fairy looking after them.

We have suggested three different fairies below; when you are familiar with the technique, try experimenting with more species!

Snowdrop

As snowdrops always grow in clumps, the indications for materials are given for three fairies.

You will need:
White felt 8cm x 7cm
Dark green felt 8cm x 6cm
Flesh-coloured stockinette for heads 5cm x 15cm (an old white T-shirt soaked in cold tea works well for this)
Fleece or cotton wool for stuffing

To make the head, stuff a small ball of fleece or cotton wool into a 5cm x 5cm square of stockinette and tie a piece of thread around the neck. The head should be about the size of a marble.

From the white felt cut a piece 8cm x 4cm for the dress. Sew the short sides together using an overstitch. Run a gathering thread around the edge at one end. Attach the head by tying the dress around the neck.

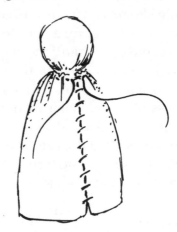

To make the hat, cut a piece of white felt 5cm x 2.5cm and shape the petals as seen below.

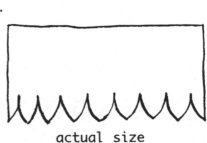

actual size

32

Sew up as for dress and gather tightly round the stalk. The stalk is made from a tiny circle of green felt.

Fix the hat to the head with glue or small stitches.

Make the leaves by cutting a strip of green felt 8cm x 3.5cm as follows:

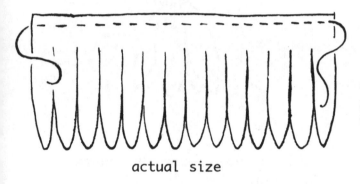

actual size

Gather the top edge with green thread and tie the leaves around the neck over the dress.

Primrose

You will need:
Light yellow felt 8cm x 7cm
Green felt 8cm x 4cm
Stockinette for head 5cm x 5cm
Fleece or cottonwool for stuffing

Follow instructions given for the Snowdrop. Make the hat and dress from yellow felt. Shape the hat as follows:

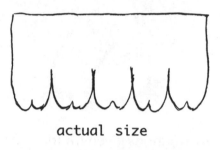

actual size

Make up the hat as for Snowdrop. (No green is inserted into the top of the hat for the Primrose.) Shape the leaves as follows:

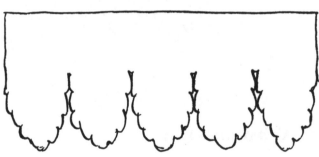

Crocus

You will need:
Purple felt 8cm x 7cm
Dark green felt 8cm x 4cm
Scraps of golden yellow felt
Stockinette for head 5cm x 5cm
Fleece or cottonwool for stuffing

To show the characteristic golden yellow colour of the stamen, cut a scrap of golden yellow felt as shown below.

Make up the hat as for Snowdrop and gather the top of the hat tightly around the yellow stamen.

Follow instructions given for the Snowdrop. Make the hat and dress from purple felt. Cut the hat in a crocus petal shape.

actual size

The leaves are the same as the ones for Snowdrop.

Valentine's Day

There were actually two St Valentines martyred in Italy on February 14th ca 270 A.D. Despite this, Valentine's Day has become a very secular feast, having more to do, perhaps, with an old belief that this was the day on which the birds chose their mates. The customs are sometimes erroneously confused with the Roman purification rites of Lupercalia held on February 15th. These survived well into the 5th century A.D. but were then superseded by the Feast of the Purification of the Blessed Virgin, celebrated forty days after Christmas (January 6th at that time). When Christmas was moved to December 25th this feast was transferred to February 2nd (see Candlemas).

The custom of choosing a 'Valentine' was established by the 15th century, and today it has become an occasion for both fun and heartache, especially among teenagers.

Younger children relate easily to the activity of bird life in spring, and they will enjoy a Valentine tree full of bird biscuits (see below). Try putting only one bird from each pair on the tree and having a hunt for the others.

Older children cannot help being stimulated by commercial pressures to want to join in the exchange of cards and presents. We suggest they try the Transparency (p182) or the spattering method (p74) to make original Valentine cards. They could also decorate the boxes on pages 228 and 229 with hearts, and use them for holding a little Valentine gift. Parents might surprise the whole family with a decorated gingerbread heart (see p152 for recipe), a red heart candle floating in a little bowl (see p28), or a single red rose on each breakfast plate. A table prettily adorned with the unexpected may just manage to distract a lovelorn heart from the empty mail box!

Valentine bird biscuits

Hang these in pairs on a branch as a table decoration for Valentine's Day. Place the branch in a stable vase.

You will need:
175g white or 81% wholemeal flour
50g ground rice or semolina or ground almonds
150g butter or vegetable margarine
60g sugar — white or soft brown

½ level tsp salt
1 level tsp baking powder
1 egg yolk

Stir all dry ingredients together. Mix the egg yolk with the sugar. Mix all ingredients together lightly with the fingers until a dough is formed. Roll out on a floured board until 5mm thick. Use bird-shaped cutters, or cut shapes free-hand using a pointed knife or darning needle. Or

transfer (see p253) bird shapes shown
below to card, cut them out and place on
the pastry as a guide for cutting. Make pairs
of birds facing each other, and place on a
greased baking sheet.

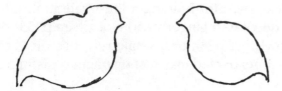

Bake until pale gold (approx. 10 mins.) in a
moderate oven 175°C. Using a large darning
needle, carefully pierce each biscuit while
hot. Cool on a wire tray. Thread with black
cotton for hanging. Decorate with royal
icing (see p152) if required. Hang on a
branch of a blossoming tree if possible, and
add small bows of narrow white ribbon to
the twigs above the biscuits.

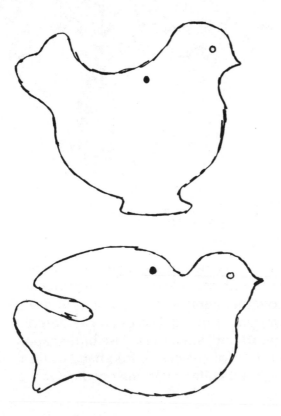

Valentine decorations

bottom end of each 'heart-pair,' sew along centre dotted line with a sewing machine or by hand. Use the thread at the top of each heart for hanging. Carefully bend the four sections of each heart so that they are at right angles to each other. Tie the smaller hearts to the bottom of the larger ones at equal distances.

Felt hearts

You will need:

Valentine pattern (see p255)
2 sheets of red card 16cm x 28cm
Matching red thread
Tracing paper (any transparent paper will
    do)
Carbon paper — optional
Craft knife or small pointed scissors
Paper clips

Trace the patterns and transfer them to the red card, (see p253). Use paper clips to hold both sheets of card together. Cut out along drawn lines with knife or scissors. To cut out the eyes of the birds, push a thick darning needle through the card where the eye is indicated. Keeping the two cut-outs *exactly* on top of each other, and starting at the

You will need:

Red felt 18cm x 16cm
Matching red embroidery cotton
Fleece or cottonwool for stuffing

Cut out the three sizes of hearts using the pattern below, two pieces per size, from the felt.

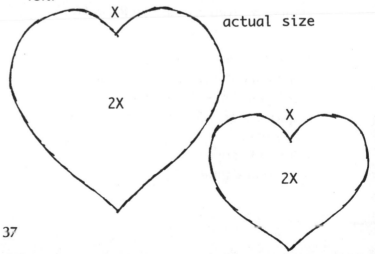

X

actual size

2X

X

2X

37

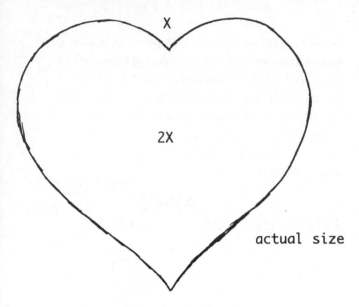

X

2X

actual size

Sew together the hearts of the same size using a blanket stitch. Start stitching at the top (point X), ending in the same place. Just before closing up each heart, stuff it lightly with fleece or cottonwool. Make a chain of hearts.

You could make several 'heart-chains' and hang them on a wreath or branch, with a little bell attached at the bottom.

Heart baskets

Pop a present into a festive heart basket for a Valentine gift that is also delightfully decorative. Hang a few on a flowering branch, or from our All Year Round Ring. (See p252.)

You will need: (for one basket)
2 strips of coloured paper in contrasting colours 5cm x 17cm each
Strip of paper, 1.5cm x 12cm, in one of the colours
Ruler and pencil
Scissors and glue

Gold thread or embroidery silk — optional

Place the two strips of paper on top of each other and fold them in half.

Cut unfolded edges to make a symmetrical curve.

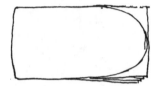

Separate the two strips. Cut two slits in each strip, approx. 1.7cm from each side, running 5.5cm up the strip.

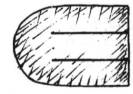 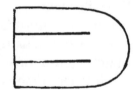

Place the strips on top of each other and at right angles to each other. The curves should create a heart shape.

Interweave the strips, alternately passing one through the other to make a chequer effect. The back view of the patterns created by this weaving process is the same as the front view shown below.

When you have mastered the weaving technique, try the following variation, using the pattern below.

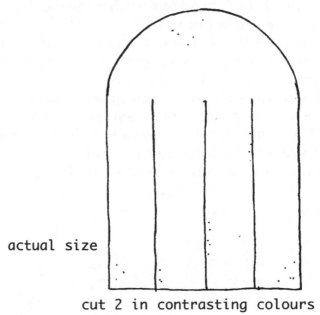

actual size

cut 2 in contrasting colours

To form a handle, glue a strip of paper (1.5cm x 12cm) in place. Alternatively, use gold thread or embroidery silk.

Shrove Tuesday

The practice of attending church to receive absolution — or be 'shriven' or 'shrove' — before the forty-day fast of Lent, has given the name to this day. Years ago, Church regulations during this fast were very strict and forbade many items of food. These items were used up before Lent began: all scraps of meat ('collops') were eaten on 'Collop Monday,' and butter, eggs and milk were used up the next day (Shrove Tuesday) in a spree of pancake making. All frivolous thoughts were used up, too, in general fun and extravagant behaviour, out of which arose the many pre-Lenten carnival traditions.

The word 'carnival,' popularly translated (from the Italian 'carne' — flesh, and 'vale' — farewell) as "Goodbye to meat," actually has an older derivation from the Latin 'carnelevarium' which suggests the meaning 'solace (or lightening) of the flesh.' This light mood has led to some curious jollifications — including the extraordinary pancake-tossing races held throughout England on this day.

Pancakes

Why not try your hand at tossing pancakes and making a fool of yourself in front of the family? Clean the floor *first* and use only a smear of oil or fat in the pan. Here is a basic recipe.

You will need:
150g flour
2 eggs
½ litre milk
Pinch of salt
Oil, or margarine for frying
Sugar
1 lemon
Butter

Beat the eggs, salt and a few tablespoons of milk together thoroughly. Pour this mixture over the flour and beat it until smooth. Add the rest of the milk. Heat a very little oil in a frying pan. Pour a little batter into the pan with a ladle, tilting the pan to spread the batter thinly. Brown the pancake on one side and turn it with a toss! Brown the other side. Place on a warm dish. Sprinkle with sugar, a few drops of lemon juice, and some melted butter. The pancakes may be prepared before the meal and kept in a warm oven.

LENT

Ash Wednesday

The name given to the first of the forty days of Lent comes from an old practice of wearing an uncomfortable garment ('sackcloth') at this time and covering the head with ashes to express sorrow and a recognition of mortality, as if the shining life of spring must call forth its companion shadow from the soul. Lent has been kept as a time of penance, of strict self-denial, and for contemplating the sufferings and temptations of Jesus Christ as he fasted forty days in the wilderness.

Nowadays, the imposed strictness of Lent has largely been relaxed, and more emphasis placed on using the time to strengthen the inner life through spiritual education or appropriate self-discipline.

The long fasts of Lent and Advent were once used to make pilgrimages or 'progresses' to holy places. The word 'progress' implies not only the outer journey, but also the inner journey of the pilgrim — his progress in self-development. The ease of Nature's progress in spring may challenge us to test our own human capacity for renewal and inner growth. Lent reminds us that we always have the opportunity to do this, and thus prepare in understanding for the archetypal picture of renewal given at Easter.

Many different religions and cultures include periods of fasting in their observances, not only to discipline the soul but also to 'cleanse' the body. Rural traditions point to suitable food, mostly with cleansing properties, to eat at this time of the year. The early shoots of wild plants: dandelion, nettle, and hawthorn (known locally as 'bread and cheese') are recommended to purify the blood. Herbs such as tansy, rue and sorrel, in small quantities, are advised for the same purpose. Leeks are considered particularly health giving: "Eat leeks in Lide (March) and ransoms (wild garlic) in May, then all the year after physicians can play." Chervil, another cleansing herb, has long made a popular soup for Maundy Thursday (see p51).

Fasting and self-discipline have little relevance for young children, even though they often attempt to 'give up sweets for Lent.' They will participate in such moral content more through the unobstrusive example of the parent or teacher, who leads them in this way through what is really an adult festival.

Easter is very much a morning festival — the women disciples came to the tomb "very early in the morning." To be properly awake to what the morning can bring, we need to have had a 'good night.' We need to have spent some time in our own quiet darkness away from outer stimulation, in that mysterious space which is yet familiar — a space which is, above all, restorative.

This is what Lent could be for all of us, a time during which we gather the forces needed to meet the vital renewal of our daily lives. For young children, who carry the joy of life so close to them anyway, their pleasure in the fullness of Easter Day can only be the greater if they have been prepared through the quiescent 'night' mood of Lent.

Because of this we must consider carefully how to lead a child through this time before Easter.

Children relate to the world about them primarily through what is *seen* and *done*. It is only later that they easily grasp abstract ideas. So in preparing festivals for children we give priority to the visual presentation and to the accompanying activity. We have found it best to avoid *completely* the temptation to explain in words anything to do with the meaning or background to a festival. It could be many years later that illuminating connections in thought are discovered by the child — but this will be a personal discovery and therefore all the more precious and inspiriting. We have never known a child demur when, in answer to the question, "Why do you do that?" we answer "Because today is (e.g.) Ash Wednesday!"

It is not always necessary to maintain a Lent mood over forty days. Choose the period of time which you feel is right for your family.

In what ways can we develop an appropriate Lenten mood for a young child? We could sit together for a few minutes each morning, listening in silence as the birdsong gains strength from the ebb of night. We could take time to watch for the moon as it unfolds its rhythmic process between darkness and light. There are many small, quiet ways in which the adult can offer certain pictures. We do not mean art reproductions of the Crucifixion, which children can find disturbing, but pictures taken 'out of the book of Nature,' or presentations of a symbolic quality. For example, if an unlit candle stands on the dining table each day instead of flowers, this can make a very deep impression. Or one might decide to decorate the Seasonal Table with bare twigs alone; (always exchange them before they put out leaves, and allow them to leaf or blossom in a different part of the house). A special herb tea could be chosen just for this time of Lent: these may seem small matters, but it is so often the small things that need attention.

If a bowl of dry earth (mixed, perhaps, with a pinch of ash) is prepared on Ash Wednesday, and stands barren on the Seasonal Table until Palm Sunday, this simple picture will have time to be well 'digested' by the child. Then, if grass seed is sown in the same bowl on Palm Sunday (or grain is sprinkled there on Maundy Thursday), and watered well, the contrasting picture of the transformed earth on Easter Day will stand out all the more.

Mothering Sunday

Fourth Sunday in Lent

This is a very old festival in England and its origins are not to be confused with those of Mother's Day in the U.S.A. on the second Sunday in May. (This was instituted in 1907 through the personal campaign of Anna Jarvis of Philadelphia, who incidentally never became a mother herself!)

As far back as medieval times there was a relaxation of austerities on the fourth Sunday of Lent. This day was also set aside for priests to visit the Mother Church of the district, and for laity to return to the church where they had been baptised. Serving girls and boys, hired at the Michaelmas Fairs, were allowed this one day's holiday half-way through their year's service to visit their homes. It became customary for employers to bake a 'simnel' cake for the mother, perhaps hoping that the good deed would bring luck to themselves:

"I'll thee a simnel bring
'gainst thou go a-mothering
So that when she blesses thee
Half that blessing thou'lt give to me."   Anon.

There were different varieties of simnel cake. The base was always a very rich plum cake, full of dried fruit and candied peel, often boiled in a cloth first before being put in a pastry case and baked. The name probably derived from the Latin 'simila,' meaning the 'fine flour,' which was mixed with water to make the pastry covering. Nowadays the simnel cake is usually prepared for Easter and has a layer of marzipan placed in the middle of the mixture before baking. Another layer covers the top after baking and is browned slightly under a hot grill. A crimped edging of marzipan may also be placed around the top of the cake, a reminder of the old pastry case seam. Eleven balls of marzipan are sometimes added for Easter to denote the eleven faithful disciples. These are browned under the grill before being added to the cake. Use our Epiphany cake recipe (see p242) as a base if you would like to try a 'simnel.'

Violets are also a traditional Mothering Sunday gift. Most likely they were gathered from the hedgerows by the weary maids on their long walk home:

"Who goes a-Mothering
finds violets in the lane."   Trad.

Why not try the Spattering technique (see p74) using violet leaves and appropriate shades of violet paint to create a very personal token of affection for *your* mother?

April Fool's Day

The custom of playing tricks on April Fool's Day goes back more than two hundred years. It commemorates the birthday, on April 1st 1752, of Olaf (Pilor) Toyou, the first-born son of Hungarian fisherfolk. When Olaf was nearly six months old, on September 12th 1752, a violent earthquake struck far out in the Mediterranean. Olaf was sleeping in a cradle slung from the branch of a tree, while his mother mended nets nearby. The turbulent sea raced up the beach so swiftly and quietly that the mother noticed nothing until it was too late. She ran to save her son but all she found in the cradle was a small fish. Demented, the mother searched for her husband, shrieking that the baby had gone. While her back was turned, a second tidal wave miraculously returned the baby to the cradle and retrieved the fish. When the husband inspected the cradle and found the boy, wet but unharmed, he berated his wife as a fool. She, however, remained convinced that her child had the power to turn himself into a fish at will. To the derision of everyone on that stretch of the coast she insisted on calling him Olaf 'Pilor' — which means Olaf the Little Pilchard.

To this day, people in France must beware of turning their backs on April 1st... They may later discover a paper fish pinned to their jacket and realise with embarrassment that they have become the 'Poisson d'Avril'.

There is one way to avoid becoming an April Fool: it is said that to hang a little cradle, carrying a fish, around your neck, or at the front door, will protect you and your family. Most practical jokers respect this code. (Of course, the cradle should be hung up very early on the morning of April 1st — busy mothers may choose to do it the evening before.)

Fish cradle to wear

You will need:
Half walnut shell
Carded fleece or cotton wool
Scrap of cotton material in pale colour
Scrap of pale blue card
Blue embroidery thread or gold string
    approx. 75 cm long
Glue

Cut the thread in half, and glue each half beneath the rim on each side of the walnut shell as seen below. Tie the ends of the thread as illustrated.

Line the nut shell with a scrap of wool. Cut out a small fish from the blue card.

Lay fish in the cradle, cover it with cotton material and glue this to the inside of the shell.

Basket fish cradle

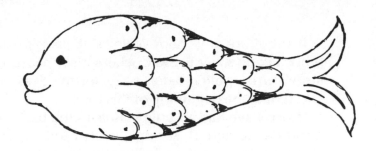

You will need:
Small oval basket — approx. 10 - 12 cm in
    length
Carded fleece or cotton wool
Scrap of cotton material in pale colour
Scrap of pale blue card
Coloured pencils
Pink or blue gift ribbon — optional

Line the basket with wool. Cut out a fish
from pale blue card and decorate it with
coloured pencils.

Lay the fish in its cradle. Cover and 'tuck' it
in gently with some cotton material. Fix a
little bow of gift ribbon at either end of the
basket.

Suspend the basket with matching ribbon
or string.

HOLY WEEK

Palm Sunday

This day recalls the entry of Jesus into Jerusalem, when He was greeted by crowds laying palm
branches in His path, (John 12: 13). The following days unfolded the sequence of events
which led to the Crucifixion.

   During this week the mood of Lent intensifies and many adults receive significant spiritual
support by setting aside a little time to contemplate, day by day, the events of Holy Week (or
Quiet Week as it has sometimes been known). The children are looking forward to Easter, so
for them also this can become a special week of preparation.

   The cockerel is a wonderful symbol to use at this time, for he announces to the world that a
new day will soon be dawning. The children will 'wake up' to Palm Sunday when they see our
Cockerel Cut-Out (see p49) hanging over the breakfast table!

   In many parts of Europe processions are held on Palm Sunday. Adults and children carry
light wooden crosses or circles, decorated with bread figures (especially the cockerel),
strings of dried fruit and streamers.

If there are any 'Palm Willows' (Salix caprea) in your neighbourhood, the family might enjoy taking some Bread Cockerels (see p50) on a picnic, and bringing back a bunch of these large, furry, pollen-laden twigs for the Seasonal Table. They will add a gleam of hopeful sunlight at the beginning of this week.

If you have had an unlit candle in the background during Lent, Palm Sunday would be a good day to light it. A single white candle in a plain holder, perhaps on a square of white cloth, can make a deep impression on a child by its very simplicity. It is a quiet signal that a special moment has been reached.

Palm Sunday could also be a good day to sow grass seed (see p48) and collect moss to make a Lenten Garden.

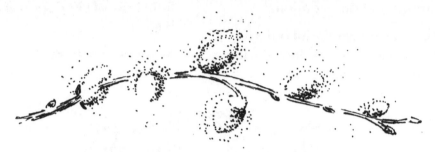

Lenten garden

Nature speaks a language which all small children understand, and we are able to use this language as a strong foundation on which the child can build coherent thoughts in later years. The concepts of 'death' and 'resurrection' may only become accessible to us in maturity, but we actually live with them quite comfortably from day to day, surrounded as we are by the manifold pictures from 'Nature's Book.' Each time a little seed swells and splits apart, giving up its own existence to grow into new life, there before us is the mystery of death and resurrection.

Such pictures are everywhere, but perhaps none is so vividly descriptive as that of the caterpillar transformed into a butterfly. The young child can unite wholeheartedly with the beauty and wonder of this picture; it is for him, and for us all, a parable of Easter. So at this time of year we build a garden within which we can lead our children from Lent into Easter, from the caterpillar to the butterfly, from night into day.

You will need:

An old metal or plastic tray, which will hold water. It can be as large as you like (drip-trays
   from old cookers are excellent), or fairly small, and other items must be scaled accordingly
Three or four mossy rocks, or large pebbles
A suitable branch for the 'tree' (see below)
Lump of clay or plasticine, or some other stable holder for the 'tree'
Shallow glass dish for the 'pond' — brown or dark green ceramic would also be suitable
A little sand, gravel or very small shells
Moss

Small flat pebbles or little stones
White candle in a holder (see p247)
You may also need: black plastic sheeting, newspaper, cloth or veil in pale yellow or green, some soil, a strip of bark or rough wood

The Seasonal Table could be a place to make this garden, especially if it catches the morning sun. Protect the table with some newspaper and a sheet of black plastic or dustbin liner and cover with a cloth. Place the tray on top and arrange a little grotto on it with the rocks. Alongside the grotto place the lump of clay, wrapped in a thin plastic bag to keep it clean. The lump should be 'mountain shaped' with the weight spread out at the base. Push the branch that you have chosen as the Lenten Tree into the lump so that it is quite stable. The branch could be of oak, ash or any other tree with a strong gesture in the twigs, and the buds should stay tightly closed for the week.

Place the 'pond' dish well forward on the tray. Scatter some sand, gravel or shells in it and fill it with water. Arrange moss over the rest of the tray, concealing the lump of clay and carpeting the grotto. If you have had a bowl of earth on the Seasonal Table (see p42) it could be incorporated into the Garden, otherwise include an area of soil between the moss, maybe at the base of the Tree. With the small pebbles make a winding path of stepping stones leading from the base of the Tree to the grotto. Span the pond with a strip of bark or wood as a little bridge. Position the candle (with the holder beneath the moss) near the grotto entrance. The Garden is now complete and should be well soaked with water. It remains throughout Holy Week as a quiet background for the Easter preparations.

Here are some suggestions as to how the Lenten Garden could be woven into the children's activities during Holy Week:

Six small white cake candles are evenly spaced along the path between the Tree and the grotto. On Palm Sunday, at some convenient moment of the day, the large candle in the Garden is lit, and from it is taken a light for the first small candle furthest from the grotto. This is allowed to burn right down. Each day, preferably at the same time, another small candle is burnt, until the very last candle at the entrance to the grotto is burnt on Good Friday. Holy Saturday is a day of waiting when only the large candle is alight — perhaps at story time.

On Palm Sunday, when the Garden has been completed, some grass seed can be sprinkled on the soil area and lightly forked in. Ideally, the shoots should only become visible on Easter Sunday so if the room is very warm this activity could be put off until Maundy Thursday. On this day it is rather special to sprinkle some wheat grains on the soil, press them down into the earth and water them well. They will sprout and shoot very dramatically in a few days.

On Good Friday a child will enjoy making a little caterpillar out of green plasticine or wax, wrapping it carefully in a small square of real silk (white or cream in colour) and placing it on the moss inside the Grotto. On Holy Saturday the caterpillar is still there, but on Easter Sunday morning only the silk remains, and a butterfly hovers in the branches of the Easter Tree (see p61).

Although the Garden must be kept damp all the time, Holy Saturday could be a good day to make more of a ritual of the watering. Choose a pretty jug to hold the water if you do not have a sprinkler.

Easter Sunday arrives, and the Lenten Garden has been transformed overnight into an Easter Garden, to the great surprise and delight of everyone (see p56).

Magic tufty cones

Here is a little surprise to include in your Lenten/Easter Garden or to have somewhere on its own.

You will need:
3 smallish pine cones
Shallow dish
Some moss (or sand or soil)
Tsp grass seed

Dry cones on a radiator so that they open. Sprinkle grass seed, not too thickly, between the scales of the cone. Arrange the moss in the dish and add water until everything is really soggy. Sit the cones firmly in moss taking care not to spill the seed. The dampness will soon cause the cones to close, concealing the grass seed.

Keep away from direct heat and water each day. If the room is very warm and dry, a twice-daily spray may be necessary to keep the cones firmly shut. After about five days, grass shoots will appear and soon the hard, dry cones will be changed into tufts of shining soft new grass. Magic!

If the dish is large enough, a small rock and a nightlight set in the moss will create an unusual centrepiece for the Easter Table.

A Palm Sunday and Easter decoration

This cut-out cockerel looks especially attractive when made from yellow card.

You will need:
Cockerel pattern (see p256)
2 pieces of yellow, thin but not floppy card
    each 23cm x 24cm
Matching thread and darning needle
Tracing paper (any transparent paper will
    do)
Carbon paper — optional
Craft knife

Fold one piece of card in half, after scoring the fold line with the back of the craft knife to ensure a neat crease.

Transfer the pattern to the card (see p253). With the craft knife cut along drawn lines. To cut out the cockerel's eye, push a thick darning needle through the card where the eye is indicated. Repeat whole process with the other piece of card. Open up both cut-outs and lay them on top of each other, taking great care that the centre creases correspond. Starting at the bottom end of the cut-outs, sew along centre crease with a sewing machine or by hand, making sure that the seam is absolutely straight. Leave enough thread at the top for hanging.

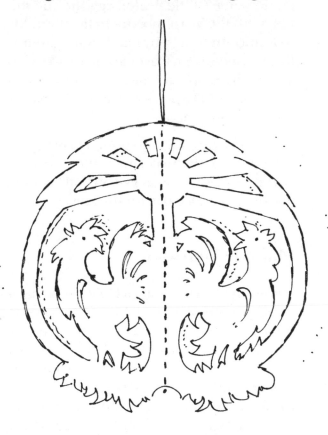

Bend the four sections so that the cockerels are at right-angles to each other.

Bread cockerels

You will need:
500g 100% wholemeal flour
1 tsp salt
1 tsp cinnamon
40g butter or margarine
250ml hand-hot water and/or milk
100g sugar
1 heaped tsp dried yeast
1 large egg, beaten

Dissolve some of the sugar with the water and add yeast. Leave in a warm place until frothy (15 - 20 mins.). Mix flour, salt, sugar and cinnamon in a warm bowl. Rub in the fat. Reserve a little beaten egg and add the rest with the yeast mixture to the flour. Mix to a smooth dough by hand, adding more flour if necessary. Cover and leave to rise in a warm place for an hour. Knead briefly and divide into 100g pieces. Fashion the pieces into cockerel shapes.

Using scissors, snip the dough to make tail feathers, comb, beak and wattle. Add a currant or clove for an eye on both sides of the head, and a clove for the feet.

Place on a greased baking sheet. Add a little sugar to the reserved egg and brush on the cockerels. Leave to rise in a warm place (30 - 60 mins.). Bake for 20 mins. in a hot oven.

Don't despair if your cockerel looks like a walrus, it will still taste delicious!

Maundy Thursday

It was on the Thursday of Holy Week that Jesus Christ gave his disciples a new 'mandatum' — commandment — which was "to love one another" (John 13: 34), and demonstrated His loving service to others by washing the feet of each disciple. This was on the occasion of the Last Supper. Another 'mandatum' was also given as He broke the bread, and commanded the disciples to "do this in remembrance of me" (Luke 22: 19). From this Latin word (mandatum) has derived the strange word 'Maundy,' which is used in Britain. British monarchs in the past performed a ritual on the Thursday of Holy Week of washing the feet of thirteen people.

This practice has been replaced by a gift of specially minted coins known as 'Maundy money' to as many of the poor as there are years in the monarch's life. In other parts of Europe, however, this day has always been known as Green Thursday, a day on which one eats green food, especially salad vegetables and herbs.

The symbolism of giving and receiving food is appreciated by all cultures in different ways. Maundy Thursday could be for us a day in the year when the simple act of sharing a meal together becomes more than the formal satisfying of hunger, but is rediscovered as a meaningful deed of fellowship. The simpler the fare the more the significance of the occasion is able to express itself. A bowl of soup, bread rolls, a jug of water and a basket of grapes — these may be all that is needed in the way of food. A plain white cloth, a white or pale mauve candle and a specially chosen grace or reading would complement the meal.

Chervil soup

Here is a recipe for a green soup.

You will need:
3 good handfuls chopped fresh chervil or
3 tbsps dried chervil
3 tbsps butter or oil
2 rounded tsps flour
100ml cold water or stock
500ml hot stock
Salt to taste
1 tbsp cream (fresh or sour)

Sauté chervil in butter/oil. Add flour and sauté again. Slowly add cold water/stock and stir to smooth consistency. Add the hot stock and salt, and simmer for 20 mins. Remove from heat, add cream and serve.

Good Friday

As children grow older and become more aware of the story of Christ's Crucifixion, many declare: "It shouldn't be called Good Friday, it should be called Bad Friday!" This is an indication of how difficult it is for a child's thinking to cope with the story of Good Friday, and how they need to orientate themselves towards the question of death and resurrection in a different way.

On the Friday of Holy Week, the day of the Crucifixion and Burial, it is possible to meet such Mysteries through the mysterious processes of Nature. This is a day to dig over a new plot and sow seed potatoes, or take a handful of largish seeds (sunflower, marigold, nasturtium) and push them here and there into flower beds or into prepared flower pots. The seeds are buried, but from their earthy grave a new and fruitful life will spring. Such are the secrets of life and death to which a child is privy. Likewise, the riddle of the caterpillar's transformation is easily accepted by the smallest child, who will usually find great joy on Good Friday in preparing his own caterpillar to be transformed in the Lenten/Easter Garden (see p48).

Good Friday is the day to make and eat Hot Cross Buns. These delicious spicy buns, marked with a cross and eaten warm with butter, were made in England in pre-Christian times. Then, the bun was a symbol of the moon, and the cross divided it into its four quarters. As with so many folk customs, the advent of Christianity added a new significance to the old symbols: nowadays, for Easter Sunday to be celebrated, one must have seen the first full moon of spring and have recognised the Cross of Golgotha.

Hot cross buns

Busy mothers may find it easier to make the dough the day before and store it in an oiled plastic bag in the refrigerator overnight. Knead the dough briefly in the morning, form into buns and leave to rise in the usual way.

You will need:
1kg plain flour
1 egg, beaten
100g sugar
100g butter or margarine
35g fresh yeast
600ml warm milk
200g currants
Grated rind of one lemon
Generous pinch of nutmeg
1.5 tsp mixed spice
Pinch of salt

Sift together flour, salt and spices in a large warmed bowl. Mix in currants and lemon rind and most of the sugar. Cream the fresh yeast with a teaspoon of sugar and a drop of warm milk. Gradually stir in the rest of the milk, and allow to stand in a warm place for 12 mins. Melt fat over very low heat, remove from heat and add sugar. Pour yeast mixture into the flour together with melted fat and sugar, and the beaten egg. Mix to a dough by hand and knead well until the bowl is clean. Cover and stand in a warm place for 30 mins. Knead very briefly, and leave for a further 30 mins. Knead briefly again and remove 50g of dough. Divide rest of dough into pieces (approx. 50g) and form into round buns. Space them well on a greased baking sheet, and brush them with milk. Mix the reserved 50g of dough with an equal quantity of marzipan and roll out very thinly on a board. Cut into narrow strips and, with these, form a cross on each bun, dividing it into four quarters. Leave to rise in a warm place for about 30 mins. Bake for approx. 10 mins. in a moderately hot oven. Boil a little water with a spoonful of sugar in it. Brush this syrup over the buns when they are done but before they are taken from the tins. Return to the oven for a few more minutes to glaze.

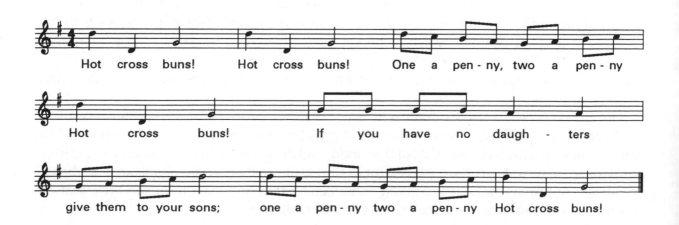

Holy Saturday

As with the swing of the pendulum, when the moment of stillness is the most decisive, so it is on Holy Saturday. This is the quiet day of waiting, of stillness, where seemingly nothing happens but a momentous change of direction is being prepared. That which descended into the earth on Good Friday is preparing to rise into a new era on Easter Sunday.

Both for children and adults it can be a day of practical preparation: the decorating of eggs can now be completed, the dough mixed for Easter bread, and Easter baskets lined and decorated.

If you have a family garden, there is the possibility of enticing the Easter Hare to visit with his gift of eggs! One way is to prepare a little nest in a secret spot on the ground, lining it with hay or washed sheep's wool. (A clean carrot or other tasty snack could be placed there to refresh the Easter Hare on his long journey.) Alternatively, a small basket lined with hay, or a paper box from our pattern on page 228 serves the purpose well. The basket is then placed somewhere in the garden before it gets dark on Saturday. By sunrise on Sunday morning the Easter Hare, we hope, will have passed by with his message of new life — the Easter Egg.

There may be an opportunity on this day to make a special breakfast bread for Easter. Use the directions below to prepare a Bread Ring with empty 'pockets' in it. In the evening, before the children go to bed, lay the table for breakfast placing the Bread Ring in the centre. The surprise comes on Easter morning, when the middle of the Ring is filled with flowers surrounding a yellow, red or light green candle, and the 'pockets' are filled with dyed eggs.

Easter bread ring

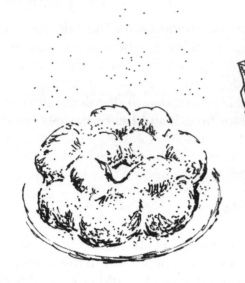

Use the recipe of the Festival Bread (see p250).

You will also need:
Pebbles, about the size of an egg, at least one for each member of the family
Aluminium foil or baking paper

Plait the dough and shape it into a ring. Part the dough to make little pockets, one for each member of the family. Wrap pebbles in foil or paper and settle them in the pockets.

Bake bread as directed. Remove pebbles to leave the pockets empty. They are now ready to receive coloured eggs from the Easter Hare! (P.S. No-one has ever yet seen the Easter Hare colouring his eggs…)

A small piece of dough can be used to make a 'nest' for a coloured egg: an attractive and tasty gift for a child, or friends who live on their own. (The baking time will be shorter for these 'nests.')

Easter

There is no fixed date for Easter. It moves in the calendar between the middle of March and the middle of April, and the festivals of Lent, Ascension and Whitsun (Pentecost) move along with it. The moment of Easter arises when the four great rhythms which we use to order our lives meet as they have run their course. When the sun has moved through a full year from one spring equinox to the next, then the monthly lunar cycle must be fulfilled with the sighting of the full moon. After that, the rhythm of the week must draw to a close. Finally, the moment which marks one day from the next — midnight — must have passed before the Easter Festival of Resurrection can truly be celebrated.

It seems appropriate that something of this kind of stately celestial dance should accompany a Festival which marks the triumph over death of Christ Jesus, who speaks in the words of the old carol:

> "Then up to Heaven I did ascend
> Where now I dwell in sure substance
> On the right hand of God, that man
> May come unto the general dance." (The Oxford Book of Carols No.71)

Eostre was the goddess of spring to the people of ancient times, and she brought new life and light to the world. She has lent her name to what is today the most important Christian festival of the year. The long weeks of Lenten 'night' have passed and the light of a new day breaks the darkness. Easter is truly a 'morning' festival. On Good Friday the body of Christ was laid into a tomb "hewn out in the rock" (Matt. 27: 60). On Easter Sunday the tomb was empty, but in the garden nearby the Resurrected Christ appeared to Mary Magdalene (John 20: 15). She mistook Him for a gardener — one who works in the realm of plants where the sap flows in a living stream, a nourishing revitalising 'Water of Life.' On Good Friday we relate to the Christian story by way of the cold darkness of the rocky element of Earth. However, on Easter Sunday we have left this behind and emerged into the sunlit watery world of plants.

The theme of water has recurring connections with Easter. In the earliest centuries A.D. the baptism of new converts (by immersing three times in water) was a central feature of Easter celebrations, and even today the blessing of the water is a part of many Christian rituals on Easter morning. The old custom of visiting a well or spring and drinking or washing one's face in 'Easter water' points again to the renewing, revivifying associations of the Water element.

In the plant, the life energies of the sap are quickened with the rising sun. Could it be the imagery of the golden sun yolk hidden in the hard lifeless shell, that has contributed to the widespread and ancient use of the egg as a symbol of new birth? In the creation myths of many cultures the egg plays a central role, and even in pre-Christian Egypt eggs were being coloured and exchanged between people in the spring.

So it is entirely fitting that on Easter Sunday morning we should seek in a garden for the hidden source of renewal, of new life. Whether eggs have been tucked into prepared nests or baskets by the Easter Hare, or scattered in the park as he bounded on his way, an Easter egg-hunt is an activity enjoyed by everyone.

May we here make a plea for the reinstatement of the Easter Hare? He is fast becoming an endangered species, owing to the increasing popularity of the 'Easter Bunny.' The rabbit, with its established communal life and reputation for timidity, presents a very different picture from that of the hare. The hare is a loner, creating the most transient of abodes. He is said to be a bold and courageous creature, and his upright stance is characteristic. His long ears suggest a wide and intelligent interest in the world, and in legend and folklore he is invested with the virtue of self-sacrifice. Because of all these attributes it is he, and not the 'Bunny' who makes the more suitable 'Messenger of Christ' who roams the earth to bring to those who actively seek it, the sign of new life in the Easter egg.

To step out quietly on Easter morning while it is still dark, to hear the birds begin their dawn chorus, to see the sky lightening and the rich blaze of the sun lifting above the horizon, this can be an Easter Festival in itself. If circumstances do not permit this then it is still possible to see the sun rising over your own Easter Garden.

The Easter garden

As the week swings from an ending to a new beginning, from Saturday to Sunday, so the Lenten Garden (see p46) is transformed into an Easter Garden. Flowers blossom from hidden vases, primrose and violet plants and charming little 'weeds' (daisy, celandine, shepherd's

purse) nestle between the mosses. Tiny creatures emerge from their Lenten 'hibernation': hens and their chicks, rabbit families and lambs, even tortoises (see p136) can be seen making their way along the path and over the bridge. Butterflies hover over the pond. The grotto is empty but for the small piece of silk, and above, hanging in the Easter Tree is a special butterfly, quite different from all the rest. The Easter Tree is a graceful birch or hazel branch, just breaking into leaf; on it hangs a shower of coloured eggs. The Easter Hare loiters discreetly beneath the tree with a tiny basket of sugar eggs, and here and there in the moss the glint of coloured foil suggests another egg-hunt in the offing!

The wheat grains have sprouted with clear green blades, and the morning light catches an almost transparent fringe of new grass over the patch of bare earth. Carrot tops beneath the moss have sprouted little plumes and the whole Garden is refreshed with a fine spray of 'dew.' A golden-yellow candle stands at the grotto, and its joyful flame reflects in the golden disc of the sun, (hanging from the Tree), that is now rising above and behind the grotto.

Easter candles

These egg shaped candles set in a moss-lined saucer will add a nice touch to your Easter breakfast table.

You will need:
1 blown egg (see p67)
A little oil and a small paint brush
8cm candle wick in narrow size
Some plasticine
Melted candlewax (see p246) enough to fill
   an egg shell
Metal skewer
Egg box

Enlarge the hole at the round end of the egg by chipping the edges with a skewer, or snipping carefully with scissors. Oil inside

of the egg thoroughly, using a small paint brush. Add colouring to the hot wax if required. Dip the wick once in the wax and pull straight. When cold, thread the wick through both holes in the egg. Seal the small hole around the slightly protruding wick with a little plasticine. Stand egg in the egg box (large hole on top). Fill egg shell with melted wax, holding the wick in the middle. Keep wick in place with two matches while wax is cooling. If a well has appeared around the wick, break the surface skin of the wax with the skewer and top up with more hot wax. Repeat topping-up process if needed as the cooling wax shrinks.

Leave candle to set overnight, then crack the egg shell and remove it. The place where the wax was poured in will become the base of the candle, so trim the wick and level the wax to ensure that the candle stands upright.

The egg can be decorated by glueing on small pressed flowers, applying flowers in modelling wax, or painting on a motif with melted wax crayon. (See p143.)

Hare

Sew bottom edges together, drawing them in slightly.

 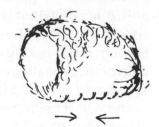

Stuff body with fleece and sew up the open end, again drawing edges together. (One can place a pebble inside the fleece to weigh down the Hare.)

To indicate the Hare's front legs, model them with a few stitches.

You will need:
Approx. 25g brown or grey mohair wool
3mm (2US) knitting needles
Fleece for stuffing
Tuft of white fleece for hare's tail
Length of black embroidery cotton
Pebble — optional

The Hare is worked in garter stitch.
Body: Cast on 20 sts. and knit a square.
        Cast off.
Head: Cast on 10 sts. and k. 20 rows.
        Cast off.
Ears: Cast on 6 sts. k. 1 row.
        2nd row: k. 5 sts. Turn.
        3rd row: k. 5 sts.
        4th row: cast off all 6 sts.
        Repeat for other ear.

Run a gathering thread along one edge of the body-piece and draw together.

Fold head piece in half (the knitting rows run horizontally) and sew long sides together. Run a thread through the edges at each end.

Draw one end together, stuff the head and draw in the other end.

Sew the head to the body in the appropriate place. Sew ears to the head. With embroidery cotton, make a couple of stitches on each side of the head to mark the eyes.

For the Hare's tail, take the white fleece and make a knot in it. Shape it into a neat little ball and sew it to the Hare's rear end.

Cockerel, hen and chick

Chick

You will need:
3mm (2US) knitting needles
Small amount of yellow double knitting
   wool or mohair (for a fluffy chick!)
Scrap of orange felt
Length of blue embroidery thread for eyes
Fleece or cotton wool for stuffing
One button 1.5cm diam. for foot

Cast on 3 sts. with the yellow wool and work in garter stitch. Knit 1 row. On next and every alternate row increase one st. at each end. When you have 17 sts. on your needle, knit one row. On next and every alternate row decrease 1 st. at each end until only 3 sts. are left. Cast off. Fold square in half Y to X.

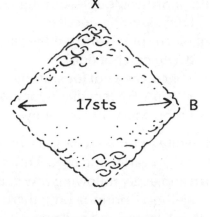

Sew up one open side of triangle X-Y-B and put in the filling. Sew up the other side of the triangle. Pull one top corner slightly inwards to make a more rounded shape which will form the head. With a few stitches around the neck, shape the head.

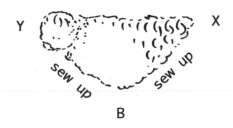

Cut the orange felt for the beak and sew beak to the head with small stitches.

beak

A stitch on each side of the head with the blue embroidery thread will mark the eyes. Sew on the button with hollow side facing downwards, to make the Chick stand.

Hen

You will need:
White or brown double knitting wool
3mm (2US) knitting needles
Small pieces of red and yellow felt
3mm (CUS) crochet hook
Fleece or cottonwool for stuffing
One button 1.5 - 2cm diam. for foot
Black embroidery thread for eyes

With white or brown wool cast on 22 sts. and work in garter stitch. K. 3 rows. In fourth and every following row k. the first 2 sts. together. Continue until there are 6 sts. left. Break thread and pull through the 6 sts. Fold this triangular piece in half and sew up one side.

Stuff triangle and sew up other side. Where the thread was pulled through 6 sts., pull slightly inwards to make a rounded shape which will form the head. From red felt cut the chicken's comb and wattle. Cut beak from yellow felt and sew everything into place.

Embroider the Hen's eyes with a stitch on each side of the head using black thread. For the tail use the same wool as for the body. Crochet four rings with 7 - 8 chain sts. each. For the wings cast on 6 sts. Knit one row. In the next row k. 4 sts. and turn. Knit back. Next row, k. 3 sts., turn and knit back. Next row, cast off over all 6 sts. Sew wings and tail to the Hen.

Sew on the button as for the Chick.

Cockerel

You will need:
White or brown double knitting wool
3mm (2US) knitting needles
Small pieces of red, yellow and green felt
Fleece or cottonwool for stuffing
One red button 1.5 - 2cm diam. for foot
Black embroidery thread for eyes

Knit and make up Cockerel exactly in the same way as described for Hen. The only differences are the tail and the posture. From the green, red and yellow felt cut some tail feathers and sew them into place.

To give the Cockerel a proud attitude, use some of the body-colour wool to model him, by pulling his head and tail upwards with a few internal gathering stitches.

Butterflies

Paper butterflies hanging from a branch or the ceiling will flutter in the slightest breeze. Fixed to a thin wire, they will appear to hover. What a surprise and delight when a new kind of butterfly appears on Easter Sunday, hovering over the Easter Garden (see p56) or resting on a branch of the Easter Tree!

The simplest butterfly is easily made by taking a rectangular piece of tissue paper and twisting it in the middle. The butterfly is then hung from a cotton thread.

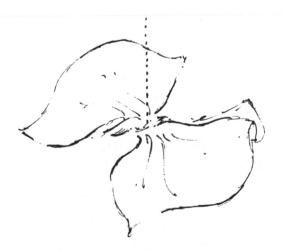

It is possible to use a pipe cleaner as a body. Two layers of shaped tissue paper make the butterfly more colourful.

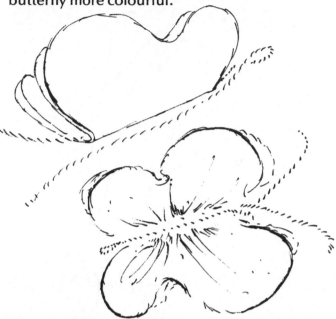

The following three examples of butterflies are a little more complicated to make:

Cut-out butterfly

You will need:
Coloured paper 8cm x 12cm (writing paper thickness)
Glue
Nail scissors and craft knife
Approx. 25 - 30cm of thin wire (florist's wire)

Fold the paper and draw a butterfly outline with antennae and patterns for wing decorations.

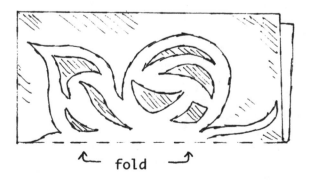

fold

Experiment with your own design or trace one of the examples below:

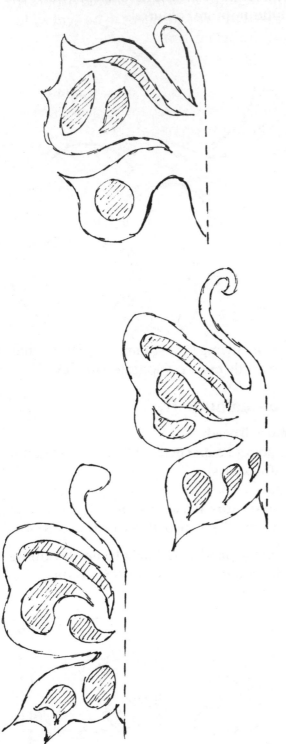

Cut the butterfly out. First cut away shaded-in areas on the wings with a craft knife and then cut outer butterfly shape with nail scissors. Measure length needed for the butterfly from the tail-end to the head, and cut out a triangular piece of the paper for the body as below:

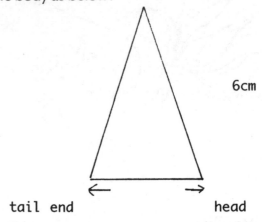

6cm

tail end   head

Roll the body piece tightly, starting from broad end of the triangle. Secure end with glue. Open up butterfly and glue the body to the inside of the fold.

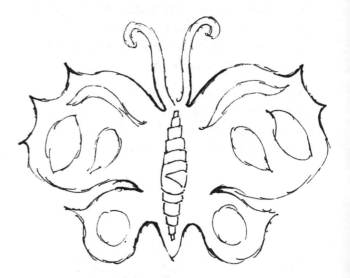

Push the wire carefully through the body and bend it over at the tip to hold it in place.

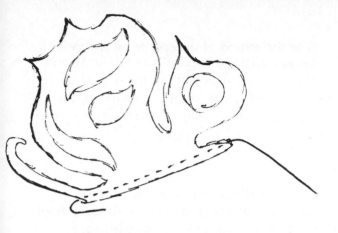

Make a body as described above for Cut-Out Butterfly from the coloured paper. The base of the triangle needs to be 4cm wide and the height 8cm.

Bunch the tissue paper shape together in the middle and glue body in place. Spread out the wings evenly.

Tissue paper butterfly

You will need:

Tissue paper 10cm x 12cm (writing paper thickness)
Paper in a matching colour 4cm x 8cm
Glue
2 stamens — available in craft shops for making artificial flowers
Needle and thread

Cut out butterfly shape from the tissue paper using the pattern below.

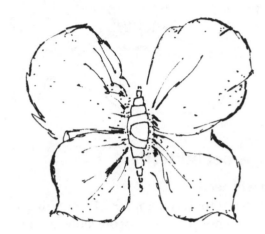

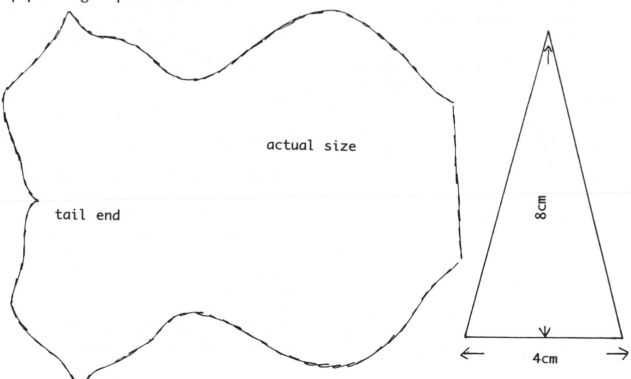

actual size

tail end

8cm

4cm

Insert stamens into the front of the body for antennae. Bend the body into a slight curve to make it more graceful. To hang the butterfly, push a threaded needle through the body.

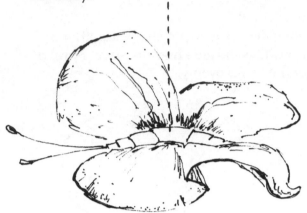

Dress-net butterfly

You will need:

Dress-net material approx. 10cm x 10cm
Twist of sheep's wool, preferably dyed in a
    colour matching the dress-net
Sewing thread in matching colour
Wax candle

Cut out a butterfly shape, as below, from the dress-net and sew a gathering thread along the middle.

Fold the strand of sheep's wool and twist it as seen below:

Draw the dress-net together with the gathering thread and sew the sheep's wool body underneath the wings with a few stitches. Use the end of the thread for hanging the butterfly. Rub ends of sheep's wool twist across a lump of beeswax, or on the side of a candle, to stiffen the antennae. Curve the antennae outwards.

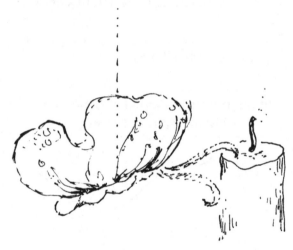

Easter eggs

How does an egg become an Easter Egg? Because we 'wrap it up in joy' — we decorate it! There are many ways to help the Easter Hare with decorating eggs. We shall just describe a few. When choosing the eggs, try to find the palest available. Some free-range chickens still lay the old-fashioned white ones, but not many. Duck eggs are larger but very suitable for decorating. The hunt starts here!

The traditional eggs are hardboiled. After boiling they can be dyed in egg dye or food dye to which a dash of vinegar is added. After the eggs are dyed, let them dry thoroughly and then rub with a drop of oil to make them shiny.

Onion skin dye

3 variations on the same basic theme:

You will need:
Pale uncooked eggs
Onion skins
Small flowers, leaves or grasses
Small piece of white cartridge paper
Scissors
Fine cotton thread
Vinegar
An old nylon stocking

Method (a):
Wrap egg with onion skins, laying smaller pieces on the egg first and finishing off with larger ones. Tie the skins in place with thin thread and then put the 'parcel' inside a piece of nylon stocking. Tie stocking at both ends with thread or kitchen tie-twists, so that the onion skins are firmly pressed against the egg.

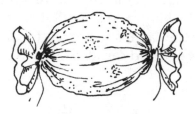

Fill a medium-sized saucepan (enamelled saucepans might turn brown!) with enough water to cover the eggs. Add the wrapped eggs and a dash of vinegar and boil for 10 mins.

Remove eggs from the saucepan and cool under running water. Unwrap the eggs and discover the delicate patterns which are printed on them. Polish eggs with a little oil.

Method (b):
From the cartridge paper cut out an Easter Hare to fit on an egg.

Wet the Hare and lay it on the egg. Now follow the same process as described above for Method (a), covering the Hare with onion skins.

When you unwrap the egg you will find the Hare hiding in a dappled landscape!

Method (c):

Cut out a Hare or Chick from the cartridge paper as in Method (b). Take some small flowers, grasses or beautifully formed tiny leaves, and wet these. Wet the Hare or Chick, lay it on the egg, and surround it with flowers or leaves tying them in place with thin thread. Put the egg carefully into the nylon stocking, add a handful of onion skins to the water and proceed as in Method (a). This method can also be used on blown eggs.

Batik eggs

In Eastern Europe the batik method of decoration is often used for both blown and hard-boiled eggs. Use very simple decorative motifs on hard-boiled eggs; after all, they have a very short life! For the more complex batik eggs you will need a proper batik tool (pychanki) obtainable from craft shops. Instructions for these are included with the tool.

You will need:
Very fine artist's brush (not your best one, you will not be able to get it clean again!)
Or — Pencil and a pin with a coloured plastic head
Or — 'Pychanki' (very fine batik tool)
Eggs
Small quantity melted wax (see p246)
Candle flame
Red egg dye (or food dye) in a small glass bowl
Paper towel
Lots of newspaper to cover work surface

If you choose to work with the 'pinhead tool,' stick the pin into the end of the pencil.

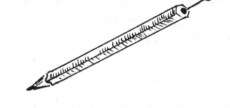

Dip the pinhead into the melted wax and draw a dot, or drop shape, on the egg. The pinhead has to be dipped into the wax for each dot or other shape.

If you prefer to work with the batik tool or brush, draw or paint an Easter motif on the egg with the hot wax.

When the picture or pattern has cooled, the egg is dyed in the red dye. Turn the egg so that the dye is taken up evenly. Allow egg to dry. Hold the egg next to a candle flame — not *above* it, or *in* it, otherwise it will turn black with soot. Let the wax melt off. As soon as the wax starts to run, wipe it off with the paper towel. Continue until all the wax is melted away. This process gives the egg a warm, glowing polish.

Scratched eggs

This method is not so easy, but older children manage it with some care and patience. If the egg is boiled for half an hour, and there is no crack in the shell, it will last (as decoration!) for many years.

You will need:
Pale hard-boiled eggs
Food colouring or batik dye — dark colours only
Sharp knife or nail — a dentist's drill-bit is ideal (ask your dentist for old ones) held in a large-headed clutch pen available from art shops
Black pencil and rubber band

Dye the eggs and dry them. Draw a pattern on the shell in pencil. While scratching through the design, hold the egg in the palm of the hand to prevent it from cracking.

Using the sharp point of the tool you have chosen, gently scratch away the pencil drawing to reveal the white underneath. The traditional design divides the egg in halves horizontally. If you do not have a steady hand, use a rubber band to guide you. (Put the rubber band around the egg where you want the line to be.) Mark this line with a pencil and scratch it away with the tool. Then divide the egg vertically. Repeat this vertical division at right angles to the first vertical line.

Now you have eight parts. To finish the basic structure of this design, make a triangle in each part and fill these triangles with pictures or patterns, using your own imagination.

When this is done, polish the egg with furniture wax or transparent shoe polish.

Pace-egging

With a hard boiled egg, you can go 'Pace-egging!' On Easter Sunday or Monday, take your egg to the top of the nearest hill and roll it down. Only when the egg cracks are you allowed to stop and eat it. If you cannot get to a hill, sit on the floor, or the grass, with a partner and roll the eggs between you.

Pace-egging is a very ancient custom, (the word comes from 'Paschal,' and derives from the Hebrew word for Passover). In Christian times it reminds us of the moment when the stone rolled away from the tomb on the first Easter Day.

How to blow an egg

Pierce the egg at the top and bottom with a sharp needle or a metal meat skewer. Make the top hole slightly larger. Break the yolk inside with the needle. Hold the egg over a bowl and blow into the smaller hole until all the egg content has run out into the bowl. (Use up the eggs promptly in an omelette, or cake, etc.) Wash the shell well in soap and water with a dash of vinegar added. To avoid smelly shells, direct a jet of water into the shell. Shake well and blow all the liquid out.

How to hang an egg

You will need:
Matches
Thread
Blown and decorated eggs

Break off the head of the match to reduce the length of the matchstick to about half its original size. Tie the thread firmly around the middle of the matchstick. Push the match into the egg and pull it gently back. Make a loop at the other end of the thread to suspend the egg.

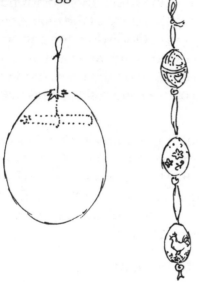

Another way to hang one or more eggs at the same time, is to suspend them with a ribbon. Thread a length of ribbon through a large darning needle and pull it through the egg. Make a knot at the bottom end and let the egg rest on it. You can hang an egg from the other end of the ribbon in the same way.

Crêpe and tissue paper decorations

Some of these techniques are especially useful when working with very young children or large numbers of children, e.g. in a playgroup.

You will need:
Blown eggs
Small pieces of different coloured crêpe or tissue paper
The same number of small bowls as you have colours
Vinegar
Egg box
Overalls and newspaper

The paper can release a very strong dye when it is moistened. Protect the work surface with newspaper, and wear rubber gloves if necessary. Half fill each bowl with water and a dash of vinegar. Dip the pieces of paper into water and lay them on the egg. (Use each bowl for only one colour of paper.) Wrap up the whole egg with these wet paper bits. Leave egg to dry in the egg box. When dry, peel off the paper.

The secret with this method is to keep to a few related colours per egg. For instance, use yellow, orange and red, or green, blue and yellow.

An even simpler way to work with tissue paper is the 'dabbing method.' Crumple a small piece of tissue paper and dampen it on a wet rag. Dab the egg with the damp paper. This creates a very delicately dappled egg.

You will find that some colours and types of paper release their dye much better than others. Have fun experimenting!

Batik eggs for children

This is a very straightforward way of using the batik technique on eggs. Children from 6 - 7 years can use this method — well supervised of course, as there is a lighted candle involved.

You will need:
Blown eggs
Candle
Egg dye or food colouring in three different but harmonizing colours
Paper towel
Thin knitting needle, and Blu-tack or plasticine

Run the knitting needle through the holes in the blown egg and use Blu-tack to hold egg in place. Light the candle and let a few drops of wax fall on the egg, either to form dots or, by turning the egg, allowing the wax to run in streaks. Let the wax dry and dye the egg in a light colour (e.g. yellow). Drop more wax on the egg (now on the yellow ground). Dye the egg again, in a slightly darker tone (e.g. red). Repeat the wax dripping process once more and then dye the egg in the darkest tone (e.g. violet). Let the dye dry. Now hold the egg next to the candle flame — not *in* it or *above* it, otherwise it will turn black with soot. As the wax melts, quickly wipe it off with the paper towel. Repeat this until all wax is removed.

Painted eggs

You will need:
Blown eggs
Newspaper
Watercolour and fine brushes
Water
Varnish (can be clear nail varnish)
Brush and brush cleaner for varnishing

It is difficult to hold an egg while painting it! To make this easier, put the egg on a fine knitting needle, holding it in place with Blu-tack or plasticine. Simply colour the egg thickly and freely with the paint. Use blue and green carefully as they tend to muddy the final effect. When dry, varnish the egg.

If you wish, dye the egg first in very pale yellow and paint your design on top.

Eggs can be decorated very effectively with wax crayons, felt-tip pens or the kind of coloured pencil which can be dipped in water. Modelling wax, used very thinly on the egg, also gives good results.

To present a decorated egg as a very personal gift, you could set it in its own little moss garden laid out in a basket.

More things to do with eggs

For a special Easter gift, create a miniature garden inside an egg or make a 'Surprise-Egg-Box.' Patience is needed, and we seldom make these while toddlers are playing around us! Nevertheless, these egg gifts are much easier to make than one would think.

Miniature garden in an egg

You will need:
One egg (duck or goose eggs are especially suitable because of their size)
Darning needle
Sharp craft knife or razor blade
Small piece (10cm x 10cm) of pastel coloured silk cloth or tissue paper
Glue and pencil

Moss and small silk or paper flowers
Modelling wax and 15cm of narrow ribbon
— optional

Pierce the narrow end of the egg with a needle. Draw an oval shape, in pencil, on the egg to mark the 'window.'

With the knife or razor blade scratch gently but persistently along the pencil line, holding the egg in the palm of the hand. It takes about ten minutes of unhurried scratching for the shell to be penetrated and the window lifted out. Empty the egg content into a bowl and wash the shell in soapy water. If you wish, colour the shell delicately with tissue paper using the 'dabbing' method described on page 68.

Push a needle and thread through the hole in the top of the egg for hanging, securing the end of the thread inside the egg with a knot or small bead and a dab of glue. The egg does not have to be lined but it certainly looks pretty if it is. For a lining, manoeuvre the silk or tissue paper into the egg. The material does not need to lie flat but will crumple and fold. Secure the lining around the outside edge of the opening to form a frame for the window.

If you choose not to line the egg, the edge can be neatened by a delicate frame of modelling wax, or tissue paper glued on. Alternatively, glue some narrow ribbon all the way around the outside surface of the opening.

Create your own small world inside the egg with some moss, flowers, or a tiny chick or Easter Hare made from modelling wax. If there is no lining, a sky landscape with sun and clouds can be created with very thinly applied modelling wax.

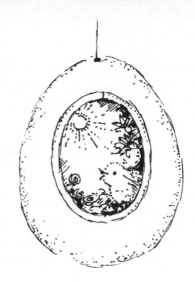

Surprise-egg-box

You will need:
One large egg (Goose eggs are the best for this project)
Sharp craft knife or razor blade
Approx. 30cm of narrow ribbon
Piece of pastel coloured silk cloth or tissue paper (approx. 10cm x 20cm)
Glue

With a pencil draw a line dividing the egg in half lengthwise (if necessary, use a rubber band stretched around the egg to guide the line). With the knife or razor blade cut the egg in two, in the way described above for Miniature-Egg-Garden. Empty the contents into a bowl and wash both halves of the shell in soapy water.

To make hinges, cut a small piece of silk or other thin cloth (approx. 1cm x 2.5cm) and glue it from one half shell to the other, bringing the edges of the shells together.

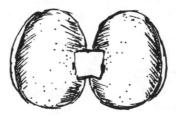

Line each half with silk cloth or tissue paper as described above for Miniature-Egg-Garden. Neaten edges with ribbon as described above.

The egg-box is now ready to be filled. Moss, felt or paper flowers, a little Easter chick, a tiny egg or other gift will bring delight on Easter morning. Close the lid and tie with matching ribbon. The traditional Easter colours are red, yellow and green, and combinations of these always look festive.

Settle the egg-box on a small bed of moss or muslin remnant.

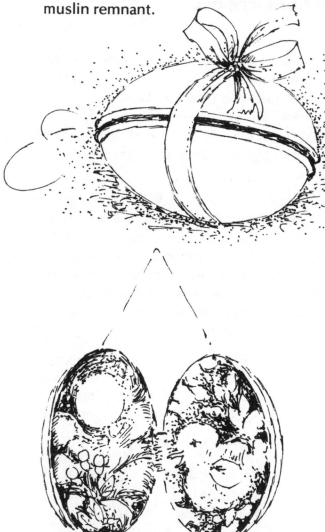

Egg with seeds

This is a wonderful Easter gift for children, as they can crack the egg and sow the seeds. It is best to choose seeds which germinate and grow easily so that the child can follow the whole process day by day. Calendula (marigold), sunflower or nasturtium seeds are very suitable.

You will need:
Egg
Flower seeds
Small amount of wax or plasticine
Egg decorating materials of your choice

Blow the egg as described on page 67. Make the hole at one end large enough to allow the seeds to be put inside the egg. Decorate the egg using any of the methods described above. Neatly block the smaller opening in the egg with wax or plasticine. Pop the seeds into the egg and close off the second opening.

Pop-up Easter egg card

Cards with moving parts fascinate children. The movement brings magic, and what can be more magical than the Easter Hare popping up in front of one's own eyes?

You will need:
White card — not too thick or glossy (a good quality watercolour paper is ideal) approx. 40cm x 10cm
HB pencil and pair of compasses
Watercolours, fine brush, jar of water
Craft knife or scissors
Glue
Cartridge paper — optional

Draw a large egg on the card, about 12cm high. The plumper the shape, the better. This is side A — the front. Repeat to make side B — the back.

Use the compasses to draw a circle of 4.5cm diam. on A and B, 1cm from the top. Draw insert C as seen in the diagram.
It has a slightly larger circle, 5.5cm diam., and tab 6.5 x 1.5cm.

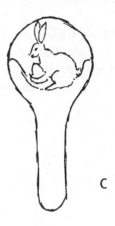

C

Cut out eggs A and B, and tab C. Cut out window D on egg A.

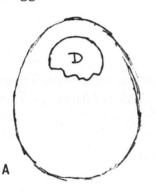

A

Cut background E away from the Hare on the tab.

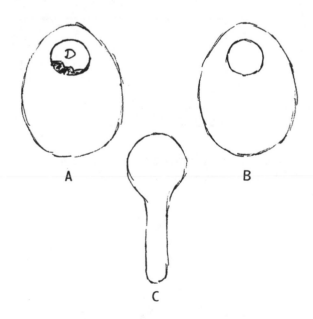

A

B

C

Draw an Easter Hare on the tabbed circle.

Colour the various parts. Yellow and pale green are colours which capture the spring mood, so try these as a background colour for frame A. Colour the Easter Hare in soft brown and paint a simple landscape (or sunrise perhaps) inside the circle on B. Assemble the parts when dry. Insert C between A and B. Glue along the dotted line.

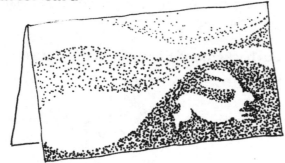

B

Gently pulling and pushing the tab will make the Easter Hare pop up and surprise us all!

Easter card

The technique used for this card is 'spattering' water colour over stencils.

You will need:
Firm white cartridge paper for the card and stencils
Craft knife, ruler, scissors, pencil
Cutting surface
Blu-tack
Watercolour paint: lemon yellow and prussian blue, preferably in blocks

Jar of water
Old toothbrush
Old kitchen knife
Newspaper
Hairdryer — optional

Measure out and cut the card, making sure that it fits your supply of envelopes. Fold the card in half — see above.

Cut out three wavy shapes, A, B and C, from a separate piece of cartridge paper, similar to the ones shown below. The overall size of these forms should be slightly larger than the card.

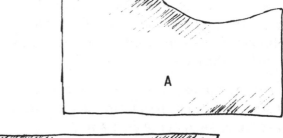

A

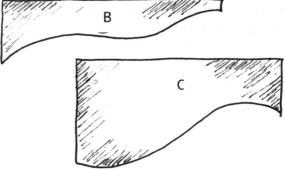

B

C

Using another piece of cartridge paper, draw and cut out a hare.

74

Cover the work surface with newspaper. Wet the toothbrush and dip it into the paint. It is important to mix the paint with the right amount of water. Too much water will produce unsightly splodges, and too little will not give the fine spray you need. Practise the technique on a piece of newspaper:

Hold the toothbrush with the bristles pointing down. Scrape the knife lightly across the bristle ends, directing your aim at one area of the newspaper. The finer (dryer) the spray the better. Be careful of drips.

Place a wavy stencil form, such as A above, on the folded card, leaving the top part X^1 of the card exposed. Now spray the card yellow.

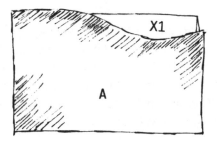

Leave to dry, or dry with a hairdryer. Move A further down, turn it slightly and cover the top of the card with B. (Either leave some of the card unsprayed between the top yellow X^1 and the next area to be sprayed, X^2, or overlap the layers.)

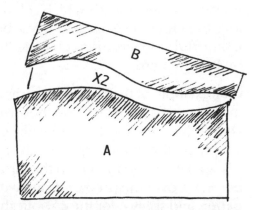

Make a pale green colour by mixing *very* little blue with some yellow, and spray X^2. Dry it, and remove A and B. Place the hare in the bottom section of the card. Fix it in place with Blu-tack. Cover the area above the hare with C.

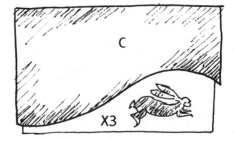

To keep the darkest tones to the bottom of the picture, spray X^3 with a darker blue-green (add more blue to the light green colour). When dry, your card is finished.

You will find that paint will be everywhere on the work surface, and, if you make more cards, you will also find that the stencils start to curl. Don't be put off! Just pin them down with Blu-tack. Place clean newspaper on the work surface for each new card.

Once you have mastered this technique, why not experiment and design your own cards, also for other occasions? As the success of this kind of card depends largely on the mixture of colours you are using, it is worth thinking ahead: which colour mixtures for which occasion? Maybe A Colourful Conversation, on page 19 could be helpful here.

Our example of the hare above was of a 'negative' shape. To achieve 'positive' shapes (i.e. shapes filled out with colour), simply cut the shape required out of a piece of paper which is larger than the card (see D below). Cover the prepared card with this paper, and spray over the cut-out shape. The design D will stand out in colour.

Simple Easter egg cut-outs

You will need:
Small pieces (approx. 6cm x 8cm) of thin card or strong paper in yellow, red or green for the egg shape
Scraps of brown and yellow paper
Thread in matching colours

Draw (or trace) the outlines of the egg shape A on the card and cut it out.

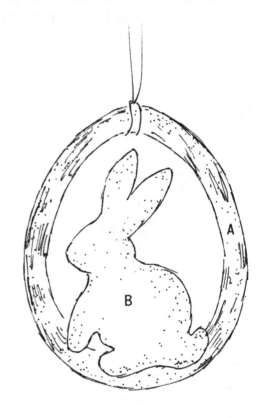

Cut out the little hare B from the brown paper and glue into the egg-shaped frame. Cut out another egg-shaped frame. (This one looks best when made from green card.) Use some yellow paper and follow the diagram below for making the flower. Cut two (C and D). Glue D to C.

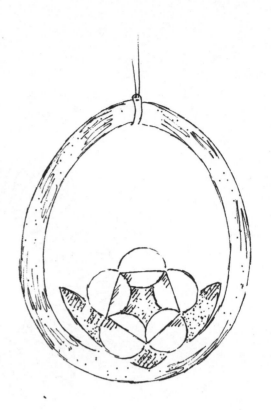

Glue flower into frame as illustrated. Add a couple of leaves made from green card. Thread a length of sewing cotton into the centre top of the egg shape for hanging the decoration.

SUMMER

"...I knew when Summer breathed —
Not by the flowers that wreathed
   The sedge by the water's edge,
      Or gold
      Of the wold,
   Or white and rose of the hedge;
But because, in a wooden box
In the window at Mrs Mock's,
There were white-winged shuttlecocks..."

From "The Calendar"
by Barbara Euphan Todd.

Summer

Past now are the morning frosts, past also is the watery lush growth of spring: summer is here. We have moved from the crystal coldness of the Earth element through the limpid freshness of the Water element, and now comes the moment when we fling our windows wide to enjoy the summer air and open our arms to the fire of the sun that fills it. Under clear skies a tapestry is already being worked — shafts of light are wrought with shadow, insects meander between threads of floating gossamer, and breezes ravel the scents of flowers and leaves. We walk the countryside and become part of this complex embroidery. Bird song and earth smell, the glitter of a dragonfly's wing, the sweetness of honeysuckle and the softness of rose petals — all are woven within us through the eager activity of our five senses. Nature celebrates a Festival of Joy.

The urge to unite ourselves with this colourful weft is strong. We cast aside the confinement of our houses, our shoes and our clothes, to lie close to the warm earth and give ourselves up to day-dreaming in the heat of the sun. Nowadays this urge is often explained by saying that we need to 'unwind' or 'wind down.' To do this we may take 'time off' or 'time out' to go on holiday, to leave behind the workaday routines and create a different space for ourselves over the hills and far away. Nevertheless, however enjoyable the holiday may be, there usually comes a moment when thoughts are drawn back to the workplace we have left, and we find ourselves planning new business initiatives or resolving to clear out the bathroom cupboard. It appears that within that 'time out,' that 'different space,' we have re-found the thread of our life, we have begun to collect ourselves, maybe even become more in touch with who we are, and what adjustments, improvements or sacrifices we must make to become more effective in the world. We are, in fact, ready to 'wind up' again and re-enter the rhythm of daily life.

The sign of the Crab (ruling that part of the heavens which the sun enters at midsummer in the northern hemisphere) is formed of two spirals, winding inwards and outwards. These spirals are not connected — to move from one to the other entails stepping into space. The summer may entice us away from responsibility, tempting us to float with the thistledown through the warm days, but we are also given the chance to find a creative space within which we can take hold of our lives in a new way.

The festivals in summer

See page 24.

April 23	St George's Day
May 1	May Day
	Rogationtide
	Ascension Day
	Whitsun (Pentecost)
June 21	Summer Solstice
June 24	St John's Day (Midsummer's Day)
July 15	St Swithun's Day

The seasonal table in summer

The Festival of Easter spans the forty days until Ascension Day. Therefore the Easter Garden, created out of the exuberance of the spring resurrection, can become for us a pathway into summer. If the moss is kept moist the garden will stay a fresh and renewing source of interest. Little weeds appear unexpectedly; they flower, and even set seed. The grass grows long and lush; it can be cut with scissors and made into hay for an Easter chicken's nest. A beautiful spider's web or worm cast may appear one morning and be greeted with delight by the children. Of course, flowers will have to be renewed, and some of the carrot tops too. The Easter Tree (if kept in water) will sprout its pretty leaves, but it, too, may need to be replaced when it starts to droop. There can only be one *real* Easter Tree, so replace it with a jug of branches and flowers. Keep a few of the decorated eggs to hang among the branches and add some more butterflies. By now, the Easter Hare has discreetly departed and the piece of silk in the grotto has also gone. The golden disc of the rising sun could be replaced by a veil of warm yellow 'sunshine' as a backdrop to the garden. Hang it in a rising curve above the garden rather than in a straight line.

May Day is usually celebrated before Ascension, and the Garden could also incorporate this. Pink and blue veils are added to the background; pink, blue and mauve flowers fill the vases. A little Maypole, set up on a mossy bank, completes the scene for the day.

With the approach of Ascensiontide, a different mood descends on the Garden. The flowers decrease in number; the animals gather their families and set off down the path to unseen summer pastures; one by one the eggs disappear from the tree. On Ascension Day, the Easter Garden is no more — only a posy of wild flowers adorns the table. However, if, like the disciples, our gaze is lifted up on that day, we shall see the butterflies from the Garden fluttering high up beneath the ceiling.

A day or two before Pentecost (Whitsun) the butterflies will have flown away, allowing us a quiet space in which to wait for this important Festival. When Whitsun (White-Sunday) arrives, the table is covered with a white cloth or muslin veil. On it stands a simple white candle and above it flutters a white paper dove. Nothing could be better for this day than a vase of daisy-like flowers. The circle of individual white petals, joined as they are by a sun-gold space which bears the future seed, tells the Whitsun story in one picture!

Summer sets her own festival table out of doors. We cannot hope to capture within four walls those special delights of high summer — the mingled scents, the mixed hum of insect life, the penetrating warmth and entrancing light of the sun on its high throne. However, June may also bring some grey days and then a Summer Table will brighten up the mood. Summertime celebrates the element of Air, and the light, the colours and the sounds that are carried by it. The strong light of outdoors will dance rainbow-coloured through the room if cut glass pendants are hung at the window and the best crystal bowls and vases put out on the Table. Wind chimes tinkling in the draught, the reflection from a jug of water dappling the ceiling — these are among the momentary joys of summer which should not be missed.

The Seasonal Table can also become the focus for the children's outdoor activities. Shells and seaweed appear after a day's outing. Pebbles under water reveal startling colours, daisy chains float in a bowl, rose petals are spread out to dry. In the centre is a beeswax candle and above, circling in the air, a gold spiral hangs glinting, coiling and uncoiling: is it winding up… or winding down?

St George's Day

As we live in England we must mark St George's Day, for he was declared Protector of England during the reign of Edward III...

St George is venerated as much for his legendary personality as for his historical one. He was born in Lydda in Palestine of noble Christian Cappadocian parents, and rose to high rank in the Roman Imperial Guard. When the Emperor Diocletian published an edict of persecution against all Christians, George resolved to confess his faith openly and plead the cause of his fellow Christians. He returned to Lydda, freed his slaves, sold his property and gave his money to the poor. Then he set off to meet the Emperor. On the way, so the legend goes, he saved a king's daughter from being sacrificed to a dragon who was terrorising the land. He subdued the dragon, the princess tied her girdle around the beast's neck and it followed her meekly into the city. There George promised to slay the dragon once the king and all his people had been baptized as Christians. That accomplished, he continued on his mission to the Emperor. His appeal was in vain, and his courageous confession to Christianity resulted in his being tortured and subsequently beheaded on April 23rd 303 A.D.

In the circle of the year, the Day of St George and the Feast of St Michael and All Angels (September 29th) stand opposite one another. In many ways we can see how George's reputation as a courageous knight and champion of the oppressed, steadfast in truth, holds up an earthly mirror to the warrior Archangel who fought the great dragon in heaven (Revelations 12).

The qualities of beauty, virtue and noble love, associate St George with the emblem of the rose, England's national flower. However, his appeal is not confined to national or religious boundaries. He has been revered by Eastern and Western Christendom alike, and also by the Moslem faith which connects him with the prophet Elijah. So if, on this day, we place a rose on the table in honour of St George, we may be reminded of his story and encouraged to broaden our love of nation into a respect for nobility of character, wherever in the world we happen to meet it.

> "To save a maid St George the Dragon slew
> A pretty tale, if all is told be true
> Most say there are no dragons, and 'tis said
> There was no George: pray God there was a maid..."   Anon.

Teenagers, or adults even, may enjoy a party on this day to celebrate 'Englishness' and share music, songs and poetry on this theme. Bearing in mind the renowned capacity of the English to laugh at themselves, this may not be an altogether serious occasion!

83

May Day

Folk traditions abound for May Day, and in Europe these usually involve flowers and often the coronation of a young girl with garlands to make her 'Queen of the May.' Such customs can be traced back to a Roman festival held at the end of April, in honour of Flora, the Goddess of Flowers and Bride of the West Wind. Incidentally, 'may' is the country name for the hawthorn flower which, before the calendar changed in 1752, was easily found on May Day. It is most likely that the old song "Here we come gathering nuts in May" was originally "Here we come gathering knots of may" — a 'knot' being a small posy.

The second division of the old Celtic year fell on May 1st and indicated the beginning of summer. The leaping flames of the Celtic Beltane fire festivals, that once marked the threshold between Walpurgis Night and May Day, have now largely disappeared. In more and more places in England today the dawn of May Day is greeted by the leaps of Morris Men. These boisterous folk-dancers trace their name back to the 13th century Spanish 'Moresco' dancers (who blackened their faces and so looked like Moors), but their origin goes back much further. They assist the great fire of the sun rise into summer, with a hearty stamping of feet, jingling of bells and waving of large handkerchiefs.

To dance in the open air is a natural expression of the freedom and exuberance of summer, and has, no doubt, perpetuated the rural tradition of Maypole dancing. Originally, the Maypole was simply a tree (sometimes up to sixty feet high) cut and stripped of all its branches, except for a few sprouting at the top to symbolise new life. It was decorated and set up in an open space, often next to the village church. The English have taken up a custom, originally from Southern Europe, of attaching ribbons to the pole. These are carried by the dancers who move in such a way that the ribbons are plaited in a variety of patterns. The dance is then reversed to allow the decorative plait to unwind itself.

To the rhythm of lively music, the Maypole dance works its magic, translating the invisible weaving of colour and light in the streaming summer air into a moment of restrained clarity. Here the pattern of things, the creative intention of the dance, is briefly revealed before dissolving again into the flowing energy of life.

English gardeners know this moment well when, at the beginning of May, the plants are crisp in their new growth, the patterns of leaf structure are well defined and give a characteristic gesture to each plant. Later, the texture of the garden loosens as the process of flowering and fruiting unfolds, until the form is lost completely in the inevitable cycle of renewal.

May Day brings promise: to the farmer, the promise of kind weather; to the girl who washes her face in the May Day dew, the promise of a fine complexion; to the young people weaving the pattern of creation around the Maypole, the eternal promise of the future.

> "The moon shines bright and stars give light,
> A little before it's day
> So God bless you all both great and small
> And send you a joyful May."

Variant of the "Bellman's Song" a traditional English May Carol.

In most years, May 1st falls between Easter and Ascension. In the forty days after Easter, the teaching of the Risen Christ gave the disciples glimpses of the Divine Pattern woven by the events of Holy Week. By Ascension, these glimpses were only a memory, but the promise to His followers remained as their consolation — the promise, "Lo, I am with you always, even unto the end of the world." (Matthew 28: 20.)

Maypole

The Maypole was often a work of art, decorated in most elaborate ways with flowers and branches. Here is a simple version for use in a family or playgroup.

You will need:

2m length of dowelling of at least 2.5cm diam. (broomstick thickness), or even a thin tree trunk

At least 4 ribbons in bright colours, each 2.5m long and about 3cm wide

Small tacks and a hammer

Base of a rotary washing line or sun umbrella — available at garden centres or hardware stores — optional

Attach the ribbons evenly around the top of the pole with tacks. The ribbons might have to overlap each other. Sink the pole firmly into the ground. Stones or bricks around the base will keep it steady. Alternatively, the base of a rotary washing line works quite well.

Each child or adult holds a ribbon and together they form a large circle around the Maypole. Now the dancing can begin. Young children (up to about the age of 7 or 8) will have enough fun simply skipping around, first in one direction and then in the other, keeping firm hold of their ribbon. Adults will find instructions for many traditional Maypole dances in specialized books.

Music can be sung or played on an instrument. A tambourine with some bells is a wonderful additional instrument, which an older child, (or grandparent sitting on a chair), could easily play, giving the dancers the beat of the music.

Tip:
To stop the ribbons from flying around and getting tangled while the Maypole is not in use, wind them around bricks which are placed at the base of the pole.

A simple Maypole Dance:
To be played on an instrument such as a recorder or violin.

Song for dancing around the Maypole:
The words can also accompany the traditional tune of "Here we go round the Mulberry Bush."

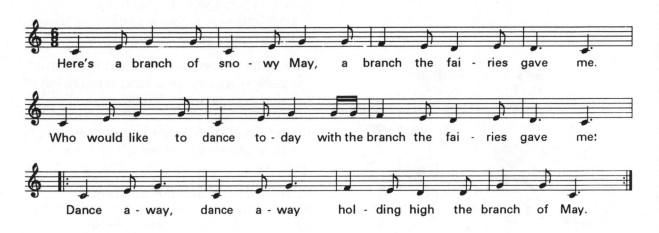

Here's a branch of sno - wy May, a branch the fai - ries gave me.

Who would like to dance to - day with the branch the fai - ries gave me:

Dance a - way, dance a - way hol - ding high the branch of May.

Arrange the flowers in a crown on top of the ribbons, and tie them on tightly by winding another ribbon around the stalks.

Small Maypole

This makes a pretty decoration for a special cake on May Day, or could take place of honour on the Seasonal Table.

You will need:
40cm lengths of narrow ribbon (about 0.5cm wide) in 6 different colours
1 extra length in any colour for tying the flowers
Wooden stick — a piece of dowelling or a knitting needle about 30cm long
Glue
Small paper or silk flowers

Glue the coloured ribbons evenly around one end of the wooden stick.

Ankle bells

Young children delight in skipping around with bells tied to their ankles. (A perfect outfit for Maypole dancing!)

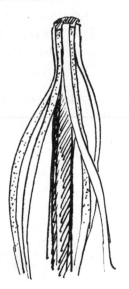

You will need:
70cm of cotton tape, 2cm wide
4 small bells

6 brightly coloured ribbons, each 25 cm long and approx. 1 cm wide
Thread

Cut the cotton tape in half and use a 35 cm length for each band. Tie each of the six coloured ribbons into a bow. Sew bells and ribbon-bows to the cotton tapes as seen below.

Mayday decoration

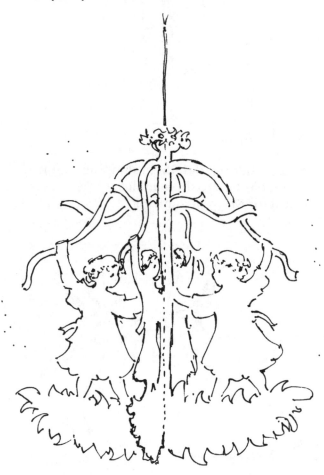

You will need:
Mayday pattern (see p257)
2 pieces of thin pink card each 24 cm x 24 cm

Matching pink thread
Strong paper or thin card (20 cm x 20 cm), light green
Strong paper or thin card (20 cm x 10 cm), yellow
Scraps of pink and yellow tissue paper
Glue
Craft knife and sharp nail scissors
Tracing paper (or any transparent paper)
Carbon paper — optional

Follow the general instructions for the Palm Sunday decoration on page 49.

Cut four 'ribbons' from yellow paper and four shorter 'ribbons' from green paper as indicated. Glue these paper ribbons in the appropriate places. Put a dab of glue on the child's hand to stick the yellow ribbon in place.

Cut out the garlands from the green paper using nail scissors. Glue one garland to each side of the child's head as shown on the pattern. Make the longest garland into a wreath by glueing the ends together. To make flowers for the wreaths, tear off little round pieces of tissue paper, about the size of a thumb nail and crumple them into tiny balls. Glue about three or four of these pink and yellow 'flowers' on the garland on each side of the child's head. Glue more 'flowers' on the little circular wreath.

Open up the Decoration. Rest the small wreath on top of the Maypole.

Rogationtide

The four days before 'Holy Thursday' (Ascension Day) were set aside by the early church as a time to ask (Latin 'rogare') for blessing on the growing crops. Rogationtide festivities often included a procession to 'beat the bounds.' This seems to have been a fusing of two old Roman festivals: Terminalia (in honour of Terminus, the god of boundaries), and Ambarvalia, a ritual beating of the ground with sticks to drive out the spirit of winter. In some parts of Britain, these days are known as 'Gang Days' from the Anglo-Saxon 'gang' meaning 'to go.' The people went about the parish calling down blessing on the crops as they passed. Often the young boys of the community would be caned with willow sticks at the parish boundaries, or even held upside down to have their heads bumped on the boundary stones. In the days before maps, it was probably an accurate belief that this unpleasant experience would imprint the memory of the parish boundaries on the up-and-coming generation!

Do you know your parish boundaries? Why not take a map and a picnic and get to know your locality on one of these days?

Dyeing fleece

In some parts of the country, a summer walk across the fields can mean pockets stuffed with sheep's wool gathered from the fences and hedges. But what do we do with it when we get home?

We offer some suggestions for washing and dyeing fleece using the simplest of methods. Consult a specialised book before dyeing large quantities for spinning and knitting.

Summer is a good time for experimenting with plant dyes, and surprising results can be obtained. No two batches of plant-dyed wool will ever be the same! The subtlety and lustre of plant colour and its aromatic fragrance cannot be matched by any chemical dye.

You will need:
Stainless steel or enamel container
Source of heat — either a cooker or open fire outdoors
Smooth wooden stirring stick
Roughly the same weight of fleece and onion skins
Muslin bag

The fleece must be thoroughly washed before being dyed. Wash it at least twice in warm soapy water and rinse afterwards until the water is quite clear. Fill the container with water. Tie the onion skins into the muslin bag and soak them overnight in the container. Add the washed fleece to the water and bring to the boil *very slowly* over a period of 45 mins. Simmer for another 45 mins. Remove dye bath from heat, take out the wool and allow to cool slowly. (For two shades of colour, remove only half the wool at this point and leave the rest cooling in the dye bath until the next day.) Before drying, gently squeeze out excess dye and rinse wool in tepid water.

You will find many uses for coloured fleece, from puppets' hair to gnomes' beards. When teased or 'carded' into a soft froth it makes a beautiful lining for a treasure box or Easter basket.

Ascension

Forty days after Easter, as described in Acts 1: 2-12, the Risen Christ was "taken up" into the heavens and "a cloud received Him out of (the disciples') sight." The story gives us the picture of the disciples as they "looked steadfastly toward heaven." On Easter morning Mary Magdalene found what she was seeking in a garden, where the Water element brings life to the Earth element. On Ascension Day the disciples' longing drew them to seek among the clouds where the Water and Air elements mingle, creating potent and ever-renewing forms charged with blessing for the earth.

> "Behold the Highest, parting hence away,
> Lightens the darke clouds, which hee treads upon
> …Bright Torch which shin'st, that I the way may see."
>
> From John Donne "Ascension."

Between the common ground of our daily life and the vaulted heights of our ideals, the longings of our heart swell like summer clouds. They may be shapeless and ill-defined at first, but if they take on form and substance they can begin to shine for us, become an inspiration, a 'castle in the air' that builds its own foundation on the earth. By freeing our thoughts into the mobile landscape of the clouds, we may find our own life-landscape refreshed and re-affirmed.

In some parts of Europe Ascension Day is a public holiday, but no longer in England. If it is possible to take an outing, try to leave the car behind and walk to a hilltop. Find a space there to day-dream awhile, to watch the mist rising, to see the showers fall, to feel one's mind and soul broadened by the boundless creative life of the far-ranging clouds.

At this time of the year, when the meadow flowers open their thousand blossoms to the sun, and the dandelion clocks give their little stars to the breeze, nature appears secure in the promise of the future. Whether the clouds overhead are black or white, we too can feel linked to the stream of blessings which unite heaven and earth.

The soft summer clouds lie beyond the grasp of little fingers, but a billowing, silken parachute is perhaps the next best thing…

Parachute games

If you are fortunate enough to obtain an old parachute from an army surplus store or a sky diving club, you have a wonderful opportunity for playing communal games with children aged five and upwards.

Use only the canopy of the parachute. Lay it open on the ground and let the circle of children grasp the parachute by its edge. When all their arms are lifted in unison, the parachute billows into a large dome. Once it is inflated, the children can walk beneath it towards the centre of the circle and back out again to their original places, holding the parachute all the time. Or, they can let go when the parachute is in the air and run into the centre to stand still while the parachute gently floats down to cover them.

In one popular game every third child in the circle is called 'Eagle,' or simply 'Number 3.' The other children are numbered '1' or '2' or called 'Lion' or 'Bull.' When the game-leader calls out "Eagles" or "Number 3s," all these children run into the middle as the other children lift their arms to inflate the parachute. The children in the centre lie on the ground facing upwards, heads together and feet pointing outwards like a star. The remaining children shake the parachute gently up and down for a short while creating a pleasant breeze. At a call everyone returns to their places and the next group take their turn running in.

Another very exciting game is to put a light ball on top of the parachute which is lifted waist-high by everyone. The aim of this game is to keep the ball rolling on top of the parachute for as long as possible, without it rolling off the edge or through the central hole.

Once they start playing parachute games children become very enthusiastic and discover that many more games can be invented...

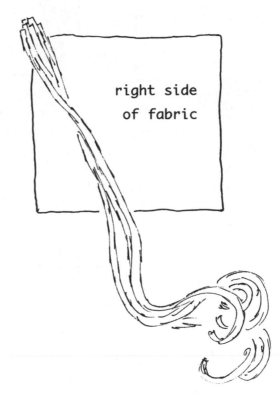

right side of fabric

Toys for summer air

Wide open spaces are best for these four toys which all make lively noises. The Streamers on sticks can also be used in a very small garden.

Flying streamer bag

You will need:
2 scraps of cotton material in a bold colour
    each 10cm x 10cm
Rice, lentils or small beans
Piece of string approx. 45cm long
6 brightly coloured strips of crêpe paper
    3cm x 1m

(Crêpe paper will stain and tear when wet — an alternative is nylon ribbon, or rip-stop nylon, available in kite shops.)

Take one cotton square and lay it right side up. Place the ends of the paper strips on one corner of the square as seen below.

Lay the second square, right side down, on top of the first square and the paper strips. Pin together on three sides and sew as shown below. Be careful not to catch the streamers when sewing the side seams. Make *small* stitches if you are hand sewing.

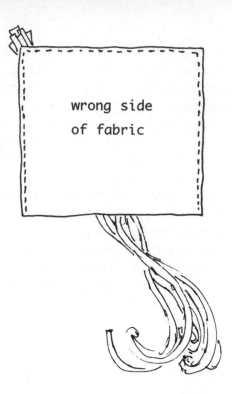

wrong side
of fabric

Now go outside into an open space, hold the bag by the string, twirl it round and round and let it go! Very young children might enjoy simply throwing the bag without a string.

Streamers on sticks

Enjoy drawing shapes in the air with these streamers, or just run about and set the paper rustling. White streamers for Whitsun, perhaps, but for a birthday party try a different colour combination for each child.

You will need:
6 crêpe paper strips — or nylon ribbons in bright colours, each 3cm x 80cm
60cm length of dowelling or straight stick (approx. 1.5cm diam.)
Glue

(For smaller children, reduce the length of stick and streamers.)

Glue strips one by one around the top of the stick. Let them dry well before using.

Turn bag inside out and fill it with rice, lentils or sand. Knot one end of the string. Turn in the open edges of the bag and sew together. Before closing the corner diagonally opposite the streamers, push in knotted end of string and stitch through it a few times to secure firmly.

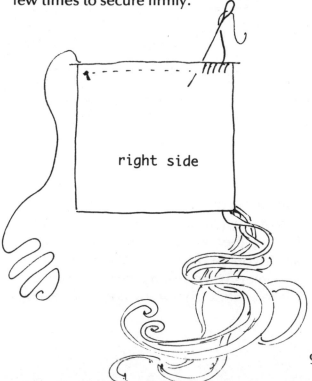

right side

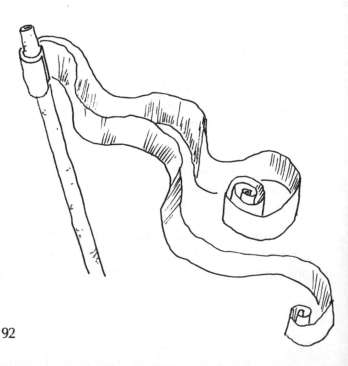

Nylon ribbon will not stain or tear in wet weather, but crêpe paper is more 'rustly' and can be made very decorative by stretching the edge of the streamer into a frill, using thumb and forefinger.

O - X	= 11.5cm
A - D	= 1cm
B - D	= 1cm
O - E	= 2.5cm
E - A	= 15cm
E - B	= 15cm

Whipper-whopper

Run with the whipper-whopper and see it twirl behind you! A nice project to do with younger children — they can colour their own whipper-whopper.

You will need:

Piece of drawing or cartridge
   paper 27cm x 9cm
Ruler and scissors
Length of thin string 75cm long
Small wooden bead
Wax crayons for colouring

Colour the piece of paper. Measure out and cut as shown below. (Dotted lines are folding lines and must not be cut!)

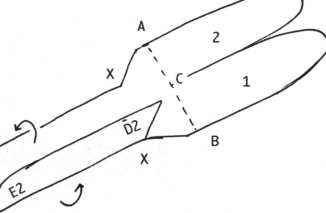

Fold section E2 - D2 upwards along folding line O-X. Then bend section E-D towards the back along O-X.

Now fold the two flaps as follows: Bend flap 1 towards the back along folding line C-B. Fold flap 2 upwards along folding line C-A. Thread and knot the bead to one end of the

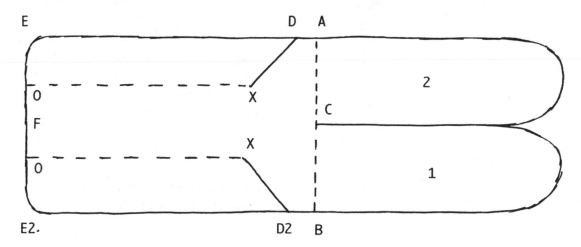

string. Fix it on the whipper-whopper as seen below. Glue an extra piece of paper at F for reinforcement. Make a hole for the string.

Now hold the whipper-whopper by its string, and run!

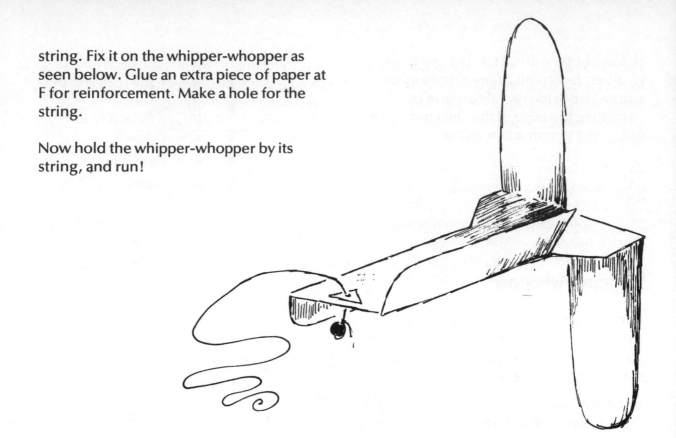

Windmill No. 1

A traditional favourite with all children.

You will need:
Windmill No. 1 pattern (see p258)
Piece of card in a bold colour, 16cm x 16cm
Scraps of coloured paper or card in contrasting colours
2 small wooden beads (approx. 5mm diam.)
12cm length of wire (approx. 1mm thick)
Piece of dowelling (6mm diam.) or other stick of similar thickness, 40-50cm long
Winebottle cork cut into length of 2cm
Knitting needle, 3mm (2US)
Craft knife, scissors and glue
Tracing paper (or transparent paper)
Carbon paper — optional
Small pliers — optional

Trace the pattern (see p253) and transfer it to the card. Cut along all the solid lines. Score along the dotted lines with the knitting needle, (these are the folding lines).

To decorate the centre of the windmill, cut two circles, one with a radius of 1.5cm and the other smaller, from some scraps of card or coloured paper. Glue them (the largest first) to the centre of the windmill. Carefully bore a hole through the centre of the cork with the knitting needle.

Make a small hole exactly in the centre of the windmill. Matching the holes, glue the cork to the back of the windmill as a stabilizer.

Take the piece of wire and make a small loop at one end (pliers are helpful here) to stop the bead from slipping off. Thread the beads and windmill on the wire as seen below. Wind the rest of the wire tightly around one end of the stick.

It is most important that the bead is not fixed too tightly between the cork and the stick. The bead must have room for movement to allow the windmill to turn freely.

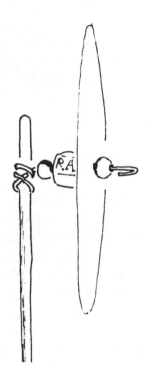

Windmill No. 2

You will need:
Windmill No. 2 pattern (see p259)
Piece of card, in a bold colour, 23cm x 23cm
Other materials as for Windmill No. 1

The pattern here needs its other half! So first trace this pattern on the card, then turn the tracing paper over, matching centre lines exactly and complete the other side.

Proceed and finish in the same way as described for Windmill No. 1, taking care *not* to cut along centre line.

Whitsun (Pentecost)

Pentecost was the name given to a Jewish agricultural festival to indicate that it took place on the fiftieth ('pente' — five) day after Passover. It was on this day that the twelve disciples of Jesus (now including Matthias in place of Judas) met with Mary, the mother of Jesus, and others. While the disciples were "all with one accord in one place… there came a sound from heaven as of a rushing mighty wind." (Acts 2: 2.) A powerful current gathered up the disciples as if on the in-breath of God, and, taken hold of by this divine inspiration, they became aware of "cloven tongues like as of fire" which "sat upon each of them." The story goes on to recount that the twelve were "filled with the Holy Ghost" and were able to speak in such a way that "every man heard them… in his own language."

It was the elements of Water and Air that hid the divine revelation from the disciples at Ascension; now, at Pentecost, it is the element of Air that brings the Fire of new revelation to the twelve. The Fire of the Holy Spirit hovered as twelve flames, one above the head of each disciple, as if singling out each for his own uniqueness. Yet the narrative emphasises that these twelve individuals were of "one accord," of "singleness of heart."

My individuality expresses itself in the way I think, but if I am able fully to share a thought that has 'lit up' for me, I discover real communication, a true communion of feeling, and 'accord' with another individual. Wherever in the world one individual honestly strives to understand another, endeavours to 'speak their language,' out of this effort genuine community arises.

The Holy Spirit is sometimes called the Spirit of Truth. In celebrating Pentecost we celebrate the insight that the singularity of the individual is sacred, that a spark of divine fire shines from each one of us, and that the accord between individuals rests on the ability truly to understand one another. To communicate in a spirit of truth is often a difficult challenge in today's world. If this challenge can be met, even in modest ways, then the vision of the dove descending — the symbol of the Holy Spirit *and* the symbol of peace — becomes a reality for individuals, for groups, for nations.

In England, the day of Pentecost is known as Whitsun, or Whitsunday, meaning 'White-Sunday.' It has long been a tradition to wear white on this day, perhaps as an acknowledgement of the purity of the spirit, perhaps as a reminder of the moment of joining a church community at baptism or confirmation. The countryside at this time of the year is also dressed in white. Trees, hedges and banks are frothy with white blossom, as if the cloud substance of Ascensiontide has now come to earth. Looking beyond the clouds we see the glowing sun. Towards this bright fire plant growth is straining ever upward, seeking the forces which will ripen the seed. To humankind, the fire of the spirit descends, bearing the seed of brotherhood to ripen in our understanding.

The symbolism of the candle draws a multitude of pictures towards it, but is not constrained by any of them. For many years we have celebrated Whitsun at home by standing twelve candles on the dining table. These are always set in a circle around a larger central candle, and everyone takes their turn in lighting them. Recently, in the middle of the Whitsun meal, a thirteen-year-old looked up, eyes bright with a new idea: "These could be the twelve disciples with flames above their heads!" "So they could!" we said. The siblings were unimpressed; they were working on their own ideas...

A candle circle can turn this mealtime into an event. Choose white candles with white holders (see p247), or holders in twelve different colours. If the table is small, use twelve cake candles. A white tablecloth (or white bedsheet) would be appropriate on White-Sunday, but if a cloth is used, look out for running wax! (To remove wax from cloth, see page 247.) It is also a good idea to snuff out the candles — to blow them out often means wax sprayed over the table. Wipe the inside of the snuffer with soft tissue occasionally, to avoid sooty drips.

If you hang a dove mobile above the table, well out of reach of the candle flames, you will see the doves flutter! Perhaps there could be some white food to finish the meal: a white cheese, yoghurt, meringues or frosted 'dove' biscuits (see p35).

We have known children who plan for weeks ahead the white outfit they will wear on Whitsunday — right down to their underwear and hair clips! All these details certainly mark the day as special.

Whitsun dove

You will need:
White card or strong paper
White tissue paper 12cm x 15cm
White or gold thread

From the white card or paper cut out a dove as shown. Cut a slot for the wings where indicated. Mark the eyes with a blue pencil.

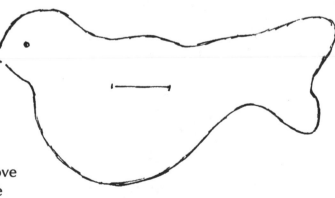

Fold the tissue paper as shown — the folds must not be wider than 1.5 cm. Trim the ends.

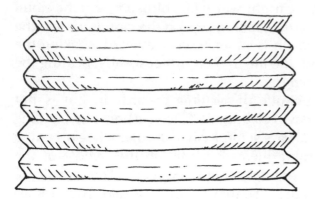

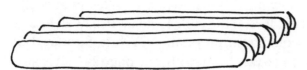

Insert the folded tissue paper through the slot in the body piece and open it up in a fan-like way. Pull the wings so that they meet in the middle. Carefully sew them together with white or gold thread, and leave a length for hanging.

It is possible to join the wings at the bottom as well as at the top and/or put a small white feather in the dove's beak.

Dove spiral

You will need:
White card or strong paper
12 pieces of white tissue paper 8 cm x 12 cm
Wooden ring approx. 20 cm diam.
White or gold ribbon approx. 1 cm wide

Follow the same instructions as for Whitsun Dove but make very small doves. For the bodies use the pattern below.

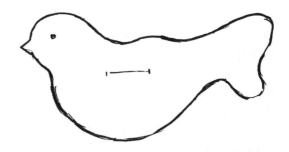

Wind some white or gold ribbon around the ring and let twelve small doves spiral towards the earth!

Ring games for Whitsun

Suitable for groups of younger children.

Fairy streamers

You will need:
White streamers on sticks (see p92).

The children skip around in a circle. Two or three children, each holding a white streamer, skip around the inside of the circle in the opposite direction. At the end of the song, as they sing "holding high the streamer gay" for the second time, everybody stands still and the children in the middle hold their streamers high in front of somebody from the outside circle. They hand their streamers over and change places with the new 'streamer-holder.' Now the song starts anew.

And so on...

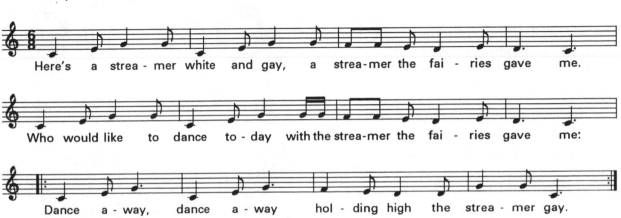

Here's a strea-mer white and gay, a strea-mer the fai-ries gave me.

Who would like to dance to-day with the strea-mer the fai-ries gave me:

Dance a-way, dance a-way hol-ding high the strea-mer gay.

White doves

You will need:
Whitsun Dove Wings (see below) for all the
   children.

Half the group hold hands and stand in a
circle, forming the 'dovecote.' The other
half are doves and crouch down in the
middle of the circle to sleep. As the first line
of the song is sung, the children making the
circle release their hands and stretch their
arms in the air, taking a step backwards if
the space allows it. The doves wake up and
fly around the outside of the circle (flapping
their 'wings' of course!).

In the second part of the song the doves fly
back into the centre of the circle to go to
sleep, and the dovecote closes up again.

This is a gentle ring game suitable for
ending an activity period on a quiet note. In
every game the 'dovecote' would also like a
turn at being 'doves.'

The dove cote now we o - pen wide and set all the white doves free
They fly a - round on ev' - ry side, up to the high - est tree. Then

they come back at e - ven - ing and close their eyes and sing: Coo - oo

coo oo coo oo coo oo.

Whitsun dove wings

You will need: (for one child)
40cm white ribbon 1cm wide
White crêpe paper
White thread

Cut the ribbon in half and use 20cm length
for each 'wing.' Cut the crêpe paper into
narrow strips of slightly differing lengths
(about 1cm x 30-40cm) and sew a bundle of
about six strips to the centre of each ribbon.
(See p101.) Then tie and fly!

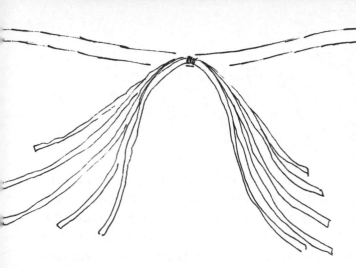

Elderflower syrup

This is a very special summer drink! The elderflowers should be gathered before noon on a dry day. Select them before they brown from areas well away from busy roads and crop spraying. Gather enough flowers to loosely fill a large bowl, stems upwards. Fill the bowl with water, covering all the flowers. Soak for 24 hours.

Strain off liquid through a muslin cloth. Discard flowers. Add 400g white sugar and the juice of half a lemon per 600ml of liquid. Bring to the boil and simmer for 15 mins. Pour into hot, sterilised bottles right up to the top. Screw on well-fitting lids tightly, touching the syrup so that no air space remains. As the liquid cools it will contract and create a vacuum seal. Unopened, the syrup will keep for months. When serving, dilute syrup with water and add some fresh lemon.

Elderflower tea

A cup of this tea mixed with a little orange or lemon juice and some honey is very comforting when you have a head cold. (It encourages the body to sweat and so is also useful for winter 'flu.) Use one heaped teaspoon of dried elderflowers per cup. Pour on boiling water and infuse for three minutes only.

You will need:
Elderflowers, picked early on a dry, sunny
    day before they begin to brown.

Dry the elderflowers by spreading them on paper in a dry, airy place away from sunlight for about a week. When the flowers are dry, store them in closed jars or tins to be used when needed.

You will need:
Large bowl
Elderflowers
Muslin cloth
Suitable screw-top jars or bottles
White sugar
Lemons

St John's Day — midsummer

Midsummer's Day has been officially fixed, not on the Solstice (June 21st) but on June 24th, which is also kept as the birthday of St John the Baptist, six months before Christmas. It is unusual for the birthday of a saint to be celebrated, but this had to do with the remarkable circumstances of John's conception and the connection with Jesus that was already established before either of them was born (Luke 1). Thirty years later, it was John who baptized Jesus in the River Jordan.

John had a very large following, and many speculated as to whether or not he was the Christ. He was a mighty preacher; his 'tongue of fire' was almost Pentecostal in the way that it sprang from the insights of his head, but it also blazed with passion from his heart. His cry was "Prepare ye the way of the Lord," (Luke 3), and it is clear that he was not speaking of a physical road but of the 'inner path' of the soul, for his preaching was of "repentance for the forgiveness of sins." (The word 'repent' could also be translated from the original Greek as 'change your thinking.') At a time when Nature rushes on, relentlessly pursuing her goal of fruiting and seeding, we are challenged by St John to pause, reassess our intentions and the direction of our life. He asks us to straighten and balance the landscape of our soul.

The summer entices us into a fairyland of lazy, dreamy days, of sweet fruits and carefree living. We seek out the warm waters, the glowing sands, the long grass of summer fields, to become part of this great Festival. Many folk tales warn of the danger of getting caught up in the Midsummer revelries of fairyland. (Shakespeare's "A Midsummer Night's Dream" is one salutary tale!) If we are to avoid 'Midsummer madness', we must not stray from the path that keeps our feet on solid ground. Those that trod this path to hear John the Baptist always brought the practical question "What shall we *do*?"

St John prophesied "He must increase, I must decrease" (John 3: 30). Summer joys are transient: the days grow shorter and the year's path leads on towards midwinter and Christmas — the Festival of Birth. Within each one of us a child waits to be born, the offspring of our efforts to overcome human insufficiency. The call of St John can stir this infant into life, in order that it may grow and 'wax strong.'

From ancient times Midsummer has been the principal season for fire rituals. These included fires of purification: noxious smoke was produced with the intention of clearing the neighbourhood of evil influences. (The word 'bonfire' may have arisen from the practice of burning bones and other rubbish for this purpose.) The customs of leaping over the fires and driving cattle between them also arose out of a belief in their cleansing powers.

The most noble quality of Fire is its ability to transform substance. In the alchemy of the soul there is always the possibility that the dross in our lives may be changed into something more precious. By 'burning up' what is unfruitful within us, we gain the strength to rise above ourselves, to jump over our own inner St John's Fire.

Summer invites us to join her celebrations, and at midday on Midsummer Day the call is strongest, so why not eat lunch in the garden? Cooking food over an open fire makes a change from the usual barbecue, and most members of the family will enjoy building a fire. They may even be persuaded to part with some 'rubbish' to throw on the flames — but please, no smelly smoke for the neighbours!

Even if we choose to eat indoors, a Midsummer ambiance is still possible. Edible flowers (e.g. marigold, borage, nasturtium) tossed in with the salad are as delicious to the eye as our Summer Pudding is to the nose! Or choose a large platter and pile it up with all the different fruits you cannot afford at other times of the year. For the centre of your table, fix a tall candle to the inside of a glass bowl and fill the bowl with water. Sink some pretty shells to the bottom, float a few little roses on top, and there you have a fairy world of scintillating light and colour. Our hanging ring of bees suspended above will add a final authentic touch to the mood!

Other little customs mark this special time of year: a bunch of cornflowers hanging from the front door, a light left burning in the porch all night, one sunflower chosen to bring indoors to shine benevolently in a corner of the home.

In the Land of the Midnight Sun, children are allowed to stay up all night at Midsummer, but in England we retire from the garden in good time, wary of the attentions of fairy folk — or is it just the gnats? Some children have not forgotten, though, that dancing is thirsty work. They lay out a tiny tea party for the fairies in some magic spot. When the fairy ball is over, the grateful little folk may leave their rose-petal cloaks behind, or even a jewel from an elfin crown...

Gold spiral

The intriguing movement of this spiral conjures the restless mood of the Air element, and the dancing gold of summer sunbeams.

You will need:
Gold Spiral pattern (see p260)
Double-sided gold foil 20cm x 20cm
Gold thread
Small bead

Transfer the pattern to the gold foil and cut along the lines. Hang the spiral with some gold thread from point X, using a small bead as a stop. The spiral turns best when it is hung above a candle (not too close to the flame!) or some other source of heat.

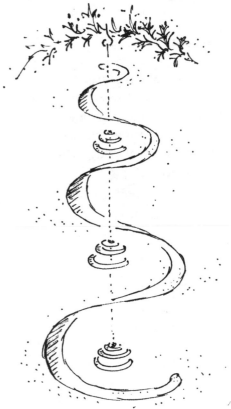

Midsummer suns

... To bring a little sunshine indoors.

You will need:
Gold foil or gold paper — double-sided if
   possible
Glue
Gold coloured thread

From the gold foil cut a strip which is twelve
times as long as it is wide, e.g. if the width of
the strip is 2.5cm then the length must be
30cm.
Fold the strip like a concertina, each fold
about 1 or 1.5cm wide.

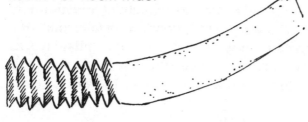

Small hanging sun

Hang several of these among large
branches of greenery and flowers in a vase.
Use the above measurements. Once the
whole strip is folded in concertina fashion,
take some thread and sew through the
centre, close to the edge.

Open up the folds like a fan, bring the first
and the last folds together and knot the two
ends of thread together, closing the circle
in the centre.

Join first and last folds together at the
outside edge with a new length of thread
leaving enough for hanging the sun.

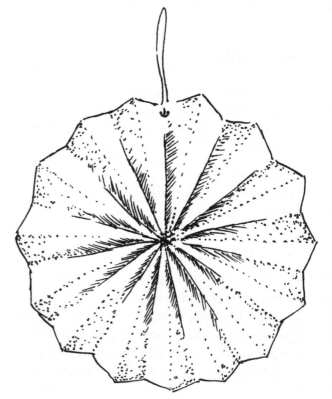

Sun around a candle on a table

Use the same proportions as described for the hanging sun (twelve times as long as the width), e.g. if you use an 8cm wide strip, it needs to be 96cm long.

When you have folded the strip as described above, glue together the first and last fold. Leave the centre open. Place your candle in the centre. Make sure the candle is properly secured on a small flat candleholder or plate beneath the 'sun.' The sun alone is *not* strong enough to hold a candle.

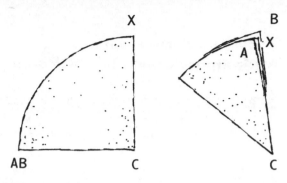

Cut the round edge of the folded circle with nail scissors as seen below:

Open up the sun and sew a gold thread through one of the 'sunrays' for hanging.

Another small hanging sun

Cut a circle of gold foil 7cm diam. Fold the circle in half, then into quarters and finally into eighths as follows:

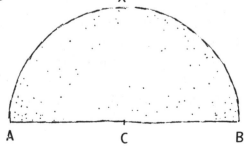

Song of the midsummer sun
Words translated from Christian Morgenstern.

I am the sun and I bear with my might, the earth___ by

day and the earth by___ night. I hold her fast and my

gifts I be - stow, to ev' - ry - thing on her so that it may___

grow. Man and stone, flo - wer and bee, all___ re - ceive_ their

light_ from me. O - pen your heart like a lit - tle flo - wer
That I may shine in it e - v'ry ho - ur

O - pen thy heart dear child to me, that we to - ge - ther one light may be.

Bees

A whole swarm of bees hanging at different heights from a branch or wooden ring, brings a summer mood into the house. They look most effective flying above and around a bunch of flowers in a vase, or perhaps around a small wicker basket in the shape of a beehive. Browsing through your local basket shop, you will almost certainly come up with a suitable shape, even if it means removing a handle. The hive can be suspended or placed on a surface. If you have the possibility of observing the shape, size, etc. of a real bee before making your own, do so. It is very helpful.

Bees from sheep's wool

You will need:
Handful of brown fleece
Dark yellow embroidery cotton
Scraps of white tissue paper or white dress net fabric
Black sewing thread

Cut out wings from paper tissue or white dress net. Bees' wings slant backwards and therefore need to be cut in a 'boomerang' shape.

Tie the wings to the body with black sewing thread and use one end of thread for hanging the bee.

More bees

Depending on what sort of cones you use, these bees may turn into bumble bees! Small cones with soft scales (e.g. larch cones) would be suitable. Alder cones make the most life-like bees. If you want to make a large bumble bee use yellow mohair wool instead of embroidery cotton.

You will need: (for one bee)
One very small cone
Scrap of white tissue paper
Dark yellow embroidery cotton (or mohair wool)
Black sewing thread

To make the bee's body, roll a little brown fleece into an oblong shape, slightly larger than a kidney bean. Take a length of embroidery cotton, tie off a section of fleece for a head, and then wrap the cotton loosely around the body a few times.

Thread each left over end of the cotton into a needle, push through the bee's body and out of the head to make antennae.

Wrap a length of embroidery cotton or wool around the cone. Knot the thread and hide the ends in the scales. Cut wings from the tissue paper as shown above for the sheep's wool bee. Tie the wings on with thread, drawing them slightly into the scales. Use one end of the thread for hanging the bee.

Antennae contribute to the 'insect look' and therefore are worth the extra trouble. Use thin slivers of natural material, e.g. dried grass or pine needles. The tiny stalk of

the alder cone makes an authentic-looking proboscis, and no antennae are needed.

Skip, jump and bounce

Rhythmical ball games, swinging or skipping, are all activities which delight most children and are ideal for summer weather. If it is possible to get hold of a few metres of rope, groups of children (ages six and over) can have endless enjoyment and fun. Two people each hold one end of the rope and stand far enough apart so that, as it turns, it just touches the ground in the middle. Children jump in and out of the turning rope, singly or in twos and threes. There is a wide repertoire of skipping games, some complicated and others very simple. For example, the months of the year can be recited, the children jumping in on their birthday month and out again when the year is over, i.e. when twelve jumps have been completed.

Why not revive games which our grandparents enjoyed? Ask them or other elderly friends if they remember skipping rhymes or games. In the meantime, here are some suggestions:

All year round skipping rhyme

January
February
March, April, May
How many months can the children play?
Count them fast
Count them slow
Count them as they come and go;
June
July
August
September
How many more can we remember?
Gather apples in October,
Light a fire in November,
Hang your stocking in December,
Twelve whole months in every year
When they're over start from here:
January
February... etc.

A counting rhyme

The children count as far as they can skip to see whose hen lays the most eggs:

If I had a cockerel I'd call him Lou,
I'd teach him how to Cock-a-Doodle-Doo,
If I had a hen I'd call her Meg,
I'd count every time she laid an egg:
One, two, three...

Skipping rhymes with actions

1

I'm off to London
To see the Queen
When you ask me
Where I've been
I'll say "Tut! Tut!   *(wag finger)*

Doff your cap.   (doff imaginary cap)
Don't let your feet go
Slap! Slap!   (jump the rope twice without a
    bob in the middle)
Mind your manners
P's and Q's
Beg your pardon   (clasp hands in front of
    chest)
Please excuse   (keep hands in position)
Curtsey ladies   (curtsey)
Men please bow   (bow)
Kiss my hand and   (kiss back of hand)
Please go now!"   (run out).

2

First place a coin near the skipper's feet.

Roses, marigold, marjoram and rue,
How many skips shall I skip for you?
A light skip   (on one tip toe)
A tight skip   (hug oneself tightly)
A skip in the dark   (shut the eyes)
A clap and   (clap)
A slap and   (slap the thigh)
A foot on the mark   (jump on one foot to
    cover the coin)
A low skip   (crouch low)
A high skip   (jump high)
A skip touch the ground   (touch the ground
    with the hand)
A wave and   (wave)
A kiss and   (blow a kiss)
A skip turn around   (turn around in the air to
    face the opposite direction).

Here is a counting rhyme to decide who
skips first:

(The children stand in a circle with their
clenched fists held inwards, thumbs
uppermost. One child counts rhythmically
touching each fist, including their own,

with each beat of the rhyme — one fist for
each line. The fist that is touched on the
word 'Men' has to be withdrawn. When a
child has withdrawn both fists they are
counted 'out.' The last child left in the circle
has the privilege of skipping first.)

Onesome
Twosome
I'll go to sea
Bail bunting
Hamaladdie
Weatherready
Sip Sop
Pennywise
Crosswise
Three fine
Men!

This can also be used as a skipping rhyme,
the first skipper running out on the last line
and the second skipper coming in to begin
again.

Wall ball

A game to be played in turn by a group of
children or by one child alone:

1. Throw ball against wall with right hand
   and catch with both hands.
2. Throw ball against wall with left hand
   and catch with both hands.
3. Throw ball with right hand and catch
   with left hand.
4. Throw ball with left hand and catch with
   right hand.
5. Throw ball against wall, clap hands
   three times and catch ball.
6. Throw ball under left leg against wall
   and catch.
7. Throw ball under right leg against wall
   and catch.

8. Throw ball, turn around and catch it facing wall again.
9. With back towards the wall, throw ball against wall over the head, turn around and catch ball.
10. With back towards the wall, throw ball against wall over the head and catch ball without turning around.

Each time a mistake is made the next player takes a turn. The game becomes more difficult when each stage has to be carried out ten times without mistake.

After your exertions, cool down with the help of a fan…

Fan for hot summer days

You will need:
Piece of card 19cm x 30cm
Paper fastener
Scissors and craft knife
35cm length embroidery cotton and large pointed needle
16 small self-adhesive stickers, e.g. stars, hearts, flowers

From the card, cut out eight sections as shown below. Cut out the shaded ornamentation with the craft knife. Pierce a hole at point Y with the needle, and enlarge it slightly with a skewer or thin knitting needle.

Lay all sections on top of each other, push paper fastener through the holes at Y and secure, but loosely enough to allow the pieces of card to move freely.

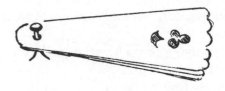

With all sections still lying in a pile, make a knot in one end of the thread and thread through all sections at point X.

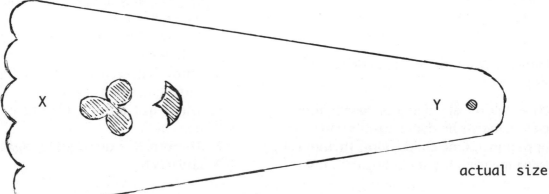

X   Y

actual size

Secure knot in place by covering with a small sticker as seen below. Spread out the fan with sections evenly spaced along the thread. Place a sticker at front and back of each hole (X). Make a knot at the back of the last section, cutting off any surplus thread.

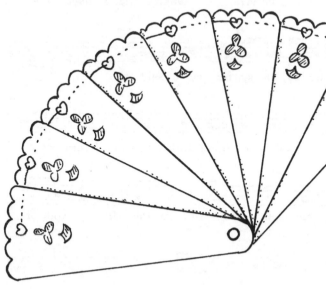

Ring game for summertime

Divide the children into two groups. One group are flowers and kneel in a circle with hands (petals) closed:

The second group are bees, and stand on tiptoe inside the circle:

1. Little bees work very hard, making golden honey
2. Taking pollen from the flowers, when the days are sunny
3. "I'm busy busy busy" said the bee "I shan't be home for dinner or tea
4. It takes me hours and hours and hours to visit all the flowers
5. It makes me rather dizzy and a little wuzzy-wizzy to be so very busy,"
6. Said the honey bee.

Actions:
1. Bees fly around on tiptoe wiggling their fingers in front of them —
2. Flowers open (hands open out) and bees dip fingers in and out of flowers —
3. Bees fly to the outside of circle and run around on tiptoe clockwise —
4. Bees turn to fly between flowers, weaving in and out of circle, anti-clockwise —
5. Each bee circles round and round one flower only —
6. Bees fly into the circle and sit down.

The groups change over and the song begins again.

Busy bee ring game

Lit - tle__ bees work ve - ry__ hard ma - king__ gol - den
Ta - king__ pol - len__ from the__ flowers, when the__ days are

ho - ney. sun - ny. "I'm bu-sy, bu-sy, bu-sy," said the bee, "I__

shan't be__ home for__ din-ner or tea. It takes me hours and hours and hours to__

vi - sit__ all the__ flow - ers. It makes me ra-ther diz-zy and a

lit - tle wuz-zy wiz-zy to__ be so ve-ry bu-sy," said the ho - ney bee.

Magic water flower

These magic flowers float gracefully on a pond or bowl of water, gradually unfolding their petals. A party of children may enjoy this as a summer activity, colouring in their own before floating them together. Dry flat for re-use.

You will need:
Stiff green paper 12cm x 9cm
White writing paper 12cm x 12cm
Scissors and glue
Crayons for colouring flower
Bowl of water

Cut out the flower from the pattern below and colour one side only (e.g. golden yellow for the heart of the flower, pink for the edges of the petals). Fold petals (along dotted lines) in towards the centre, so that the flower is closed and the colouring is concealed.

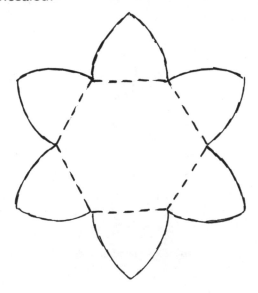

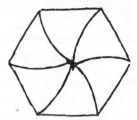

Cut out the leaf from green paper using pattern below, and cut away shaded areas. Put a dab of glue on each underside corner of the flower and fix it to the leaf.

Fill a bowl with water and gently set leaf and flower afloat.

Marije's water wheel

Most children love to play in and with water. For many years, we lived near a brook which could fill to overflowing at times, and then at others would dwindle to a trickle. Our family had hours of fun with the changing flow of water. We built dams to create lakes, and sailed improvised boats. The most memorable construction of all was the simple water-wheel we made to demonstrate the force of the flow.

You will need: (for the water-wheel)
4 pieces of soft pine (found on fruit boxes) or thin plywood, each 0.5 x 5 x 35cm
Batten, 2.5 x 2.5cm, at least 40cm long
4 galvanised large-headed nails or brass screws, 2cm long
2 galvanised nails 7cm long
Saw, hammer and chisel
Workbench — optional

The length of the batten depends on the width of the stream: for a narrow stream with firm banks, both ends of the batten can rest on the banks. Otherwise the water-wheel needs to be held by a simple stand. Instructions for a stand are given below.

Cut the four paddles from the soft pine and space them as shown:

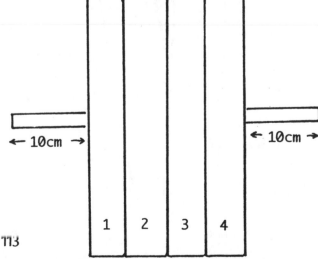

Fix paddles to the batten, using the 2cm length screws or nails. The first and third paddle lie at right angles to each other. The second and fourth paddles likewise. For paddles two and three a piece must be chiselled out to flatten the batten. Seen sideways, the water-wheel should look like this:

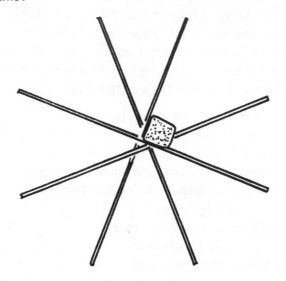

Holding one end of the water-wheel in a vice, hammer in a 7cm nail to the depth of 2cm. Repeat for other end. These two nails will act as bearings for the water-wheel. The wheel is now ready to be set into the bank of the stream.

The stand to hold the water-wheel in place in a stream is made as follows:

You will need: (for a stand)
2 pieces of pine 5cm x 7cm x 50cm
Plywood or blockboard, 76cm x 36cm
6 galvanised nails, 7cm long

Position the two pine pieces on the board, 45cm apart, and fix them by driving the nails through the base of the board and into the pine.

We indicate two measurements for different water depths, but you might have to adjust the height to suit your stream. Make sure the paddles will reach about 6cm deep into the water and at the same time hang clear of the base. Fix the 7cm nails as indicated (or use your own measurement if appropriate).

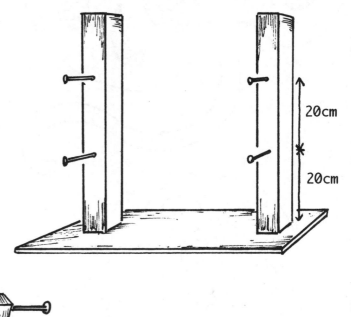

20cm

20cm

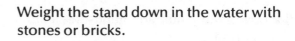

Weight the stand down in the water with stones or bricks.

Soap bubbles

Shimmering orbs of light, rainbow round, hanging in the summer air... Who can resist the joy of blowing bubbles? Use our recipe below to develop exciting new possibilities.

You will need: (for bubble mixture)
3 tbsps washing-up liquid soap
1 litre distilled water (car battery top-up)
1 tsp glycerine

Mix soap, water and glycerine. Stir the mixture slowly to prevent it becoming too frothy. Leave to set overnight.

You will need: (for various bubble sizes)
Drinking straws
Wire, 3mm diam.
Scraps of double knitting wool
Large flat dish
Dowelling 1cm diam. and 45cm long
Cotton tape approx. 1.5cm wide and 1.2m long
Curtain or keyring 2cm diam.
Drawing pin

To produce masses of tiny bubbles, dip a drinking straw into soap mixture, lift it out and blow strongly into straw. For larger bubbles cut the end of the straw as follows:

For very large bubbles use some wire to make a ring with a handle. Wind some wool around the frame as seen below:

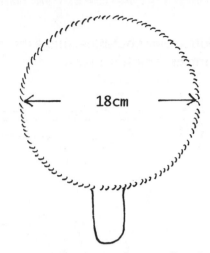

18cm

Pour some soap mixture into a flat dish and dip the wire ring in it. Raise your arm and slowly pull the soap coated ring through the air to produce a bubble.

For an interesting experiment, tie a loop of wool to one side of the ring as shown:

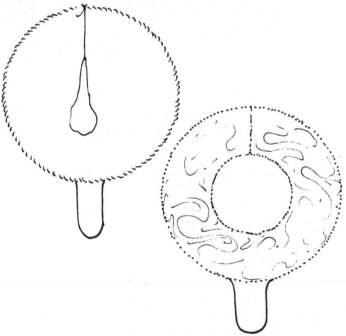

Dip ring in soap mixture as shown and use a dry object (toothpick or matchstick) to pierce the skin of soap inside the wool loop. The soap around the outside of the loop will pull evenly from all sides and form a circle of air surrounded by rainbow colours!

To produce giant bubbles, make the
following contraption:

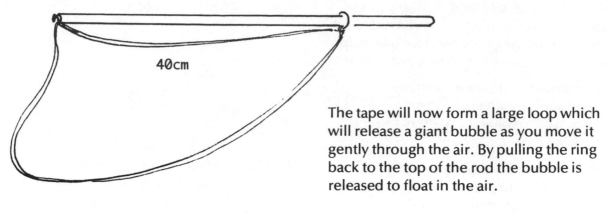

40cm

The tape will now form a large loop which
will release a giant bubble as you move it
gently through the air. By pulling the ring
back to the top of the rod the bubble is
released to float in the air.

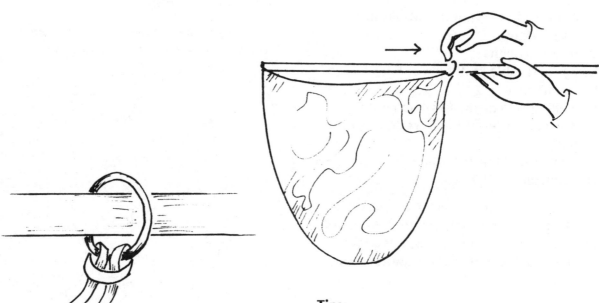

Tie the tape to the ring as seen above, about
40cm from one end of tape. Slide ring on
the dowelling rod and fix both ends of tape
into the end of the rod with a drawing pin.

Pour soap mixture into a bucket. Dip the
rod into the soap, making sure that the
whole tape is submerged. Slowly lift the rod
and pull the ring towards you.

Tips:

Washing-up liquids vary greatly and you
may have to experiment to find a suitable
one.

Any contact with dry objects will make the
bubbles burst immediately, but you can
catch and play with them with wet hands.

If the weather is hot and dry the thin skin of
soap bubbles will evaporate fast, making
bubble-pleasure very short-lived.

Drying herbs and flowers

Pick flowers for drying when they are in bud
or newly opened. Herbs are best gathered
just before they flower, unless you want
their flowers as well. Make sure the flowers/
herbs are dry when harvesting, which
should be done towards midday.

Bunch together no more than about six
stems and tie each bunch with an elastic
band. Do not pack stems too tightly but
allow the air to circulate through and
around each bunch. This helps to avoid the
risk of mildew. Cut stalks of flowers at
different lengths so that the flower heads
are staggered. Protect from dust with a
loose paper bag tied over each bunch, and
hang (stems upwards) in a warm, dry, airy
place — e.g. an airing cupboard, warm loft
or large kitchen. Remember that colours
will fade if exposed to direct sunlight, and
that a speedy drying process will retain the

colour best. When drying is completed
(after one or two weeks) the leaves should
be paper dry but not so dry that they
crumble when touched.

Flower and herb bath bags

Enjoy a fragrant flower or herb bath! Use herbs such as rosemary, thyme, sage or peppermint to invigorate and stimulate circulation; lavender, chamomile and fennel will relax and soothe aching limbs.

Rose and lavender bath bags

You will need: (for about six bags)
50g strongly perfumed rose petals, dried
30g lavender flowers, dried
Grated rind of half a lemon
15g rolled oats
Thin cotton or muslin bags (8cm x 8cm)

Mix all the ingredients and fill the bags. (Alternatively, place the ingredients in a square of muslin, draw the corners together and tie with ribbon.) The flowers provide the scent and the oats make the water creamy.

Hang the bag so that the water flows through it into the bath. The bag can be dried and used again until the scents fade.

Lavender bottle

Lavender has been popular for centuries not only for its fragrance but also for its medicinal properties. In Victorian times lavender was used to scent the linen cupboard and keep moths away. The lavender bottle is so called because of its shape. Pick the lavender on the morning of a dry day, when the flower is reaching full bloom. Make the bottle the same day to avoid working with brittle stems.

You will need:
19 heads of long-stemmed lavender, freshly
    picked
1m of narrow lavender-coloured ribbon

Tie the heads tightly together with the ribbon, just below the flower spike. Leave one end of the ribbon about 24cm long.

Bend each stem back over the flower heads so that all the stems lie parallel and make a 'cage' around the flower heads.

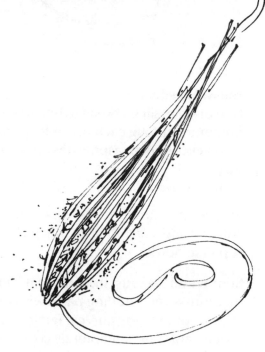

Bring the shorter end of the ribbon down alongside the flower heads, and use the long end to weave in and out of the stalks. Continue weaving until all the flowers are hidden.

Wind the ribbon tightly around the stalks a few times, and finish off with a bow, using the other end of the ribbon.

Rose water

For a special treat, wash your face and hands in delicately scented rose water! Maybe the children could rinse their hands with rose water before lunch on Midsummer-day. It is quick to prepare; stored in a screw-top jar and kept in the refrigerator, it will last at least a fortnight.

You will need:
Saucepan, with lid, full of strongly scented deep red rose petals.
Water

Cover the rose petals with water and bring to the boil. It is important to keep a lid on the saucepan all the time to retain the perfume. Simmer for 3 mins, remove from heat and allow to cool with lid still on the pan. Strain into jars.

P.S. If you are unable to get hold of strongly scented petals, you can help the scent along by adding two or three drops of rose oil (usually used for pot-pourri) to the bottle of rose water.

Some ingredients for a fairy tea-party

Rose-petal jam

You will need:
750ml fresh water
500g granulated sugar
250g rose petals (unsprayed!)
Juice of 2 lemons

Discard the white heels of the petals and bruise the petals lightly. Put them in a bowl and sprinkle with half the sugar. Leave overnight. Dissolve remaining sugar in a pan with the water and lemon juice. Add the petals mixed with sugar and simmer for 20 mins. Then boil for about 5 mins. until thick. Pour into jars and seal.

Rose petal sandwiches

An unusual treat which one can only have in summer when the roses bloom.

You will need:
Loaf of wholemeal bread at least 24 hrs. old
Butter
Rose petals from a large, strongly scented, deep red 'cabbage' rose (unsprayed, of course!)

Remove an end crust of the loaf. Butter the bread and cut the buttered slice as thinly as possible, removing crusts if preferred. Make as many slices as you need. Discard the white heels of the rose petals as they have a bitter taste. Cover slices with rose petals, allowing the petals to peep out at the edges of the sandwich. Pile the sandwiches on a plate and decorate with a rose bud.

Summer pudding

This dish is a 'must' for Midsummer time.

You will need:
Loaf of stale, sliced bread (white if possible)
Minimum of 100g each of: redcurrants, blackcurrants, raspberries, strawberries
Sugar
Double cream

Simmer the various fruits separately until soft and add sugar to taste. Keep in four separate bowls.

Remove all the crust from the loaf and line a medium-sized pudding basin with bread slices, cut to fit the curves. Put in the redcurrants, and completely cover with bread. Repeat for the raspberries and strawberries. Cover the last layer with a plate, and place a weight on top. Leave overnight in a cool place. Next day, carefully turn it out on a serving dish. Collect excess juices and pour over the top. Serve with sweetened cream.

Fruit ice

Soft fruit often comes in a glut, so you may be glad of this delicious variation on the theme of fruity desserts.

You will need:

1 part puréed fruit — if it is at all bland add a
    dash of lemon juice
Sugar to taste — be careful to use no more
    than one part sugar to four parts liquid
4 parts water

Mix the ingredients thoroughly. Freeze in a covered container. Stir the mixture every half hour to reduce the size of the ice crystals. When it begins to set, transfer to individual containers. (You may like to try using the hollowed-out shells of oranges and lemons.) Move the ice to the refrigerator 20 mins. before serving.

St Swithun's Day

St Swithun was Bishop of Winchester in the 9th century. He was respected by the Saxon King Egbert who made him tutor to his son. During his life he was well known for his humility and kindness of heart. The story is told of a market woman who, when jostled in the street, dropped her basket and broke her eggs. The Bishop promptly mended them for her!

When Bishop Swithun died he asked to be buried modestly outside the cathedral. About a century later the cathedral was rebuilt and it was decided that the Saint's remains should be enshrined within. This was accomplished only after a delay for, it is said, it rained so hard for forty days that the project had to be abandoned. This doubtful story has given rise to the old jingle:

> "St Swithun's Day, if thou dost rain,
> For forty days it will remain;
> St Swithun's Day, if thou be fair,
> For forty days 'twill rain na mair." Anon.

It is more likely that an ancient day of augury has come to shelter under the protection of this Christian Saint, but you will be able to test the assertion of the rhyme at a glance if you keep our Weather Tree up to date!

The weather tree

"We weather the weather whatever the weather whether we like it or not…"

As a child one can be particularly sensitive to the weather. Remember those endless hot summer days, or waking up in wintertime, aware of a deep hush hanging over the world as it began to snow and snow?

On our Weather Tree there is one leaf for each day of the year. Decide on your own colour-code and colour in each leaf at the end of the day according to the progress of the weather. Some days the leaf will be just one colour, other days need a mixture of several colours. At the end of the year you will have an impressive colour diary of the past year's weather. An older child may enjoy taking this on as a daily task.

If you find the given example too small, why not make a larger one yourself?

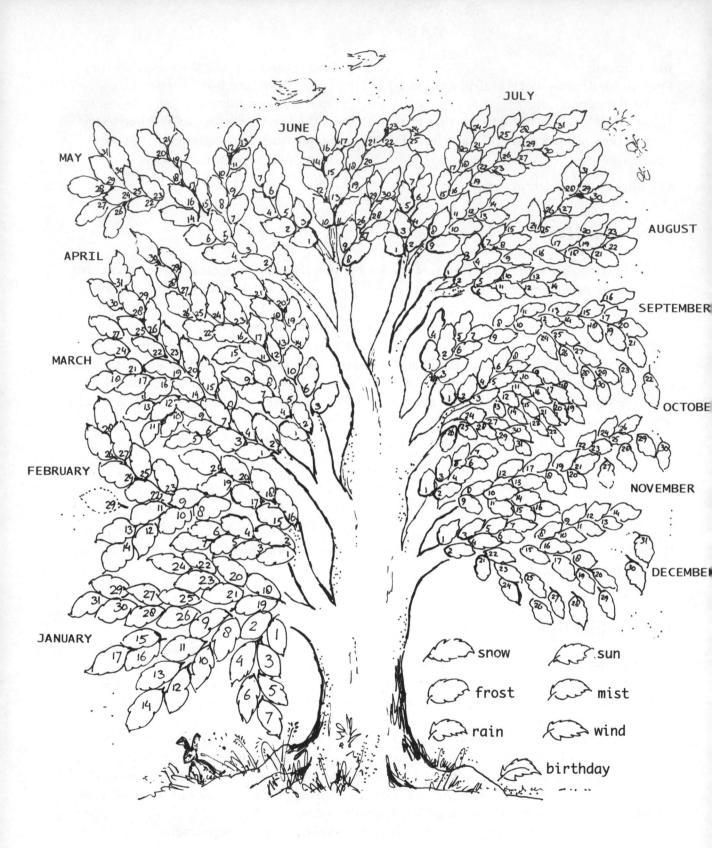

snow   sun

frost   mist

rain   wind

birthday

122

AUTUMN

"...I knew when Autumn came —
Not by the crimson flame
   Of leaves that lapped the eaves
      Or mist
      In amethyst
   And opal-tinted weaves;
But because there were alley-taws
(Punctual as hips and haws)
On the counter at Mrs Shaw's..."

From "The Calendar" by Barbara Euphan Todd.

Autumn

It is the sun that leads the dance of the year along pathways of light and warmth, which may rise to celestial heights or wind deep into the chambers of the heart. Our joy in the seasons carries us along this path, and the festivals wait for us on the way, each one opening up a particular view of life's landscape, each one helping us to assess the progress of our life's journey.

In spring we follow the languorous steps of the pale sun as its watery beam casts a glimmer of hope before us. The dance quickens with the up-beat of Easter, until the sun's fire soars above our heads, clear and brilliant, opening hearts and minds to far distant places. With this crescendo of light in early summer, the dance swings around and a new motif takes hold. The light's energy is diffused over hazy horizons, and a steady penetrating warmth flows beneath the skin, warming the 'cockles of the heart.' Little by little, summer's green fruit is changed, ripened, brought to a fullness of being.

Now summer is declining into an Autumn mood and the steps of the dance become more purposeful. The ripe heads of grain curve gracefully over, and the fruitful boughs of the apple tree lower their burden to the ground. The equinoctial point is soon passed and the earth begins to inhale one long, mighty breath towards winter, drawing the sun's fire downward to set the leaves aflame and cook the fruit to perfection. An infinity of seeds falls like ash from this great autumnal oven; like little puffs of smoke, the crane flies rise and fall in the grass.

With a flourish of fiery leaves, the dance breaks into a reel, urged towards a climax by the seasonal gales. At last the ripened leaf, fruit and seed — the past, present and future gifts of the sun — are gathered in the resolving embrace of Mother Earth. A final chord sounds and this cascade of sun-bright offerings is received into the life-giving depths.

Like an answering resonance from the furthest regions of the heavens, the Autumn meteor showers burst upon the night sky. Bright stars of iron-fire are born, and as they die towards the earth they become, for a brief moment, our fellow travellers. They accompany us as we step into the unknown, and confirm our loneliness with blessing. For the passing of autumn can leave us bereft, solitary as the trail of wood smoke rising in the November air, yet aware of a spark within that is ready to kindle new fire, to light a new star to be our companion and guide. The flame of our own Being, so easily lost to sight in the glare of the summer sun, begins to shine against the darkness of approaching winter. As Nature dies, we come to life.

Already winter's intermezzo is beginning to be heard in the creaking of frosty grass, the rattle of bare twigs. With a deep curtsey, the sun closes the dance and withdraws behind a curtain of mist.

The festivals in autumn

See page 24.

August 1	Lammas
September 21	Autumn Equinox
September	Harvest Thanksgiving
September 29	Michaelmas (Feast of St Michael and All Angels)
October 31	Hallowe'en (All Hallows' Eve)
November 1	All Saints' Day (All Hallows)
November 2	All Souls' Day
(Sunday nearest to November 11)	Remembrance Day
November 5	Guy Fawkes Night
November 11	Martinmas

The seasonal table in autumn

The August fields and hedgerows are yellowing with dried grass, and seed heads can be found everywhere in a variety of beautiful forms. The more abundant of these can be gathered without harm to the countryside if only a few are picked from one area and any ripe seeds are shaken out on the spot. Then they can be used in creative projects at home. A very simple autumn wreath can be made for the Seasonal Table by padding a wire ring with dried grass and binding it, first with thread and then with ribbon. You will probably need much more grass than you think! Posies of dried flowers or seed pods, bunches of oats or corn dollies can be pinned on as decoration. Or, using the Advent Wreath technique (see p173) one could make a nice fat ring of mixed ripe grains — wheat, barley, oats, etc. — to hang above the Table until the end of November when it can be placed outside to feed the hungry birds. Extra grain could be bound into a Harvest Sheaf and tied with red ribbon; leave any dropped kernels lying on the Table for the teasel mice to nibble...

The grain harvest gives way to the fruit and vegetable harvest. A large platter or basket will make a space for all the many coloured wild fruits, berries and leaves, or the produce gathered from your own garden plot. What variety! And how beautiful they all are! Even a simple bowl of apples, when they have been polished and decked out with autumn leaves, are a worthy celebration of the harvest. We can join in Nature's festival with a candle and a harvest song.

Autumn brings a treasure trove into children's pockets — nuts, acorns, coloured leaves and 'helicopters' from the sycamore tree — so many things to admire, to collect and to play with. However, much of autumn's intense activity is out of sight: plants are extending their root systems, bulbs are preparing to shoot, and in the warm, moist soil, the worms are busy pulling the first fallen leaves down into the earth. All the forces of Nature are at work to ensure that the seed of the future is nurtured, that life will go on. We can bring this hidden world to the child's awareness in an imaginative way, by making an Autumn Gnome Garden.

Autumn gnome garden

By tradition, the gnome or dwarf is the guardian of the earth's minerals, both the solid rock with its metallic seams, and the fine distribution of mineral salts in the soil that feed the roots of every tree and plant. Their area of work is always in connection with the earth, whether close to the surface above ground, or deep underground in mysterious passages. A large twisted tree root or piece of lichen-covered bark could make an ideal gnome's cavern in the centre of the Seasonal Table or some other suitable place. A few branches of dead wood draped with a yellow-brown veil would also create the dimly-lit 'underground' mood. In this setting it is possible to bring about an atmosphere in which a gnome might feel at home.

Gnomes like the warm earthy colours of autumn, the craggy lines of different kinds of rock; they delight in metals, in the green streak of copper oxide in the stone, and the gleam of iron pyrites. At this time of the year they are busy receiving new seeds and giving them life, so they welcome all kinds of fruit, seeds and seed pods into their store rooms. They look upwards and wait for the rowan berries to fall, for the squirrel to bury a few nuts, for the 'helicopters' to whirr through the air. Sometimes they rest for a while with their acorn cups and tell stories, while the hedgehogs, the mice and other small creatures creep up close to listen.

At Michaelmas time, it may be that a dragon is seen flying down towards the earth, but the gnomes take care not to let this interfere with their work. The leaves of sun-gold have to be stored, the seeds must be guarded and the roots nourished. It is a daily task to carry the light of the sun, moon and stars down into the darkness of the earth, and so there will always be some gnomes who are never without their lantern. Time passes quickly when there is so much to do. The gnomes are surely aware that the fiery Michaelmas candle has made way first for the orange glow of the turnip lantern and then for the coloured paper lanterns of Martinmas. But if a witch passed by at Hallowe'en, or fireworks crackled on Guy Fawkes Night, they were simply too busy to remark upon it. For they are looking forward to mid-November when most of their work is done and they can relax and enjoy *their* Bonfire Party (see p157).

The autumn landscape is flushed with sunset colours, enveloping the whole day in an evening mood. Autumn festivals bring us evening celebrations: a Harvest Supper, a Michaelmas story in the lamplight as the first fire of the season warms the hearth, the evening offering of soul cakes, the bonfires and lantern walks at dusk. Such festivals round off the day, even as autumn is celebrating the close of the natural cycle of the year.

At the end of November a new cycle of festivals begins with Advent. It is especially important, therefore, that the Seasonal Table should make a right transition at this point. If you are lucky enough to have an open fire in your house, or if the weather allows a small camp fire in the garden, you will be able to celebrate the end of autumn with the Gnomes' Bonfire and 'wind down' the Seasonal Table in a thoroughly enjoyable way.

Lammas

The old Celtic year had four major festivals: Imbolg, February 1st; Beltane, May 1st; Lughnasadh, August 1st; and Samhain, November 1st. These celebrated the female principle of the Earth in four guises: the Virgin, the Bride, the Mother and the Wise Woman. The Festival of Lammas has its origin in Lughnasadh — a feast instituted by the sun-god Lugh in honour of his stepmother. This was a harvest festival, celebrating the fruitfulness of the Earth Mother, and took the form of a 'first fruits' offering. The Anglo-Saxon Christians transformed this into the 'Hlaf-Maesse' or 'Loaf-Mass' which has given us the name Lammas. A loaf was baked with grain reaped at the very beginning of the harvest and not allowed to stand for the customary three Sundays; this loaf was offered at the Mass.

St John the Baptist sowed the seed for a change of heart at Midsummer, and since then, this seed has had time to ripen into a resolve. An initiative is always needed to turn a resolve into a deed, but when are we ever *really* ready to take an initiative? Forty days after Midsummer, the Festival of Lammas reminds us that it is possible to bake a loaf with grain that is not fully mature, and offer it with trust at Life's table.

The rest of the harvesting will continue, and the tempered seed will finally be gathered, sifted and weighed before being cast in future seasons. Meanwhile, let us value even the immature offerings of our heart, for their spontaneity and vitality!

Here is a recipe for a wholemeal loaf, where the maturing process only takes three days...

Yeast free loaf

You will need:
30g rolled oats
200g wholewheat flour
20g barley flour
30g rye flour
1 tsp fine sea salt
1 tbsp freshly ground nuts (hazelnuts and/
    or almonds)

127

Scant tbsp. honey (unheated)
250ml lukewarm water (blood heat)
Approx. 50g 81% brown flour to work the
    dough
Loaf tin (oiled)
Metal foil to cover

On the first day, before 11am, mix the dry ingredients well. Dissolve the honey in the warm water and add to the mixture to make a soft dough. Cover and keep warm! In the afternoon before 5pm, knead the mixture again, adding just enough flour to make a smooth dough. Form into a loaf and place in the oiled tin. Cover with foil and continue to keep it warm.

On the second day, at about 10am, bake for approx. 2 hrs. in a moderate oven, removing foil for the last 30 mins. Take loaf from tin and cool on a wire tray.

On the third day the bread is ready to eat. Slice thinly and eat within three days. Store in an airtight container in a cool place.

Harvest thanksgiving

Since the first Neolithic farmers began their work, the agrarian cycle has always been accompanied by festivals and ritual acts, some even involving human sacrifice. Today, all over the world, different forms of harvest festival are observed wherever there is a major crop to be gathered, although, with the spread of technology, many old customs are dying out.

The cutting of the last sheaf of grain, in particular, has been accompanied by rituals designed to nurture the life force of the field and preserve it for the following year. In pre-Christian Europe, for example, it was common for the reaper who cut this 'heart' of the field to offer his life's blood in return. Other rituals, such as those centred around the 'corn dolly' (a 'corn idol' in fact, an image of Demeter, the corn goddess) have persisted even into this century. The last sheaf to be cut was fashioned into the figure of a woman and carried back to the farm with great ceremony. There it would hang throughout the winter, a safe lodging for the spirit of the field. In the spring, the grain of this sheaf would be sown along with the rest of the stored seed. A wide variety of corn dollies are still made throughout Europe, only a few now bearing any resemblance to a woman. They are charming examples of local folk art and, for the most part, have only a decorative function.

Today, modern transport, storage and preserving techniques ensure that most foodstuffs are available when needed, and the lives of many of us no longer hang so precariously on the vagaries of the climate. However, another question still arises wherever people have to face a dark, cold 'wintry' season in their lives: how do I preserve the life of the heart through the periods of trial which I must reckon with from time to time? How do I maintain the spirit to see these difficulties through?

Gratitude is an enlivening force always bringing us warmth and peace, and the motivation to be active in return, to place our own small seed in life. Not everyone finds it easy to receive, and be grateful. In giving thanks each year for the gift of the world's harvest, in giving thanks each day for the bread on our table, we can keep in touch with the heartwarming experience of gratitude — with the living seed-bed of the future.

> "Thanks to our mother, the earth, which sustains us;
> Thanks to the rivers and streams and their water;
> Thanks to the corn and the grain fields that feed us;
> Thanks to the herbs which protect us from illness;
> Thanks to the wind and the rain for their cleansing;
> Thanks to the bushes and trees and their fruiting;
> Thanks to the moon and the stars in the darkness;
> Thanks to the sun and his eye that looks earthward;
> Thank the Great Spirit for all of his goodness."

Adapted from an Iroquois Indian address of thanksgiving to the Great Spirit.

Drying apples and pears

Harvest time is not only for farmers; even a small garden can produce enough fruit to give the household a busy time if they wish to preserve it. Home drying of fruit can be an alternative to freezing or bottling. The drying process is interesting to watch, it is easy to do and needs no expensive equipment.

You will need:
Apples (or pears)
String or thin lengths of clean dowelling or
    bamboo

Peel, core and slice the apples thinly into rings. Thread the apple rings in such a way that they do not touch each other on the string or the sticks, and suspend them in a dry, airy place (above a stove or in an airing cupboard). Pears are dried in a similar way, but quartered and cored first, then sliced thinly. The slices can be threaded with needle and cotton, or spread out on a wire tray and turned occasionally.

String of onions

If you are able to get hold of onions with leaves still on them, then try your hand at making an onion string. Not only is this an excellent way of storing onions, but it also looks very decorative hanging in the kitchen.

You will need:
Onions with leaves
1 metre of strong string
Hook strong enough to take the weight of a
    few pounds of onions hanging in a free
    space, i.e. not against a wall. (The branch
    of a tree serves extremely well.)

After harvesting the onions, allow them to dry for several days out of doors in the sun. Peel off any discoloured onion skins. Tie the two ends of the string together and suspend the loop from the hook. Grade the onions from large to small and start working with the largest. Follow diagrams below for tying the onions to the string.

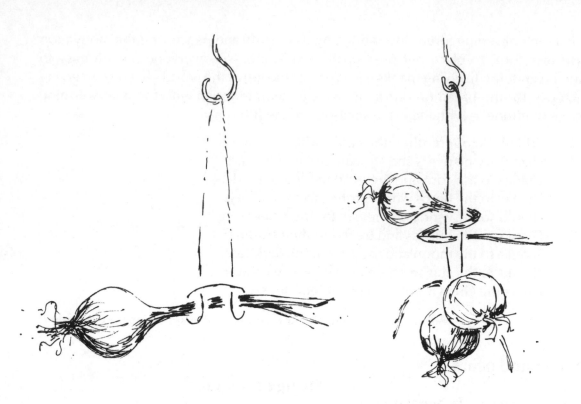

Work your way along the string, adding
onions. To produce a nice even onion string
takes practice, but you'll soon get the hang
of it! To finish, knot the string at the top of
the last onions and trim off any protruding
stalks.

Corn dollies

The tradition of corn dollies goes back 5,000 years! They are found in various forms all over the world, in fact wherever the sun is warm enough to ripen a crop of corn. Many festivals and celebrations feature corn dollies as fertility symbols or offerings at harvest time. They are made from the hollow-centred stalks of wheat, oats, rye or barley. The ears of the corn are retained as an integral, and very beautiful part of the dolly, and vary widely in their form. Barley, rye and oats have whiskery heads which are most decorative but not as easy to work with as wheat. Wheat is the best straw for plaiting. If you are lucky enough to live in a grain growing area, ask the farmer for a bunch of wheat. He may allow you to harvest the stalks left along the edge of a field, out of reach of the combine harvester. If you live in a town you might be able to buy some corn dolly straw in a craft shop, or contact a straw plaiter who could help.

There are many different traditional corn dollies — in Britain almost each county has its own design. Only a few very simple ones are described here, for there are plenty of good books available to take you further on the subject.

Before plaiting the straw, soak the stalks in warm water for at least an hour to avoid splitting. If you are making a number of corn dollies, wrap the straw in a damp towel after soaking.

Countryman's favour

You will need:

3 long straws of equal length, complete with ears
Thread in matching colour
Red gift ribbon

Tie the three straws together firmly just below the ears with some thread. Now plait the straws as you would plait a little girl's hair.

Plait for 15 - 20cm and tie the end with thread. Twist the plait into the shape of your choice. Join ends with red ribbon, tied in a bow.

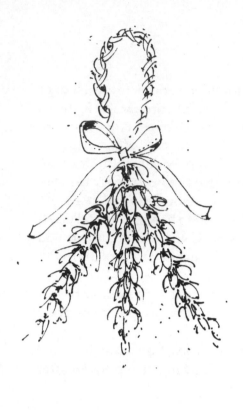

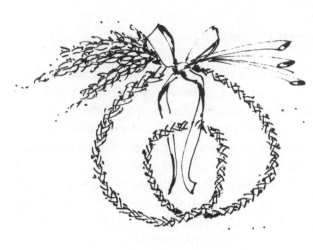

For a stronger, three-dimensional plait use four straws and plait as follows: Tie the four straws together just below the ears.

Hold the straws between the first two fingers of the left hand, ears pointing down and stalks up. Spread the stalks to the points of the compass and put the left thumb down on the centre where the stalks meet. (As you work, the left thumb has the task to keep the plait tight.) With the right hand fold the north stalk to the south and south to north. Press down with thumb. Now fold east to west and west to east.

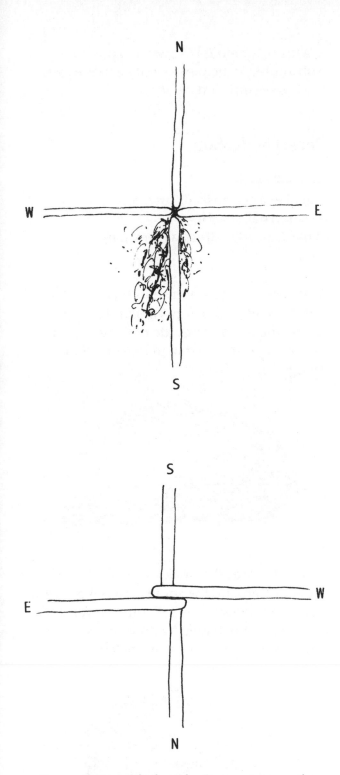

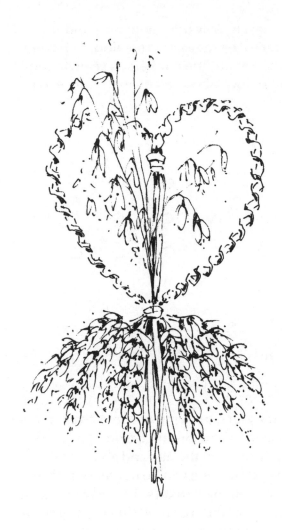

Press down with thumb. Carry on repeating this process, always moving the straws in the same order.

Conkers

Who can resist collecting chestnuts? Gather a basketful of these shiny, silky-smooth 'conkers' and stir them up with your hand — what a real autumn delight!

Conker skittles

You will need:
15 conkers (Aesculus Hippocastanum)
Piece of string or chalk
1 extra conker for each person playing

It is best to play this game on a smooth surface such as a concrete floor or paving slabs. Set out the conkers as seen on the plan below (about 10cm apart from each other).

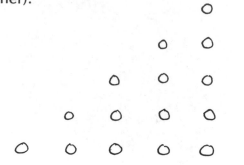

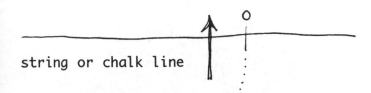

string or chalk line

With a piece of string or some chalk, mark out a line some distance from the conkers. Depending on the age and ability of the players, this line will be nearer or further away from the conkers. The players take it in turns to stand behind the line and roll a conker towards the 'skittles.' If they manage to hit or move any of the conkers, they may claim them. The game ends when all the skittles have been taken, and the winner is the one with the most conkers.

Teasel hedgehog and mouse

Families of teasel mice and hedgehogs can be made using different sizes of teasel heads. Their prickliness is usually a deterrent to a two-year-old's fingers, and the use of pins make these little creatures unsuitable as toys for young children. Black plasticine or modelling wax is a possible substitute for the pins — but keep the eyes and nose small and dainty.

Teasel hedgehog

You will need:
Small teasel (Dipsacus fullonum)
Pointed nail scissors
3 black-headed dressmakers' pins
Glue

Cut away the stem and spiky bracts of the teasel. With nail scissors begin clipping away prickles on one side of the teasel to make a flat surface (the underside of the hedgehog).

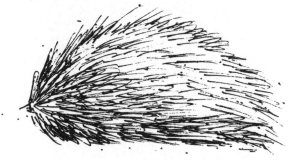

Then clip away the prickles, as short as possible, around the snout area. Take care to clip some away beneath the chin, and to create a heart-shaped 'widow's peak' around the eyes, (see diags. below).

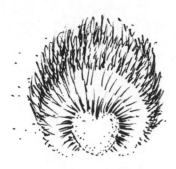

Insert the pins firmly as snout and eyes. Experiment with placing the eyes, as this can affect the whole expression and character of the creature.

Teasel mouse

You will need:
Small teasel (Dipsacus fullonum)
Pointed nail scissors
3 black-headed dressmakers' pins
Pine cone
7 cm length of cotton string in a natural
    colour
Glue

Cut the stem of the teasel to just over 1 cm in length, and clip it to a point with scissors.

With the point of the scissors, snip out some of the spiky teasel bracts, leaving two or three on each side as below:

Clip the prickles of the teasel very short within the shaded area of the diagram, to shape the head of the mouse. Halve the length of the prickles on the underside of the body to make a flat surface. Round off tail end of the mouse.

Use two small 'leaves' from the pine cone as ears — put a dab of glue on each and push them firmly into the clipped prickles just above the whiskers. Insert the pins firmly as snout and eyes. Finally, put a dab of glue on one end of the string and poke it (the pointed scissors are a help here!) down into the prickles at the tail end of the mouse.

Walnut shell tortoise

You will need:
The half shell of a walnut (opened with the help of an old knife)
Brown modelling wax, or plasticine

Press a lump of brown modelling wax into the walnut shell, allowing sufficient wax to be available for modelling the head, legs and tail of the tortoise.

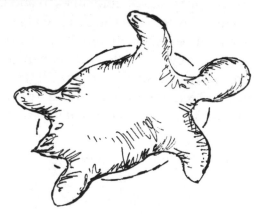

Raise the head of the tortoise a little off the ground and make sure the legs are curving slightly backwards.

A family of tortoises playing Follow-My-Leader are irresistible to the small child and adult alike!

A very quick and festive ring

This ring is made with dried flowers and seed pods. It looks stunning and is very easy to make if you don't mind using florist's foam. It can lie flat or hang on the wall.

You will need:
Ring of florist's foam for dry arrangements
Lots of dried flowers and seed heads (for drying see p117)
Florist's wire (medium thickness) and pliers
Thin florist's wire for brittle flowers

The florist's foam tends to be rather crumbly, so work on an appropriate surface. Cut a piece of wire, about 20cm long. Push it through the ring as illustrated to form a loop for hanging the ring.

Omit this wire if ring is to lie flat. Cut the flower stems 3cm long and push them into the ring. Make sure that the colours and shapes are balanced. The secret of a perfect ring is to over-fill it, packing the flowers together as densely as possible.

Some brittle flowers may need wiring. Cut a short length of wire and make a very small loop at the top. Pierce the centre of the flower with the wire, pulling through just far enough to hide the loop.

Two graces

Both are rounds in four parts.

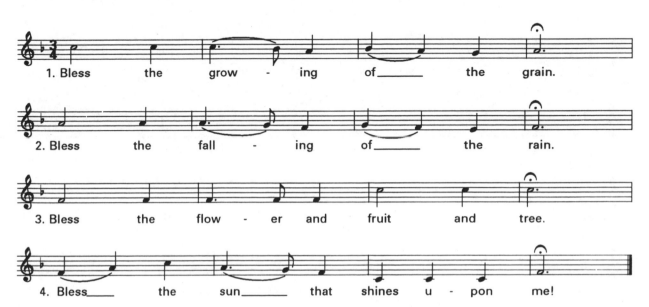

1. Bless the grow - ing of_____ the grain.

2. Bless the fall - ing of_____ the rain.

3. Bless the flow - er and fruit and tree.

4. Bless_____ the sun_____ that shines u - pon me!

1. For the seed of love with - in us.

2. For the beau - ty all a - round us.

3. For the strength of truth be - fore us.

4. Prai - ses sing to God!_____

Michaelmas

The Feast of St Michael and All Angels commemorates the deed of the Archangel Michael as described in Revelations 12: 7-9. "...there was a war in Heaven: Michael and his angels fought against the dragon; ...and the great dragon was cast out, that old serpent, called the Devil, and Satan, ...was cast into the earth."

Michael has been the Champion of both Christian and Jew; hundreds of churches in Europe have been dedicated to him. He is a well-known figure in icon painting — usually shown with a shield and lance, or fiery sword, gazing outwards while subduing the dragon underfoot. Sometimes he is shown holding a balance, with which he weighs the souls of men; again he looks outwards with his characteristic questioning gaze.

September 29th comes within the astrological sign of the Scales (Libra), and very near the perfect balance point of daylight and darkness in the year. To achieve balance between that part of us which belongs to nature, and the part which strives for goals which are not to be found in our 'human nature,' we have to outweigh the decline into death and darkness to which autumn would lead us. Through our own efforts, we must discover new inner resources which can help us to grow towards life and light. Easter was a time for contemplating the resurrection of the body, and now, at the opposite pole of the year, a resurrection experience for the soul is needed as a counter force to autumnal decay in the world.

As one of the English Quarter Days, Michaelmas has long been a time of new beginnings, when contracts were renewed between landlord and tenant, between employer and employee. In the past, hiring fairs were held at this time, where farm labourers and domestic servants offered themselves for work. Universities still begin their year at Michaelmas. So, 'taking up a new task' has long been a theme for this season, and the task Michael offered us all when he cast the great dragon into the earth, can become very real in our lives whenever we wish to take a new step on our inner journey — to raise ourselves a little above our nature. Then we discover that 'into the earth' means into *us* also, for we are immediately caught up in a battle with the weight, the inflexibility and the intractability of the hidden 'dragon' in our own being.

Michael beckons us to find the spirit to come alive through the dying year. The flashing meteor showers are said to be the sword he wields for us; each falling star is made of iron — the iron we need to strengthen the resolution of the heart. The seed-thoughts of the summer can be harvested now as deeds — to find their place in the world among people, to generate a life of their own that goes on into the future.

Michael calls us into the future with a question. What is the question? It is, in fact, his name: Mi-cha-el: which means 'Who is like God?' This is the question which leads us now from the autumn equinox into the dead of winter. In vain do we search for an answer along the way: We do not find it on earth among the fields of wet stubble or the heaps of blackened leaves. We do not find it among the lofty ranks of all the saints, nor even on All Souls' Day among the countless legions of those who once lived. Do we find the answer among the noblest of warriors or the most devout of priests? No, Michael's questing gaze reaches beyond Martinmas, beyond St Nicholas Day, beyond even Adam and Eve Day, to a helpless child lying in a cattle stall.

As we become aware of Michael, and of his question, we might recall that he is known also by another name: the Countenance of Christ. Through his beckoning gaze, Michael leads us to the contemplation of Christ; not only to the Word Made Flesh, but also to the living spirit born from the humblest dwelling of what St Francis liked to call 'Brother Ass' — our own flesh and blood. Michael reveals to us the Holy Child that seeks to be born in each human soul.

Harvest loaf

There is still time at Michaelmas to enjoy a harvest loaf, if you have not already done so. The main ingredient in this loaf is a story — it imparts its own special flavour! For the other ingredients:

You will need:
1kg wholemeal flour
500ml warm milk (blood heat)
Large tsp brown sugar
25g (approx. 5 tsps) dried yeast
50g melted butter
Scant tsp sea salt
75g white sugar
150g currants
1 egg yolk
25g sesame and/or sunflower seeds
A little beaten egg, or milk

Measure the flour into a large, warm mixing bowl. Dissolve the brown sugar in the warm milk and sprinkle the yeast on top. Stir mixture and leave in a warm place until frothy (12-15 mins.).

Prepare a clean table in the kitchen for the breadmaking; create a festive mood with a lighted candle and some flowers nearby. Place the mixing bowl with the flour on the table, and arrange the following ingredients around it in saucers or little bowls: white sugar and salt mixed; currants; egg yolk; seeds. When the yeast mixture is frothy, add the melted butter.

Now you are ready to tell The Story of the Harvest Loaf. (It is far easier to tell it by heart than to try to read and work at the same time.) No doubt the children's fingers will want to be active too, so they can be encouraged to join in. They may like to spend some time creating a landscape in the flour while the preliminary preparations are made in the kitchen.

When the story has been told, the dough can be covered and set aside in a warm place for half an hour to rise. Then knead briefly, place on a greased baking sheet and brush with beaten egg or milk. Leave in a warm place to prove (approx. 30-40 mins.) and bake in a fairly hot oven for about an hour. (The loaf should be golden brown and give a hollow sound when tapped firmly on the base.)

The story of the harvest loaf

(Begin to model a landscape in the flour.)

Once there was a fair and beautiful land. It was difficult to say whether the hills were fairer than the valleys, or whether the plains were more beautiful than the forests, but the people who lived there were happy and busy and their faces shone as they worked so that the whole land glowed with a bright light.

(Pour in yeast mixture.)

But the time came when darkness fell upon this land, for through its valleys writhed a mighty dragon, foaming and lashing his tail.

It was not long before he had laid everything to waste and disappeared to his cave, leaving the country barren and frozen hard with ice.

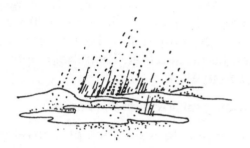

(Sprinkle on salt and sugar.)

All the people living there were frozen too, and they were unable to work or do anything at all.

Now the Archangel Michael looked down from the heavens to this sad and frozen land, and his heart was full of compassion for its people. He stretched forth his right hand, plucked a handful of stars from the firmament and flung them down to the earth.

(Throw in currants.)

With his left hand he gathered sungold from the sky and sent that, too, on a journey to the earth.

(Add whole egg yolk.)

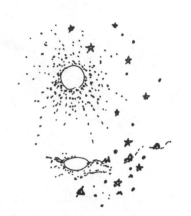

(Knead dough on a floured board.)

"Bake it in the oven until it is done. Place the loaf in the centre of your table and share it with your family and friends. For this will be the Harvest Loaf: each slice that is cut in friendship will warm your hearts, and each slice that is eaten will give strength and power to overcome the dragon."

When the stars reached the earth they became lumps of black iron, and entered deep into the ground. When the sungold reached the earth the ice was melted and men once more felt the blood warming their hands and feet. Then the people began to work.

(Begin mixing with the hands.)

The farmers took out their ploughs and ploughed the barren land and sowed it with seeds.

(Sprinkle with seeds.)

This the farmers did, and when the Harvest Loaf was placed on the table they sat with their families and friends and sang this song:

"Earth who gives to us this food
Sun and stars who made it good
Dearest Earth and
Stars and Sun
We will remember what you have done."

The iron in the earth gave strength to the crop as it grew, and soon the grain was ripening on tall, straight stems. When autumn time came, the Archangel Michael bent near to the earth and spoke to the farmers. "Harvest the good grain," he commanded them, "grind it into flour. Mix a dough and knead it well."

Earth who gives to us this food Sun____ and stars who made it good. Dea - rest earth and stars____ and sun, we will re - mem - ber what you have done!

Michaelmas candle

In the heat of summer we rarely have a fire in the fireplace. Similarly, while the daylight is still so very strong, our family tends not to light a candle on the table at every meal. However, on Michaelmas Day a brand new candle stands on the dining table, which is to be lit every day thereafter. As St Michael is often depicted fighting a dragon, we use this motif for our candle. The flame becomes St Michael's fiery sword subduing the dragon day by day until he is banished completely.

You will need:

Large candle about 5cm diam., in an
  autumnal colour (or white)
Modelling wax, preferably in green, red,
  orange and yellow

Note: If modelling wax is unavailable, melt wax crayons (in an old spoon over the flame of a candle) and paint on the candle with these melted colours.

Take small pieces of wax and knead them until the wax becomes warm and soft. Stick small pieces on the candle and model them into shape. Spread the wax quite thinly as you work. We usually use green wax for the

dragon, which curls around the candle and spits flames (red, yellow, orange) from its open mouth.

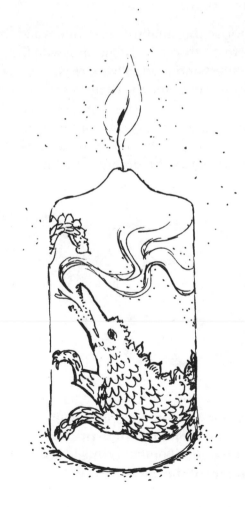

A conker dragon

(Pull-along toy.)

You will need:
61 fresh conkers (Aesculus Hippocastanum)
Strong cord (approx. 2m) red, if possible
Metal skewer or similar to pierce the
    conkers
Sealing wax — optional

Pierce a hole through every conker, taking care not to split them. Knot one end of the cord leaving 3cm of cord below the knot. (Make sure all knots are large enough not to pass through the conkers, and always leave a 3cm end.)

Choose the smallest six conkers and thread them on the cord, beginning with the very smallest and gradually increasing in size. This will become the dragon's tail. Continue threading thirty more conkers. Count back ten conkers and tie the cord in a firm knot behind the tenth conker, making a loop which will be the dragon's head.

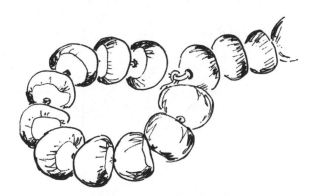

Cut away the end of cord neatly. Knot the end of remaining length of cord and thread on three conkers. Knot these above the six conkers of the tail as below:

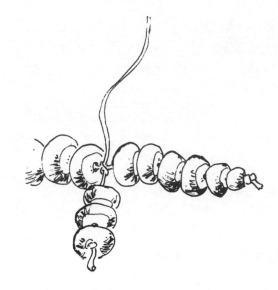

Thread on three more conkers. Make a firm knot and cut off remaining length of cord. Your dragon now has a pair of legs.

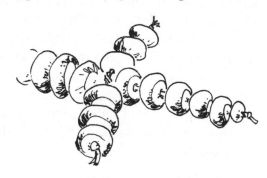

Repeat this process three more times, always keeping six conkers of the body between each pair of legs. Attach a leading cord of suitable length to the front of the dragon. Make a knot 10cm from the free end and thread on last conker. Knot cord firmly above the conker to hold it in place. Seal all knots with sealing wax if available.

Now, take your dragon for a walk…

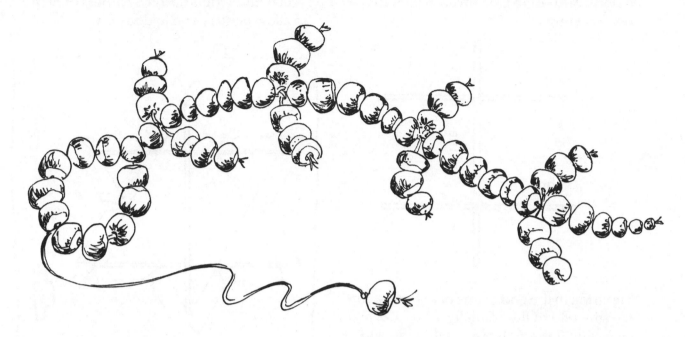

Shooting star kite

Kites have been flown for over 2,000 years and although many excellent ones can be bought, there is still nothing to beat the satisfaction of flying a kite you have made yourself. To hold a kite flying high in the autumn wind gives a wonderful feeling of 'letting go' with the power of the wind and at the same time remaining in control, with both feet firmly on the ground.

Kites are made in many different shapes and sizes; we show only a simple one here. Highly specialized books can be found on the subject, should you want to take it further.

You will need:
60 cm length of split bamboo cane or 3 mm dowelling for spine
Two 51 cm lengths of split bamboo cane or 3 mm dowelling for spars

50 m strong, thin string (preferably nylon for lightness)
Glue
Large plastic carrier bag in a bright colour (or tissue paper)
2 plastic carrier bags, in contrasting colours, for tails
PVC adhesive tape (in GB known as insulating tape)
Small keyring or curtain ring
Sharp knife and scissors
Short piece of large dowelling or a stick (to use as reel for the kite line)

Cut notches in the ends of each of the sticks.

Tie sticks firmly together with string as seen below. Add some glue on each joint for extra security.

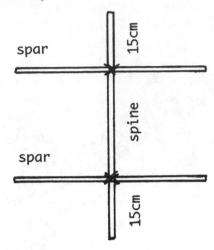

Tie string to the end of one of the spars, run it to the end of the spine furthest from that spar. Run it through the notch at the end of the spine and back to opposite end of original spar.

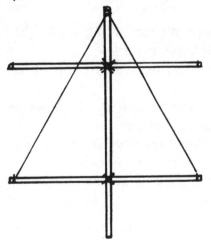

Repeat with the other spar to achieve a star-shaped frame. Cut along one of the side seams and bottom of the large carrier bag to open it out. Lay the plastic (or tissue paper) on a flat surface and position kite frame on top. Use kite frame as a guide to cut out

plastic covering. When cutting, allow for a 3cm hem all round. Notch corners of hem to allow plastic to be folded down.

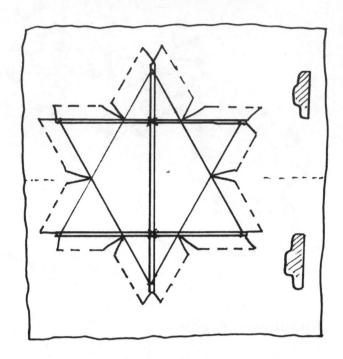

Attach cover to frame by folding edges over frame and fixing with PVC tape. Any string which runs across the kite should also be stuck to the cover with tape. Turn kite over to front side and cut a tiny opening at X1 and X2 for tying on bridle string. Cut 1.68m length of string for bridle. Thread it from front to back through the tiny openings at X1 and X2. Tie bridle string as seen below. Tie the ring with a 'lark's head hitch' knot as shown, 73cm from X1:

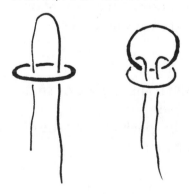

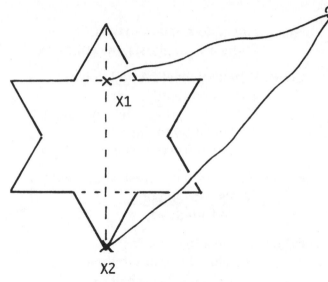

X1

X2

Cut nine streamers, each about 90 cm x 3 cm (in three different colours if possible) and tie them to kite as shown:

Tie rest of string to the short length of stick or dowelling which will become a handle for the kite. Wind the string on the stick and tie free end of string to ring. The kite is now ready for flying — invite a friend to help with its launching. One person unwinds half the length of line while the other stands facing the wind, holding the kite up with out-stretched arms. Keep the line taut. When the kite is ready to go, give it a slight upward push. Unwind more line when the kite is well up in the sky.

N.B. Never fly a kite in a thunderstorm. Never fly a kite near power lines, across a road or railway lines. Trees have a habit of devouring kites, so keep clear of them also. Observe local regulations concerning kite flying, i.e. height restrictions, etc.

More Michaelmas dragons

Involving older children in a festival may not always be straightforward. Resistance can sometimes be overcome when there is food involved!

You will need:
Dough as for Festival Bread on page 250.

After the first rising, each person uses a handful of dough to create their own dragon. These can be decorated with currants and sliced almonds. Leave to rise again. Bake for 20-30 mins. in a hot oven.

Invite someone along to guess who made which dragon…

Concerning dragons

Child: Are all the dragons fled?
     Are all the goblins dead?
     Am I quite safe in bed?

Nurse: Thou art quite safe in bed,
     Dragons and Goblins
       All are dead.

Child: Are there no witches here?
     Nor any giants near?
     Nor anything to fear?

Nurse: Who put such nonsense in thy head?
     Witches and Giants
       All are dead.

Child: Nurse, have you seen the ghost
     Which comes to Jacob's Post?
     I *nearly* did, almost —

Nurse: Hush, do not talk so wild,
     There are no ghosts, my child.

Child: When Michael's Angel fought
     The dragon, did it roar?
     (Oh, Nurse, don't shut the door)
     And did it try to bite?
     (Nurse, don't blow out the light.)

Nurse: Hush, thou knowest what I said,
     Saints and Dragons
       All are dead.

Father (to himself);
     O child, Nurse lies to thee,
     For dragons thou shalt see,
     And dragons thou shalt smite —
     Let Nurse blow out the light.
     Please God that in that day
     Thou may'st a dragon slay,
     And if thou dost not faint
     God shall not want a Saint.

Hilary Pepler

Hallowe'en, All Saints' Day, All Souls' Day, Remembrance Sunday

Let us consider these four days together, as they each contribute towards that moment in the festival year when our thoughts are turned towards those who have died.

The First World War came to a final end with the Armistice, signed at the eleventh hour of the eleventh day of the eleventh month of the year 1918. On the Sunday nearest to November 11th, Britain celebrates a national Day of Remembrance for all those who have died in conflict. This festival underlines an ancient tradition of celebrating the dead at this time of the year.

In the Christian year, those who have died are remembered particularly on All Souls' Day. In many places in Europe graves are decked with flowers and candles, processions are held and night-long vigils kept at the graveside. The previous day, All Saints' Day or All Hallows, is an important festival in honour of the Christian martyrs. It was in the 9th century that this festival was moved from May 13th to November 1st, with the intention of supplanting the pagan Celtic rite of Samhain.

Julius Caesar commented that the Celts reckoned their calendar in nights rather than days; indeed, all their Quarter Days were celebrated on the Eve. The Eve of Samhain later became All Hallows' Eve, or Hallowe'en, but many of the pre-Christian beliefs connected with this night have their echoes in customs which have endured until the present day.

Samhain marked the beginning of the New Year in the Celtic calendar, and it was an especially sacred and significant time. There was a feeling that, on the eve of this feast, time belonged neither to the Old Year nor to the New. The lack of definition in time implied also a blurring of the boundaries of space — in particular the boundary between this world and the next, between the living and the dead, between human beings and the gods or nature forces. These worlds intermingled: threatening supernatural beings walked abroad, and the souls of the dead came to visit their old homes.

In most pagan cultures, great respect was paid to the dead. Folk perceived them as hungry and in need of nourishment. Customs arose of providing food and fire for the souls of departed relatives at this time, and the offering of 'soul cakes' to the dead on the Eve of All Souls persists in many places. In Christian times, however, although the need is recognised, it has been considered more fitting to offer this food and warmth in spiritual form — as regular, heartfelt prayer. Whatever the form that is chosen, these festivals give us the space to develop a healthy and more conscious relationship to relatives and friends who have died, and to that aspect of Life which must include Death.

It is not only the little 'ghosts' of the dead that one sees nowadays stalking the streets of Britain and America on Hallowe'en, but many companies of witches, goblins and naughty sprites who threaten to 'trick' if they are not 'treated' properly. Folk tales have always warned that soured milk or some other domestic calamity would be the price to pay for not giving the 'little people' their due respect, but it is only in recent years that such phenomena as acid rain and depletion of the ozone layer have brought home to us what ugly 'tricks' we must expect if we disregard the wise forces of Nature.

It was the wisdom of the Earth that was celebrated at Samhain. The Earth goddess was pictured at this festival as an Old Wise Woman in black who stands at the dying of the Old Year, on the threshold of the New. She has come into our culture as a witch figure, but there is perhaps more in common with Hecate, the Greek goddess of the Dark Moon, who, although a fearsome guardian of her knowledge of the underworld, could also be of help to human beings earnest in their life's task.

Three questions are today becoming more and more central to the task of living: How do we treat the forces of life properly? How do we find the right relationship to death in the face of mass famine, euthanasia issues and life support systems? Have we the courage to recognise evil, not only in the world but also in ourselves?

So when the bell rings to announce the 'trick or treaters' on Hallowe'en, or those begging for soul cakes on the Eve of All Souls, maybe we can see through the corruptions of folk custom, and the distortions of the supermarket masks, and open our doors to the real issues which stand on the very threshold of our life situation.

Technology is becoming especially powerful in areas which lie beyond the grasp of our knowledge, and, in many cases, our morality. There are some mysterious aspects of life experience which increasingly demand recognition and understanding. A giggling huddle of ghouls and ghosties on the doorstep may remind us of forgotten corners of existence that could become a source of suffering through our neglect.

Dabbling in the occult is a dangerous practice, and many people shun Hallowe'en because of this association. 'Trick or treating' also, is often frowned upon for its antisocial excesses. But it would be a shame if this festival were to disappear, for its contribution can be a valuable one. The Christian martyrs, whose lives are celebrated on the following day, have been venerated as examples of those who confronted the fear, the superstition and the baleful influences in the world around them with courage. Hallowe'en challenges us to face with strength, with perception, with understanding, these negative forces as they appear unexpectedly on the doorstep of our own soul.

Turnip lantern

These lanterns can also be made from a swede, mangold-wurzel or any other large root vegetable. They keep for about 3-4 days in a cool place.

You will need:
Large turnip
Sharp knife and a spoon
Metal skewer
Nightlight candle
Thin wire (approx. 30cm) for handle

Slice a lid off the turnip about 5cm from the top. With knife and spoon, scoop out the inside of the turnip, leaving about 1.5cm thickness of wall. Decorate the outside of the turnip by scraping shapes and figures into the skin. Cut 0.75cm deep into the skin only, and not through the wall. Place the candle inside the turnip and pierce an air-hole with the skewer through the base near the candle. Pierce two small holes about 2cm from the top edge on opposite sides. Thread the wire into these holes and secure.

Traditional Hallowe'en Colcannon

Colcannon is, by old tradition, eaten on Hallowe'en and usually conceals a few prophetic charms similar to the ones buried in a Christmas pudding.

You will need:
1 kg boiled potatoes
A few spring onions finely chopped
A little milk
25 g butter
350 g boiled green cabbage or kale
Salt and pepper

Mash potatoes and mix with milk and spring onions. Finely chop the cabbage or kale. Heat the butter and toss cabbage in it. Stir cabbage into the potato mixture and serve.

For an extra tasty dish, form the Colcannon into a flat but thick pancake and fry on both sides in some bacon fat until the outside is crisp and brown.

Hallowe'en witch

Why not make your own Hallowe'en decoration? Older children could try this one, (possibly with some help when it comes to the sewing of the card).

You will need:
Hallowe'en Witch pattern from page 261
2 pieces of thin but not floppy card in a
    'witchy' colour, each 23 cm x 24 cm
Thread in matching colour
Tracing paper (or any transparent paper)
Carbon paper — optional
Craft knife

To make up, follow the instructions for the Palm Sunday Decoration on page 49.

Hansel and Gretel gingerbread house

This house, covered with delicious treats, reminds us of the witch's house in the fairy tale of Hansel and Gretel. When the nightlight within shines in a darkened room, it brings an additional touch of magic!

You will need:
Gingerbread House pattern (see p262)
Cake board approx. 36cm square or 40cm diam.
Sharp knife
Some red tissue paper or cellophane
Nightlight candle
Icing bag and small plain nozzle
Stiff paper for pattern

For the gingerbread:
300g sugar
4 tbsps syrup
100ml water
180g butter
0.5 tbsp mixed spice
2 tsps ground ginger (or cinnamon if preferred)
1 tsp baking powder
1 tsp bicarbonate of soda
750g plain flour

Royal Icing:
(Water icing is not really strong enough to 'cement' the house together.)
1 egg white (from a reputable source)
150g icing sugar
Pinch cream of tartar or 1 tsp lemon juice
0.5 tsp glycerine

Mix ingredients and beat well until glossy. Add more lemon juice if necessary but keep the icing reasonably stiff.

For decoration:
Quantity of tiny sweets (jelly beans, chocolate drops, etc.)
Quantity of cake decorations (silver balls, sugar strands, etc.)
Blanched almonds, hazelnuts, sultanas, raisins, etc.

Melt sugar, syrup and water in a saucepan over low heat. Add butter and spice and allow to cool for 5 mins. Add flour, sifted with baking powder and bicarbonate of soda. Mix to a soft dough and leave overnight.

Measure out and draw house pattern on stiff paper. Roll out dough to 6mm thickness on floured surface. Lay patterns on top and cut dough accordingly. The door, windows and chimney are not cut out at this stage. (Cut trees, animals etc. out of leftover dough.) Place on greased baking sheet and bake in middle of moderate oven for 10 - 15 mins., or until pale gold. Do not remove gingerbread from the baking sheet, but immediately start cutting out the door, windows, etc. with a sharp knife. Lay the pattern back on the gingerbread to do this.

Cut carefully, keeping the door and window shapes intact. Now cut each window along the dotted line. (This will give four curved ridge-tiles for the roof and enough material to build a chimney.) Allow all pieces to cool on a wire rack. On the underside of sections (a), (b) and (d), cover window areas with red paper, using dabs of royal icing. Using the icing as 'cement,' now build the house, fixing it to the cake board as you work. See below for arrangement of pieces:

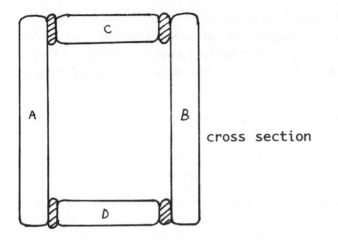

cross section

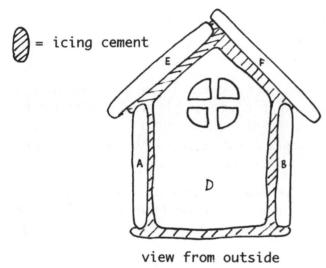

= icing cement

view from outside

Use some of the window offcuts to construct a square chimney around the

hole in the roof. Arrange the four ridge-tiles upright along the ridge of the roof. If more are needed, fashion them out of the window offcuts. Position the nightlight directly below the chimney before attaching the door, which must stand well ajar to allow access to the candle. (The easiest method of lighting the candle is to use a taper.)

Now we wish you a lot of fun decorating the Hansel and Gretel house.

Suggested approach:
a) Use light pressure only.
b) Soften the icing mixture a little with lemon juice.
c) Using icing bag and nozzle, outline door, windows and all edges and seams.
d) Affix sweets, etc. with small dab of icing.
e) Do not coat walls or roof with icing or the house may collapse!
f) Icicles add a special touch. Extrude a length of icing from the nozzle before pressing end of the nozzle against the roof to fix it. It's much easier than you think.
g) Decorate extra trees, animals etc; and fix them to the board surrounding the house.
h) Finally, dust the whole house and board with dry icing sugar 'snow.'

A Hallowe'en party

Each party guest has to bring a trick along. Treats, of course, are provided by the host! The tricks could be card tricks, juggling tricks, magician's tricks or games like these:

— The player who brings this game must have an accomplice amongst the other players. He leaves the room and the others decide on a word which he has to guess on his return. The word, as previously arranged, is the one mentioned after any four-legged thing, e.g. the accomplice in the room asks: "Is it a book?" "No!" "An apple?" "No!" "A candle?" "No!" "A cat?" (four legs) "No!" "A milkbottle?" "Yes!"

— Peter says to Jane, "Here is a piece of paper. You write something on this paper, a word, a sentence or even a few lines. I also take a piece of paper and leave the room. You must write very carefully and slowly with clear letters and I'll write exactly the same on my paper." Peter leaves the room and when he comes back, the words "exactly the same" are written on his piece of paper!

— Three chairs stand in a row. Mary tells everyone that Sophy would know without fail which chair out of the three had been sat upon. Sophy leaves the room and one of the other children quickly sits on the chair in the middle for a few seconds. Sophy is called: "Come in." She looks at the chairs, feels them, points to the middle one and says "This is the one!"

— Mary and Sophy had quietly agreed beforehand which chair would be the first one in the row. Sophy just had to listen to how Mary called her in: "Ready," one word for first chair; "Come in," two words for second chair; "We are ready," three words for third chair.

— There are three hats and one chocolate. John eats the chocolate and announces grandly: "Under which of these hats shall I magic the same chocolate?" The middle one is being pointed to and John immediately puts it on his head!

— A large and heavy book lies on top of the table. Joe is asked to practise by first touching it with his right hand: "Now touch it and press your hand hard on it… Now hit it with the palm of your hand." He is congratulated on doing well. Surely he wouldn't be able to do this blindfolded? While he is being blindfolded someone quietly replaces the book with a large plastic bowl of water. Joe is asked to hit the book with his palm right away!

— Who can crawl through a postcard? — Easy! Take a pair of scissors, fold the card lengthways in half and cut it as seen below. Take care never to cut right through the edge. The final cut is made lengthways, along the fold where indicated. Open up the card and wriggle through!

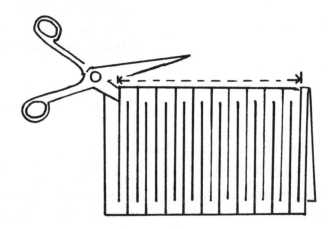

— Prepare as many slips of paper as there are players. Ask each player in turn to give you the name of a famous person, which you write on a slip of paper. All the slips are folded and put in a hat. One of the players is now invited to draw a slip out of the hat and hold it without opening it up. All the other slips are thrown away — or even burnt. You then pretend to concentrate very hard and to everyone's astonishment you tell them the name written on the slip!

How? — As they call out the names, you write the first name down on every single slip of paper!

Spear the apple

You will need:
Large plastic bowl of water
Some eating apples
Chair and fork

Float 6-10 apples in the bowl on the floor. Place a chair alongside the bowl. Each child in turn stands on the chair facing the bowl. They hold the fork loosely in the mouth by the very end of the handle, so that the fork is hanging vertically with the prongs pointing at the floating apples. Then the fork is dropped. Any apples that are speared are claimed and eaten.

P.S. The floor and furniture will get a little wet!

Punch

This is a festive, warming drink for a cold Hallowe'en night, or for any other winter evening party.

You will need:
4 lemons
2 oranges
(Use unsprayed fruit if available)
250g sugar
400ml water
10 cloves
Piece of root ginger
Cinnamon stick

Put the water in a heavy saucepan. Add spices and the peel of one thinly peeled orange and lemon. Simmer for an hour. Strain. Dissolve the sugar in the liquid and add juice of oranges and lemons. Before serving, mix one part punch with two parts boiling water.

Traditional old Sussex soul cakes

For hundreds of years, all over Northern and Central Europe, these cakes have been made for All Souls Day to offer to departed souls who, it is said, visit their old earthly abode at this time. The food was left in the kitchen the evening before, where a large log burned in the hearth all night. The tradition has now largely disappeared, but some Sussex children still enjoy calling at houses on the eve of All Souls to be given a hot Soul Cake.

You will need:

500g flour
1 level tsp baking powder
175g butter or margarine
3 eggs
300ml milk
⅓ tsp each of ground cinnamon, cloves and
    nutmeg
175g sugar
Some currants
Cup-cake cases

Cream butter and sugar until very light and fluffy. Beat in the eggs, one at a time, keeping the mixture as fluffy as possible. Sieve in the flour, baking powder and spices. Carefully fold in the milk and mix but don't beat, to allow the mixture to stay as airy as possible. Fill mixture into the cupcake cases and mark out a cross on top of each cake with a few currants. Bake at 200°C for about 15 mins. or until golden.

The saying goes that for the best results one should work in the light of an east-facing window and sing hymns during the mixing of the batter!

Guy Fawkes Night

"Remember, remember the fifth of November,
Gunpowder, treason and plot.
I see no reason why gunpowder treason
Should ever be forgot." Anon.

In the year 1605, a plot was hatched to blow up the Houses of Parliament in London in an attempt to assassinate King James I. Barrels of gunpowder were positioned in the cellars and Guy Fawkes was to light the fuse. However, suspicions were aroused, the cellars were searched and Guy Fawkes was arrested. He and the other conspirators were all sent to their deaths.

This sorry tale has been preserved in British folk culture ever since, with an evening of fun on November 5th. An effigy of Guy Fawkes is burned on top of a large bonfire, and the night crackles and sparkles with fireworks.

On the days before November 5th children make 'Guys' from old clothes stuffed with paper or straw, and wheel them on little trolleys or old prams to a street corner where they ask passers-by for "a penny for the Guy." The pennies are saved to buy fireworks. This custom is dying out, however, in areas where the bonfire and firework display has become more of a municipal responsibility.

In pagan times, the transitional moments of spring and autumn were always celebrated with fire rituals. The Beltane fires of May 1st ushered in the summer, and at the end of the Celtic year (October 31st) all old fires were extinguished and new ones kindled from the ceremonial bonfire on Samhain (November 1st). These ceremonial fires persisted well into Christian times, and the enthusiasm for the Guy Fawkes bonfire may well be due in part to the folk memory connected with this time of year.

Most people enjoy an occasional bonfire; it's a good excuse to clear up garden rubbish, to roast potatoes and chestnuts, to stay out late and gaze at the stars, to dream into the flames and the flying sparks. If you can't manage a large bonfire, why not gather one or two small children and organise a bonfire party to celebrate the end of autumn with the gnomes?

Gnomes' bonfire party

Prepare a small fire (either indoors or outdoors) and allow it to establish a good bed of hot embers. Seat all the Autumn Garden gnomes comfortably at a suitable distance from the fire and then gather every pod, leaf, cone and other scrap from the Autumn Garden that the gnomes have not been able to use, and feed them into the fire one by one. They will each burn in an individual way — some with a bright flare, some with a crackle, some with a shower of golden sparks. (Chestnuts and acorns that have not been pierced with a knife may explode, so be sure the fire is guarded.) Take time to enjoy each 'firework,' but leave the pine cones until last — if the conditions are right and they are undisturbed, they might turn to gold before your very eyes!

This event will be most successful if it can be kept small and intimate.

Knitted gnome

Arms:
Cast on 8 sts. and knit 12 rows g.st. Cast off. Repeat for 2nd arm.

Feet:
Cast on 5 sts. and knit 18 rows st.st. Cast off. Repeat for 2nd foot.

Jacket:
Cast on 13 sts. Knit 2 rows in g.st. 3rd and 4th row: K. 10 sts. turn, K. to end of row. K. all 13 sts. for next 2 rows. Then K. a short row again (as 3rd and 4th rows). Continue in this way until there are 50 rows (25 ribs) at the wider end of the jacket. Cast off.

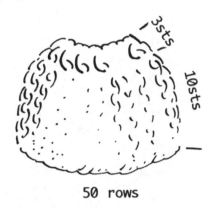

50 rows

You will need:
1 pair 3mm (2US) knitting needles
20g of double knitting wool/or mohair for gnome's clothes
10g of double knitting wool/or mohair for gnome's body
Fleece for beard and stuffing
Small piece of cardboard for feet
Flesh-coloured stockinette 8.5cm wide x 7cm long
White stretchy cotton (an old T-shirt is ideal) about 13cm x 13cm
Strong white button thread
1 very small round bead for nose

Head:
Stuff a small ball of fleece into the white stretchy square of cotton. Tie a length of strong thread tightly around the neck and form a 'head' about 3.5cm high.

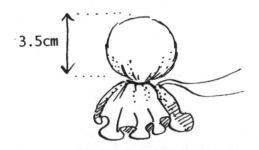

3.5cm

Tie a length of strong thread around the middle of the head to make an eye line.

Body:
Cast on 24 sts and knit 20 rows st.st. Cast off.

Hat:
Cast on 22 sts. Knit 4 rows g.st. Continue in st.st. and knit together the first 2 and last 2 sts. of the next and every alt. row. When only 2 sts. are left, break yarn and thread through the sts.

Sew a tiny bead just below eye line for the nose.

Now cover the head with stockinette. Stretch fabric horizontally around head and pull across the face tightly. Sew up at back of head. Tie thread around neck and close up top of head with running stitch drawn in around top edge.

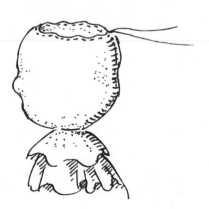

To make up:
Sew together body piece.

Sew up bottom edge of body so that the vertical seam is centred at the back. Divide legs with a few stitches (O - X). Stuff body with fleece.

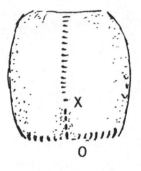

Attach head by gathering top edge of the body with a running stitch and drawing it in around the neck. Make sure that the nose is centred and faces forwards! Sew on the head. Make a beard and hair with fleece and sew into place. Draw eyes and mouth with a coloured pencil.

Sew up the hat and attach it to the head with a few stitches. Put the jacket around the shoulders like a cape and secure it at the front with a stitch. Roll up armpieces and sew in a little fleece for hands, pulling the thread slightly to make them curved.

Sew arms to the sides of the jacket. To prevent them sticking out at right angles, sew them down on the jacket with a few stitches under the armpit. Cut out two feet from cardboard.

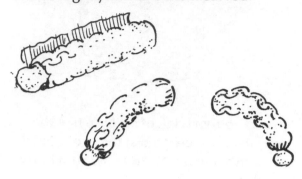

actual size   2X

Cover cardboard pieces with knitted foot pieces and sew them on the gnome to make him stand.

Simple felt gnomes

You will need:
Piece of felt (9cm x 11cm) in autumn colour
Embroidery cotton in matching colour
Fleece for stuffing

Cut out gnome's cape from felt using pattern :

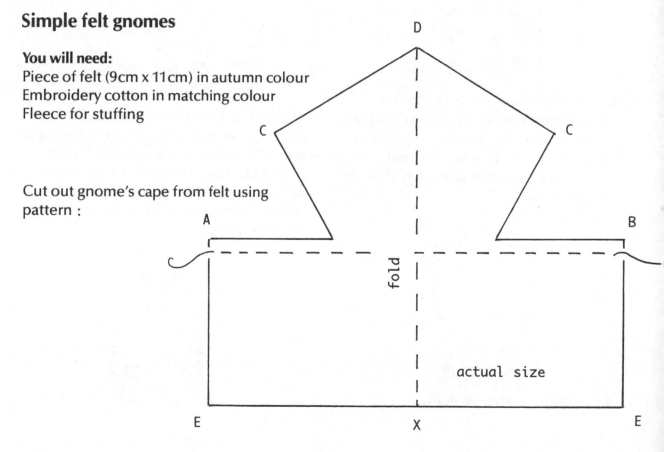

actual size

Use embroidery cotton to sew A-B with running stitch, leaving a thread of 2cm at each end as seen above. Fold cape along dotted line D-X, and sew together D-C with overstitch or blanket stitch to make gnome's hat. Stuff fleece into hat and cape to make the head and body. Draw thread A-B together and tie a knot. The front of the cape A-E and B-E can be stitched together in the same way as the hat. Gently tease out some fleece from gnome's face for a beard.

Make sure that the pine cone can stand upside down without falling over. You may need to trim one or two scales. Roll wax into a ball with warm hands. Press the ball on top of the cone for a head.

Fashion a hat from felt: Y-X-Y must fit around gnome's head. Fold on X-P and sew together P-Y.

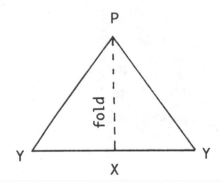

Gnome from a pine cone

You will need:
One pine cone
Small amount of wax for head (about hazelnut-size)
Scrap of felt and some thread, or the seed vessel of the Cape Gooseberry (Physalis)
Tiny twist of sheep wool for beard

Put hat on the head and press fleece on the wax face for a beard.

Alternatively, try using one of the smaller seed vessels of the Cape Gooseberry. Cut away the stem to create an opening large enough for the gnome's head.

Saw branch into length of about 4cm, and make sure that it will stand upright. Use knife to make gnome's face and beard. Cut off bark in triangular shape as seen above. Sand face and beard very lightly with sandpaper.

Gnome from a branch

You will need:
Straight piece of a small branch approx.
  2cm diam. seasoned if possible
Saw and fine sandpaper
Scrap of felt for hat
Pocket knife or small sharp, kitchen knife

Round off top (head) end of branch at back and sides with the knife.

Make a hat from felt and sew as seen below. Glue hat to head of gnome.

Indicate eyes and mouth with coloured pencils.

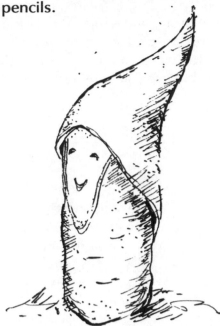

Martinmas

This day celebrates the burial of St Martin of Tours (316 - 397 AD) who devoted much of his life to establishing Christianity in France, and became one of her patron saints. He was born in Pannonia, and began life with a career in the Roman army, but eventually realised that he was 'Christ's soldier' and asked for a discharge. The legend tells that, when he was then accused of cowardice, he offered to stand unarmed between the opposing lines of battle.

St Martin is remembered especially for an incident which occurred while he was still taking instruction in the Christian faith before being baptised. While serving in the army at Amiens, Martin met a poor beggar at the city gate, who shivered half-naked in the cold. Drawing his sword, he cut his warm cloak in two and gave one half to the pauper. The following night, Christ appeared to Martin, dressed in the piece of cloak that the young officer had given away, and said: "Martin has covered me with this garment."

H. D. Thoreau wrote about autumn in 1854: "The season of hope and promise is past... We are a little saddened because we begin to see the interval between our hopes and their fulfilment. The prospect of the heavens is taken away, and we are presented only with a few small berries." We stand as paupers at the gates of winter. Martin's half cloak brought hope and comfort to the beggar — his compassionate gesture may warm us also, and protect us from wintry despair.

The traditional way of celebrating Martinmas is with lantern walks or processions, accompanied by singing. St Martin recognised the divine spark in the poor man of Amiens, and gave it the protection of his own cloak. When we make a paper lantern, we, too, may feel that we are giving protection to our own little 'flame' that was beginning to shine at Michaelmas, so that we may carry it safely through the dark world. It may only be a small and fragile light — but *every* light brings relief to the darkness.

Small lantern

This lantern shows the last glow of the autumn sun especially beautifully when it is made from deep corn-yellow card and orange tissue paper. We want to emphasize that great care has to be taken with candles. *Whenever a candle is alight it must be supervised by an adult at all times.* If you can get hold of a flame-retardant spray it is possible to make the lantern safer.

You will need:
Lantern pattern on page 263
Piece of card 20cm x 47cm
Tissue paper for the windows 12cm x 45cm
Glue
Scissors and craft knife
Approx. 20cm of plastic-coated florist's wire for handle
Nightlight candle in metal container

With ruler and pencil, measure and draw the dividing lines on the piece of card.

With scissors cut along solid lines and lightly score dotted lines to make folding easier. Draw the outlines of an autumn motif in each window space, using one of our designs or inventing your own.

Cut out design with craft knife. Cover cut-out shapes by glueing tissue paper over them on the inside. Bend the five sides of the lantern and glue overlap to the inside.

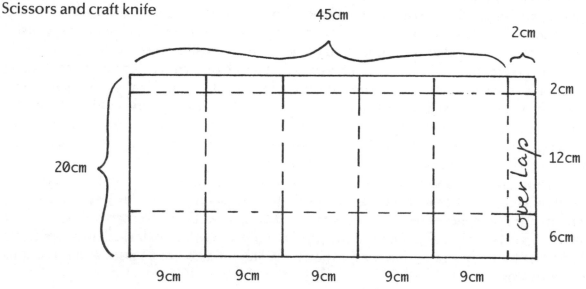

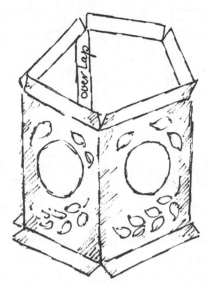

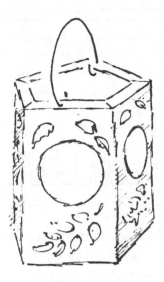

Bend and glue bottom pieces to form base of lantern as follows:

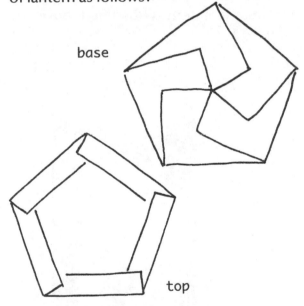

base

top

Make a neat top edge by bending and glueing edge pieces as for base.

Glue metal cup of nightlight candle securely to centre of lantern base. Bend the piece of wire to make a handle. Insert handle into top edge of lantern, and make a small loop at each side to secure it.

There are many more ways of making lanterns. One can simply glue some pieces of coloured tissue paper over a clear glass jar (an old honey jar), put a nightlight candle inside and hang it by tying some string around the top edge of the jar.

Lantern windows can also be covered with white greaseproof paper coloured with wax crayons, painted with strong water colours or decorated with pressed autumn leaves.

Two simple table lanterns

Lantern 1

You will need:
Piece of coloured card 25cm x 40cm
Scraps of tissue paper in various colours
Glue and paperclips
Craft knife and scissors
Circular piece of card 11.5cm diam.
Candle in a glass jar

Fold 1.5cm of the top (long) edge of the card and glue it down. Draw a line 5cm from bottom edge and cut a 'fringe' as shown.

165

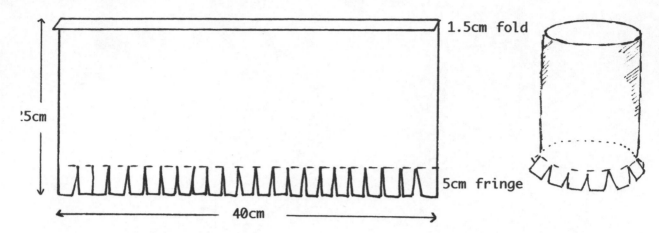

1.5cm fold

:5cm

5cm fringe

40cm

Cut some figures or shapes in the card with craft knife. Glue tissue paper over cut-out shapes. Glue short sides of card together (overlap 3cm) to form a tube with the tissue paper on the inside. Use paperclips to hold glued edges together while drying.

Put the circle of card into the bottom of the lantern and glue the fringe over it to make a strong base.

Put jar with candle inside the lantern.

Lantern 2

You will need:
Piece of strong drawing/
    painting paper 25cm x 40cm
Wax crayons
Cooking oil
Scissors and glue
Circular piece of card 11.5cm diam.
Candle in a glass jar

Draw a line across the paper 1.5cm from top edge. Draw a line 5cm from bottom edge and cut a 'fringe' as shown for Lantern 1. Draw a picture with wax crayons over whole centre strip of paper. Alternatively, cover the area with beautiful autumn tones

(yellow, gold, orange, red, maroon — not too much brown). Turn the drawing over and with a soft cloth rub the back of the paper with oil. The paper will now become transparent. Wipe off all surplus oil. Finish making the lantern as described above for Lantern 1.

A Martinmas meal

Choose a simple meal — a bread roll, baked potato or any other food which can be cut in half. At the start of the meal, divide your food and pass half to the neighbour on the left. Gift food really does taste different!

166

WINTER

"…I knew when Winter swirled —
Not by the whitened world,
   Or silver skeins in the lanes
     Or frost
     That embossed
   Its patterns on window-panes:
But because there were transfer-sheets
By the bottles of spice and sweets
In the shops in two little streets."

From "The Calendar" by Barbara Euphan Todd.

Winter

After the frenzy of the autumn dance comes the hibernal sleep. Exhausted and spent, Mother Earth rests in the peace of a 'little death,' her old bones jutting in rocky outcrops free of the withered skin of summer grass. Everywhere the relics of leaves rot beneath skeletal trees. The heart of the land grows cold.

But is this death, or the spell of enchantment? Has the ground beneath our feet been turned to stone? Do the web-weaving spiders, busily netting the evergreens, hold the whole countryside in thrall? Perhaps the earth, like one of its hibernating creatures, is alert even in sleep — listening, waiting for the coming of the Sun Prince, for the loving salutation which will quicken the lifeless. Here and there, a little blossom opens; like an eye of the world, it spies on the turning heavens, watching for the star-coded runes that will lift the spell of darkness.

With the first fall of snow we *know* that magic is at work! The morning light behind the curtains is strangely different; there is an uncommon hush in the streets. We try to concentrate on everyday tasks, yet are drawn back to the window to listen with our eyes to the soundless drifting of the snow. For some, this wizardry is unwelcome. Others rejoice as life is transformed, as an echo of this evenness creeps over the inner landscape, lightening and liberating the heart.

Now is the time to be a child: to rush outside with a piece of black velvet and catch a snow star; to look up and see what 'a million' looks like; to put out a warm tongue and taste frozen sweets from the Ice Queen.

A snow blanket covers the slumbering earth. Nature has 'gone to ground;' the cattle are shut in the barn and the snail in its shell. Human beings 'wrap up,' hug themselves for warmth and withdraw into their houses. Retreating from the cold we move ever more inwards, seeking a warm hearth. It can be a surprise to find that the most sustaining warmth comes from that inner 'fire' which seems to burn more brightly during this time of the year. We discover a fiery enthusiasm for projects to be done in time for Christmas; we bask in the glow of flickering imaginations as we curl up with a good book. We may find our mind ablaze with new ideas, for winter clears the head too, allowing thoughts to rise in clarity, like stars in a frost-polished sky.

Who has not traced the contours of light in the marvel of a winter sky, and rejoiced in its familiar geography? For the astrologers of old, the December sun illumined the celestial picture of the Archer (Sagittarius), half-horse, half-man, with bow drawn and arrow ready to fly. In this centaur figure, they saw the human struggling to rise above a lower nature, and aiming always at a remote goal. In the depths of winter, when the lower kingdoms of nature have withdrawn, it is possible for us to awaken to a rich experience of the world, to raise our hearts to the glory of God on high, and to celebrate that spiritual revelation which is, at the same time, a goal for all humankind — the birth of the Son of Man.

From ancient times, the solstices and equinoxes that quarter the year have each been celebrated as a culmination of part of the sun's rhythmic journey. Folk customs indicate the general feeling that these were critical moments of transition, that the natural forces of the heavens alone might not meet the needs of the time, and that therefore the support and involvement of earthly communities should be invoked.

With the coming of Christianity, a new force enters the world — the power of resurrection. The Christian Festivals which stand at the four cardinal points of the year — Easter, St John's, Michaelmas, Christmas — each bring their own spirit of resurrection, of new life, and they bring it always a few days after the ancient nature festivals. The universe is carried by natural forces towards the four sun-junctures, towards these moments of testing, of turning point. There, like cosmic midwives, the Christian Festivals oversee the transition, bringing the breath of new life into world harmonies.

At Christmastime we celebrate the new life of the earth's own sun — the Light of the World — that which, through the good will of men and women, forever shines in the darkness, and will not be overcome.

The festivals in winter

See page 24.

Fourth Sunday before Christmas
       Advent begins
December 4 St Barbara's Day
December 6 St Nicholas Day
December 21 Winter Solstice
December 24 Adam and Eve Day
       (Christmas Eve)
December 25 Christmas Day
December 26 St Stephen's Day
       (Boxing Day)
December 31 New Year's Eve (Hogmanay)
January 5   Twelfth Day of Christmas
January 6   Epiphany (Three Kings' Day)
First Monday after Epiphany
       Plough Monday

The seasonal table in winter

The dry husk of autumn has been burned on November fires and only the ash remains — the mineral, the element of Earth. In the play of winter the Earth element has a leading rôle, extending its crystallizing force beyond the usual boundaries. Ponds become solid walkways for the ducks, crystal snowflowers cling to the twigs and ice ferns condense on the windows, the washing on the line becomes rigid.

The Seasonal Table can reflect this theme with veils of snow white, palest mauve and blue, with crystals of calcite, quartz and amethyst, with glass vases and candleholders. Although there are are still some blossoms and many glossy evergreens for picking, nature's gifts can be justly replaced at this season with the children's (and their parents') own creativity. There are paper stars and snowflakes to be made, wax animals and snow fairies, simple transparencies in five and six-sided 'crystal' shapes: all these will, through their translucent quality, contribute something to the refreshing clarity of the winter mood.

The festival of Advent brings new possibilities for the Seasonal Table. It could be transformed into an Advent Garden, or Mary's Star Path (see p174), both of which serve as Advent Calendars and guide the children in wondering anticipation towards Christmastide.

For a simple Advent Garden, prepare the Table with a dark blue cloth. Set a white or red candle in the centre and a small bowl of stars cut from gold card, one for every day of Advent. Each evening the candle can be lit and one gold star taken from the bowl and placed on the cloth. During the night a little angel made of tissue paper alights on the star — each day a new angel, each week with wings of a different delicate hue. As the days go by and the bowl grows emptier, the Garden fills with angels. When Christmas Day arrives a veritable host of heavenly beings is assembled to rejoice in the birth of Jesus! (Angelic inspiration may be found on page 201.) This Garden might also incorporate a crib scene, brought together during the last days of Advent. The Child would, of course, appear in the manger only at the appropriate time.

A traditional Advent Wreath is not hard to make if you have a good supply of spruce twigs. Hang it from the ceiling, or place it on a tray in the centre of the Table. The candles can be lit at mealtimes or storytime (one candle in the first week of Advent, two candles in the second week, and so on) bringing a glow both to the room and to the heart. If greenery is difficult to obtain, an everlasting wreath of pine cones is a good substitute, or simply create a circle of stones, pine cones and a few evergreen sprigs on the Table including the four candles. (Remember, never leave lighted candles unattended!)

As Christmas arrives, the Advent Wreath gives way to the light-bearing Christmas Tree. Beneath its branches, if possible, the Seasonal Table has been transformed into a crib scene. The Holy Family is there, an angel hovers above, the shepherds and their sheep are approaching to greet the Child who lies on the straw. A long way off, the three Wise Men have begun their journey (see p239) which will bring them to the Child on January 6th. By this time the shepherds have returned to their flocks, and a large and beautiful gold star hangs in place of the angel. The Tree and all other greenery have gone, for this is the day after Twelfth Night, and tradition demands that Christmas decorations be taken down promptly. Only a few gold stars will remain to accompany the festive mood of Epiphany. How long does that last? Well, after the Wise Men have offered their gifts they are led away (by an angel, perhaps?) and the nativity scene also disappears the next day. The Table may then be covered with a plain cloth of rich fabric, e.g. silk or velvet in a 'royal' colour, and three candles in strong red, blue and green with gold holders (see p171) placed there to remind us of the three Wise Men. These can remain for the greater part of January as a memory of the richness of Christmas-tide.

The course of the Winter Festivals seems to take us on a journey away from the moribund earth to another reality which is filled with starlight and angel voices, with wonder and with hope. The Seasonal Table will reflect this celestial space and support the child's need for devotional expression towards all that lies above and beyond the visible world. Nevertheless, we all need to 'have our feet on the ground' and as Candlemas approaches (which once marked the end of the Christmas festivities), we move away from the wonderland of Winter Festivals and turn our attention once more to the earth we care for, and which cares for us.

Advent

As the cycle of the natural year comes to a close, the Festival of Advent opens a new Christian Year. We move from a season of remembrance for the dead, into a time of preparation for that which is to be born. Our dictionary explains the word 'Advent' as: "the coming of an important person or event." If we are expecting visitors, or an important occasion is approaching, we usually like to prepare ourselves — to "trim the hearth and set the table" as the old carol expresses it. So Advent is more of a time for making ready, than for celebration. Years ago it was used for fasting, for inner reorientation, for taking the little flame that began to shine brightly at Michaelmas on an inner journey through the darkness of the soul towards the Divine Light of Christmas. Today, this long festival (23-28 days) still offers the space for peaceful contemplation, for finding oneself, even among all the outer preparations which may occupy us.

Advent begins on the Sunday nearest to November 30th, St Andrew's Day. This saint was renowned for his selflessness, and it is he who stands at the doorway through which we approach the deep mystery of God's Gift, reminding us that to receive can be a selfless deed. At the other end of our journey we come to Adam and Eve Day, December 24th, and realise that we have had to retrace our origins in order to reconnect with the purpose of Christmas.

The self-will of humankind called forth the need for redemption, and in the ideal of Christmas the answer to the deepest longings of the human heart can be found. To receive lovingly the apple, the symbol of the Fall from Paradise, to carry it willingly along Life's path, to enable the bright fire of the human spirit to rise out of it and gradually lighten the path for others — this is the reality of the Advent deed. Those who are closer to the mystery of birth — the young children — understand this without effort, and will joyfully participate in such Advent festivities as described on page 188.

It is not unusual for the adult to experience times of struggle and isolation during Advent. Then we appreciate the children's facility for confident anticipation, their innate trust in life, and are invariably strengthened by it. It is a real blessing to have little ones around who can guide us through this time in such a mood. We can build a festival of Advent on this simple confidence, and support it for the children in many small ways. When the fourth candle on the wreath is lit and the circle is joined, when all the separate and different pictures on the Advent Calendar finally come together to form a whole, when Mary reaches the last star on her path just in time to receive the Child — all these moments reinforce our children's inner expectation that life has order and harmony, that life is *good*.

The chocolate delivered by some Advent Calendars can often leave a child craving for more. Most children are content with one star picture a day — nourishment which can give strength for a lifetime.

Advent wreath

You will need:

Wire ring, approx. 30cm diam. — from florist or craft shop

Enough newspaper, moss or straw to pad the wire base

Lots of clean, freshly cut evergreen, preferably spruce

Secateurs, pliers and scissors

Green gardener's twine or very strong, dark thread

4 broad red satin ribbons, approx. 1m each (If you wish to hang the wreath you will need extra ribbon)

4 tall red candles

It is not always possible to buy candle-holders for such a wreath so, to improvise, you will need:

4 straight pieces of strong, rigid wire, approx. 10cm in length

4 metal nightlight cases

Large darning needle

Optional: hand drill with fine bit (not larger in diameter than the wire) for drilling the base of the candles.

Work on a protected surface over a floor which can be swept, for there will be needles and twigs everywhere!

To keep the wreath as fresh as possible during the weeks of Advent, prepare a moisture-retentive base:

Tear the newspaper into strips, approx. 7cm wide. Wind these around the ring, building up a firm base approx. 5cm thick. Bind it tightly with twine or thread. (Moss or straw, if available, is better for this. Make sure to tie it really firmly to the ring.)

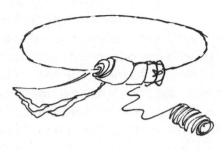

Soak the base in cold water for 15 mins. and drain well. Cut off twigs, approx. 20cm in length, from all the growing ends of the evergreen branches — discard the main stalk. Place enough twigs, side by side, to cover a section of the base, with the cut ends all pointing in the same direction. Tie them down firmly. Place a second layer of twigs similarly, but half overlapping the cut ends of the first layer. Space them evenly and wind firmly with twine. Continue working in the same direction, gradually covering the top half of the wreath, and always hiding the twine under the new layer of twigs.

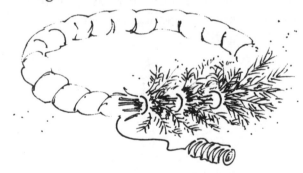

The very last twigs will need careful manipulation to insert them under the first row and complete the circle. Now turn the wreath over and prepare to work, keeping the twigs pointing in the right direction. Repeat the process building up a firm and evenly proportioned ring. Finally, conceal exposed twine by gently releasing the bushy ends of twigs, or slipping in extra twigs where necessary.

Specially designed candle holders for wreaths are hard to come by, but a strong wire spike in the bottom of each candle will hold it upright. To insert the wire, either drill a hole approx. 3cm deep in the candle to take the wire, or, holding one end of the wire with pliers, heat the other end and push *slowly* into the base of the candle. Don't rush the process or the candle may split. Reheat the wire when necessary.

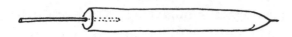

Pierce the centre of the nightlight cases with a large darning needle. Position the cases, one by one, at equal distances around the wreath and slide the candle spike through the case and deep into the wreath. The nightlight cases will catch any drips of wax and minimise the risk of the wreath catching alight. But, as with all naked flames, never leave them unattended!

Tie the ribbons in bows between the candles if the wreath is for the table. If you wish to suspend the wreath, use longer ribbons: make the bows, keeping one end of the ribbon short, knot the bows and knot the four long ribbon ends together for hanging.

Spray the wreath daily to keep it fresh. Alternatively, hang it outdoors overnight or occasionally plunge the whole wreath into water for a while, draining well afterwards.

Mary's star path

All journeys unfold through a changing landscape. They are times of expectation, of preparation, and — for a mother — the journey towards birth is no exception. During Advent we recall the path along which Mary journeyed, carrying her Heavenly Child. This path can unfold for the younger members of the family as a very different kind of Advent Calendar, developing and preparing the mood for Christmas, and allowing expectation to grow gently day by day through the children's own involvement.

A pathway of stars leads Mary towards the stable. As she journeys, the scene changes imperceptibly from Advent into Christmas, until, at last, on Christmas Day, the Child is born...

The first task is to find a place to build up the scene. A table or chest in front of a wall would be suitable, or the floor could be used if there are no very small children or pets in the house. Christine uses a deep shelf built into a niche by the side of the fireplace; the shelf is about 1m long and the wall space behind is 75cm high.

You will need:
A few sheets of newspaper
Large piece of dark-coloured plastic
Blue cloth (ultramarine/royal blue) large
    enough to cover the table or shelf and
    part of the wall behind
Gold card 40cm x 25cm
Some pieces of bark and small logs for
    making a stable
Mary and Joseph crib figures (see p210)
Collection of natural objects: stones,
    crystals, mosses, small flowering or
    evergreen branches, dried flowers, pot
    plants and fir cones
Small animals made from wood, wool,
    pottery, wax or plasticine

Protect your furniture or carpet first with a few sheets of newspaper covered with the sheet of plastic. Spread the blue cloth over the plastic and fix part of it to the wall behind. If the wall surface makes this difficult, stand a large sheet of cardboard or thin plywood against the wall at a slight slant and pin the cloth over it.

At the far side of the scene improvise a

stable with pieces of wood and bark. The construction may be covered with a blue or brown cloth if preferred.

Cut stars from the gold card. Use the pattern below and cut out four stars, one for each Sunday in Advent. Count the weekdays in Advent (the number varies from year to year, see page 171) and cut a smaller star for each weekday.

Lay out a 'star-path' winding in towards the stable. As Advent starts on a Sunday, the first star (furthest away from the stable) is one of the four large stars. Six small weekday stars follow, then a large star again and so on. The last star (Christmas Eve) lies *in* the stable. The path shows a very clear picture of the four weeks in Advent.

On the first Sunday of Advent the crib figure of Mother Mary stands on the first star and then moves day by day along the path of stars towards the stable. Every family, or class of children, will find their most suitable time each day for gathering around the star-path and moving Mother Mary; this could be in the morning or afternoon, or before bedtime.

Christine's family begin by lighting a candle and singing a song (see p177). During the song, an adult very gently and slowly moves Mother Mary from one star to the next. The star from which Mary has moved is put up in the 'sky' behind the stable with some double-sided adhesive tape, (kept ready in the hand of the adult who moves Mary and star).

As the days pass the path becomes shorter, the sky becomes bright with stars, and the scenery around the star-path grows more beautiful. In the first week stones, pretty pebbles and crystals of varying sizes are placed around the stable and path. During the second week plants are added, moss appears around the stones, flowering branches surround Mary on her way. Animals appear in the third week, and maybe some little shells. Finally, on the fourth Sunday of Advent, Joseph stands in the stable waiting to welcome Mary.

This is an appropriate time of the year to remember the Days of Creation (December 24th is Adam and Eve Day), and what better way to do this than to travel with Mary through the four kingdoms of Nature, allowing each to enrich our Advent experience!

When Christmas arrives, earth and sky are filled with beauty and are ready to receive the Child when He appears.

1. On the gol-den star - path_ wal-king, mo-ther Ma-ry tra-vels far

Brings to us the light of__ hea-ven, brigh-ter than the brigh-test star.

2. Moonbeams shine for Mother Mary,
Bells of heaven sweetly ring,
All the earth is hushed to listen
When the angel voices sing.

3. Soft her footsteps on the star path,
Stardust sprinkled in her way,
Mary brings to us the Sun Child
Brighter than the brightest day.

Advent calendar

How many children count the days until Christmas! And how many *lose* count and keep asking the grown-ups for the latest tally! An Advent Calendar will answer all these questions…

This design is for a free-standing calendar which can be placed on a shelf or table top and illuminated from behind by an electric light. It is a time-consuming project and may need two or three weeks to complete. So be sure to start well before Advent.

You will need:

3 large sheets (A1) of thinnish stiff card, dark blue
Tissue paper — as many colour shades as possible
Transparent glue (a gluepen or gluestick is best)
Craft knife, scissors, white pencil
Greaseproof paper 54cm x 59cm
Golden adhesive stars (small ones)

To make the calendar back:

First make a plan of the calendar, using the designs below as a guide. How do you choose which pictures to use out of hundreds of possibilities? We have had to tackle this question, and decided in favour of making the Calendar a 'total' experience, carefully building up day by day, instead of a collection of arbitrary seasonal associations — toys, Christmas puddings, etc. So here you will see a representation of the Nativity taking place between the heavens above and the four kingdoms of Nature (the human, the animal, the plant and the mineral) below. We did not include the Three Kings in this Calendar as, by tradition, they pay their homage only on January 6th.

Even though the number of days in Advent varies, we have chosen to have 28 windows in our Calendar so that it can be re-used year after year. During a short Advent, the children enjoy the special treat of opening two pictures sometimes — on the Sundays, perhaps.

Using one sheet of the card, measure out the Calendar plan below and draw in the solid lines using the white pencil.

Cut away all the shaded areas. Outline all the windows marked 'X' and draw the figures in each window according to the examples shown on pages 264 to 267.

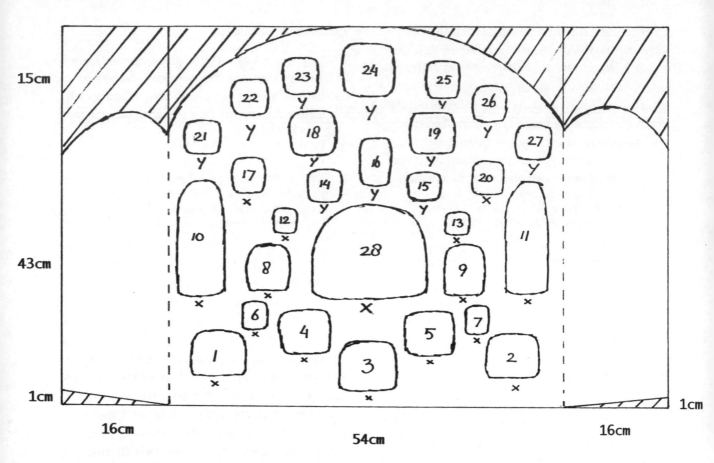

15cm

43cm

1cm

16cm

54cm

16cm

1cm

Place the card on a suitable cutting surface and, with the craft knife, carefully cut out the figures. Follow instructions for Silhouette Transparencies on page 182 for cutting and preparing each window with tissue paper. (We found that using shades of purple for the gnomes and crystals, blues and greens for plants, oranges and reds for the shepherds and animals, gives a very pleasing result.)

We do not recommend using the 'silhouette technique' for the windows marked 'Y'; these heavenly themes need to shine more brightly. So we used tissue paper alone to create these pictures, (see 'Y' figures on page 266). These are done as follows: to make a star picture, cover the whole window (on the back of the Calendar, of course) with pale yellow tissue paper. Take a darker yellow tissue and cut from it a star to fit into the window space. (To avoid spoiling your picture with pencil marks on the tissue paper, draw a star on some scrap paper, cut it out and use it as a pattern.)

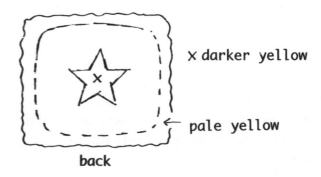

x darker yellow

pale yellow

back

For the sun, moon and star windows you may, alternatively, want to have a night sky as background. If so, first cover the window with white tissue paper, then glue the sun (golden yellow), moon (pale yellow or pale mauve), or stars (shades of yellow) in place and surround them with small pieces of blue tissue. These pieces may overlap if you wish to give more depth to the picture.

Y white   X blue

To make the calendar front:

Lay the greaseproof paper on top of the Calendar and trace the shape of each window. Using the *back* of a scissor blade, mark, but do *not* cut, the outer shape of the Calendar on the second blue sheet of card. Transfer the pattern of the windows (making sure they are exactly in place) from the greaseproof paper to the Calendar front. Do this by tracing the outlines with a hard pencil, using sufficient pressure to leave an indentation on the surface of the card. Remove the greaseproof paper, place the card on a suitable cutting surface and cut out each window. Glue the Calendar front on top of the Calendar back, matching the window openings. Trim the outer shape of the Calendar front to match the Calendar back.

To make the shutters:

Using the pattern on the greaseproof paper as before, transfer the window shapes to the third sheet of card, this time tracing only an outline 5mm *outside* the window as in the diagram below.

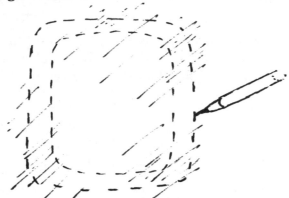

Cut neatly along the dotted line shown. The shaded area will become the window shutter. Cut one shutter at a time. As you go along, mark each shutter lightly on the inside with the 'title' of the window, e.g. 'star,' 'shepherd,' etc. to identify it, and prevent a muddle.

Attach each shutter over the window with two or more self-adhesive golden stars. Add another star to the centre of each door. (The star seals should peel off without difficulty when the door is opened, otherwise they can be eased off with a pin or a craft knife.)

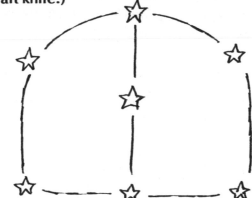

If you wish, mark each shutter on the outer side with a number (use a gold pen for this). We are setting no rules for the order of opening, except for the central 'Nativity' window which should be the last one opened.

Use the back of a knife to score along the crease line of the two side panels on the Calendar front. Fold back the panels and stand the Calendar in front of a light.

Your Calendar is complete — what an achievement! Now, at last you may sit back and enjoy it with your children as the shining colours and pictures unfold day by day.

Happy Advent!

Afterword:

Find, or make, a sturdy envelope in which to store your Calendar. Keep all the offcuts of blue card and use them to replace those shutters which become damaged or soiled. Keep a smaller envelope at hand in which to store the shutters as they come off the Calendar.

A note for teachers and playgroup leaders:

The Advent Calendar described above also works very well when hung at the window. As children are at school during the day, the daylight will light up the pictures.

Only two changes are needed: omit the two sideflaps and cover the back with some self-adhesive clear film to avoid possible condensation damage.

The whole Calendar and its pictures could, of course, be made much larger to suit the windows of the classroom.

Other Advent calendar ideas

However we choose to celebrate Advent with children, it is important to remember the motif of preparing and building up towards Christmas. Whatever we do can be regarded as stepping-stones along the 'path of Advent.' This path progresses steadily but is never quite completed until Christmas.

In our busy lives there may not always be time to make a calendar such as the one described above. We should therefore like to offer some simpler and less time-consuming Advent calendar ideas:

Advent sky

You will need:
As many gold paper stars as there are days in Advent (see pp171 and 254 for star pattern, and make your own choice of size)
The same number of small self-adhesive stars (or gold paper stars backed with Blu-tack)
Gold thread

Each morning, before the children wake up, a new star hangs from the ceiling by a gold thread. (The thread is fixed to the ceiling with the self-adhesive star or the Blu-tack.) You may wish to use an extra large star for each Sunday.

Alternatively, stick a large gold star flat to the ceiling and group tissue paper angels (see p201) around it — a new one each day. Choose a different colour for the angels each week of Advent. (These calendars are not recommended for pristine ceiling surfaces!)

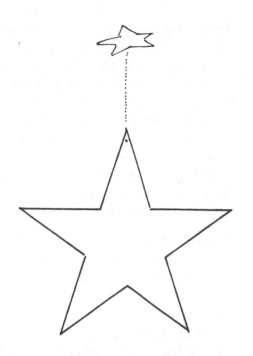

Stick the self-adhesive stars along the blue ribbon, spacing them evenly. Find a suitable place in the room where the ribbon can be suspended (e.g. from a shelf, the wall, a curtain) and allowed to trail down to a surface (a table or chest of drawers). Weigh down the lower end of the ribbon with a crystal, or pin it to a cloth on the table or chest.

Place an unlit candle on a golden, star-shaped candleholder (see p248) at the end of the ribbon. Surround it with some moss, if available, a small plant and any small pretty stones you might have. Slide a pin through the back of the tissue paper angel.

Star ladder

You will need:
Deep blue ribbon approx. 90cm long and 4cm wide
As many small gold self-adhesive stars as there are days in Advent
One tissue paper angel (see p201)
Deep blue cloth or paper for the table

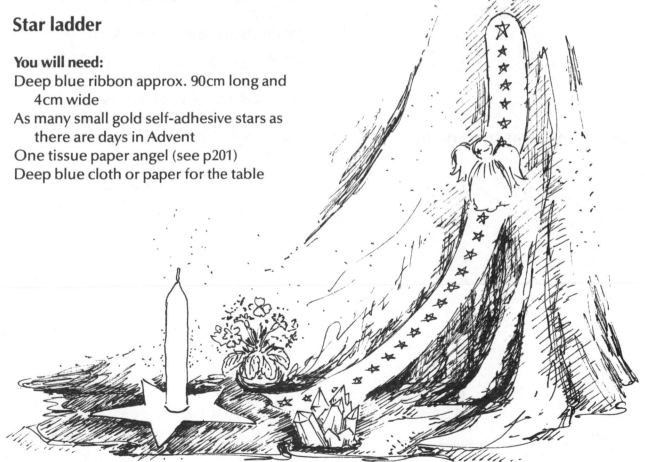

On the first day of Advent, fix the pin with the angel by the first star and then, day by day, continue to move the angel from one star to the next, down the ribbon. At Christmas the angel will have come 'down to earth' and the candle can be lit.

As an alternative to the paper angel, a large gold star could also be moved down the ribbon.

Silhouette transparencies

These transparencies remind us of stained glass windows. You can begin in a very simple way, and allow them to grow more intricate and colourful as you gather experience. Children from the age of ten upwards can make beautiful Christmas presents using this technique. The transparency needs a source of light behind it and can either be hung at a window, or set before an electric light (or protected candle) in a darkened room.

You will need:
    (for a free-standing transparency)
Black or dark blue, thinnish, stiff card 30cm
    x 14cm
White pencil
Craft knife and glue
Tissue paper in bright colours of your
    choice
White tissue paper 15cm x 13cm

Working on the wrong side of the card and following the diagram below, measure out and mark the folding lines with white pencil. Use the blunt edge of a knife to score these two lines. Cut away shaded areas.

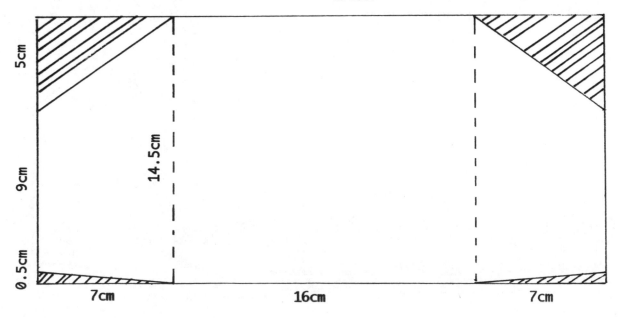

Still working on the back of the card, draw some silhouettes in the middle section. Silhouettes will often be more recognizable when drawn in profile. Leave a margin of about 2cm all around the picture.

With the craft knife, cut around the figures, but take care not to cut them out of the picture! (i.e. cut all around the top of a tree but leave the base attached to the ground. Similarly, leave the feet of people or animals attached to the ground.) Keep figures small and allow a large sky space for colour effects. Still working on the back of the picture, take the lightest shade of tissue paper — e.g. a pale yellow — and cut it slightly larger than the picture. Put a thin layer of glue around the edges of the frame and a few dabs of glue on the silhouettes. Glue tissue paper down, covering the whole picture.

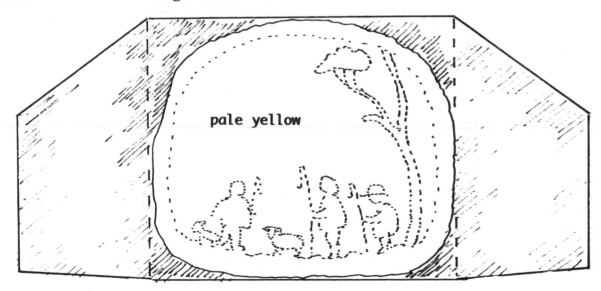

Now take a darker shade of yellow and before covering the picture again, cut out areas in the middle to let the pale yellow show through.

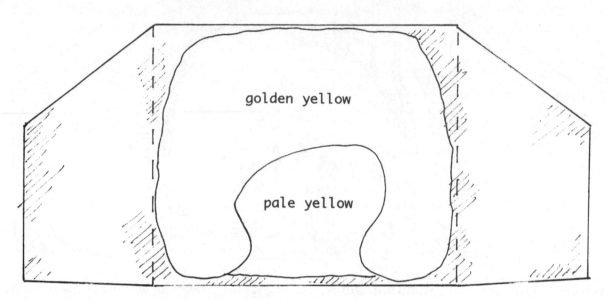

Glue the darker yellow in place keeping glue to areas backed by the card. Next, place light orange tissue paper over the picture, this time removing even more of the centre paper to reveal both shades of yellow:

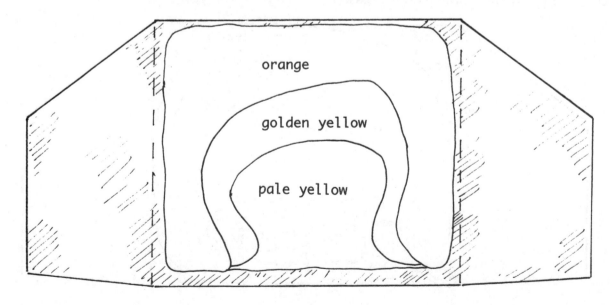

It is possible to carry on in this way using darker colours for each layer. Finally, glue a piece of white tissue paper neatly over the whole back of the picture. Bend the two side panels along the scored lines towards the back of the transparency so that it can stand. Place it in front of a light.

The above method also works very well if just one colour of tissue paper is used. With each layer the colour tones will become progressively darker. Whatever colour scheme you choose, it is important to start with the lightest shade, getting darker with each layer. Be aware that two different shades of tissue paper combine to produce a new colour. It is best to hold the tissue paper sheets on top of each other in front of a light to check your colour mixture. Sometimes the result is quite surprising!

Tip:
If you are the lucky owner of a glass table, your transparency making becomes much faster: put a lamp under the table, work on top of it and you can see straight away if the colours are correct.

To make a transparency for the window, follow the instructions above but leave out the side panels. Cover the back of the transparency with some self-adhesive plastic film to avoid condensation damage.

Rosettes for the window

Rosette 1

This is not difficult to make and very beautiful to look at. It is surprising how richly the colours of the tissue paper glow when the light shines through the different layers. It is advisable to hang window decorations made from tissue paper away from direct sunlight (choose a north or east window). Although the colours shine beautifully at first, the sunlight will cause them to fade quickly. Condensation on a window can also ruin the tissue paper, so protect the back of the transparency with plastic film.

You will need:
Red tissue paper 30 cm x 35 cm
Pair of compasses
Scissors and glue
Piece of card 20 cm x 20 cm for the frame
Warm iron

With compasses, draw five separate circles on the tissue paper, each one slightly smaller than the previous one.

Circle 1: 9 cm radius (18 cm diam.)
Circle 2: 7 cm radius
Circle 3: 5 cm radius
Circle 4: 3.5 cm radius
Circle 5: 2.5 cm radius

Cut out each circle. Put largest circle aside and fold each of the four smaller ones as follows:

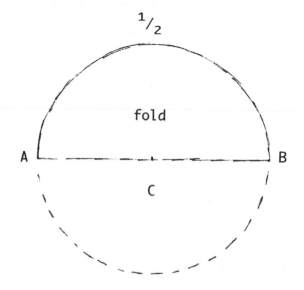

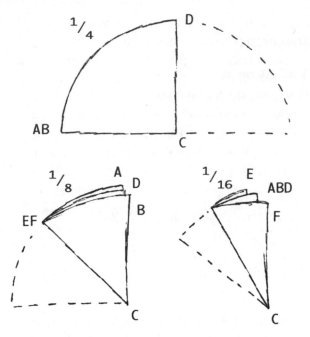

Cut outer edge of each circle as seen below.

Open up all folded circles and iron each one carefully. Glue circles on top of each other with a *small* dab of glue in the centre and an even smaller dab on three or four points around the periphery. Start by glueing circle 2 to circle 1, continue with circles 3, 4 and 5.

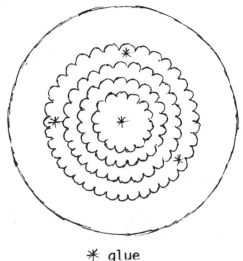

✳ glue

To make the frame, draw a circle with 10cm radius on the card. Draw a second circle inside the first one, with 8cm radius. Cut out this 2cm wide ring. Carefully position and glue to the rosette after circle 5.

A loop of thread on the back of the frame will hang the rosette.

Rosette 2

This project can't be done in a hurry! But it is well worth the time it takes, as a small work of art is your reward in the end. If you are lucky enough to find it, use 'kite paper' in three matching shades of colour as it is more durable and the colours tend to glow more strongly. However, very good results are also achieved with tissue paper.

You will need:
3 circles of tissue paper or kite paper of
    9.5cm radius (19cm diam.), one pink,
    one lavender, one purple
Nail scissors and glue
Piece of black card 20cm x 20cm for frame
Pair of compasses
Warm iron

Fold each tissue paper circle into sixteenths as shown above for Rosette 1. With nail scissors cut away shaded areas on each folded piece.

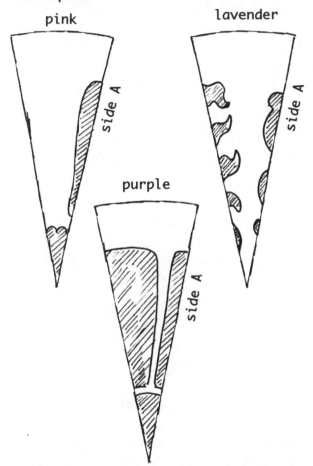

pink

lavender

purple

side A

side A

side A

Carefully open up each cut-out circle and press with an iron. With very few dabs of glue (around the edge) stick the lavender cut-out to the pink one, matching the folds of sides A. Then glue the purple circle on top, again matching sides A.

Draw a circle with 10cm radius on black card. Draw a second circle inside the first one with 8cm radius. Cut out this 2cm wide ring and glue it to the rosette (on the purple circle) to make a frame as seen above for Rosette 1.

Rosette 3

You will need:
Rosette pattern (see p268)
Piece of black card 16 x 16cm
Pair of compasses and pencil
Craft knife and glue
Tissue paper in one or various colours

Use compasses to draw a circle with 8.5cm radius on the card. Cut out the circle and draw Rosette No. 3 Pattern on the card, or invent your own design. Cut out pattern with craft knife on a hard cutting surface which can be spoiled. Place cut-out on a sheet of white paper with any pencil marks facing up. (The white paper gives clarity to the procedure.) Lay some tissue paper over the centre of the cut-out and trace the outline of the first shape with a pencil, allowing a few millimetres extra for overlap.

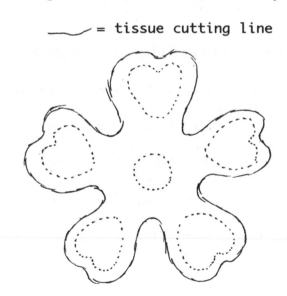

———— = tissue cutting line

Cut tissue paper along pencil line and fix carefully with glue to opening on cut-out. Use a different colour for the next section, tracing the further round of shapes and glueing as before.

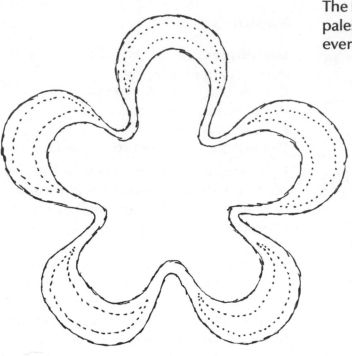

The best results are obtained using the palest colour for the centre and choosing ever darker colour towards the edge.

An Advent activity for groups of children

Many years ago some of our friends introduced us to a delightful way of celebrating the beginning of Advent:

The floor of a large room had been cleared and a path was laid out, spiralling inwards. Moss and greenery edged the path and a small tree stump stood in the centre of the spiral, bearing a tall lighted candle. Beautiful stones and crystals were set in the greenery, and stars of gold card shone at the sides of the path. The room was lit by a few candles, and as adults and children took their seats, the soft music of flute, lyre and xylophone set the mood.

The celebration began with a seasonal story for the children, followed by carol singing for everyone. During the singing, each child approached the entrance of the spiral path to receive a white candle in a shiny red apple, which they carried towards the centre of the spiral.

One at a time the children walked in, the very little ones shepherded by a parent, and reached the central candle. Here they took a light for their own candle and then proceeded outwards — very carefully, eyes fixed on the candle flame — until they found a gold star on which to place their candle and apple. When the moment came that all the children had walked the path, the whole spiral was aglow with lights, and the music and carol singing drew to a close. The doors were opened and everyone quietly left the room, many turning for a last glimpse of the shining garden of lights before going out into the crisp November darkness. There in the garden, muffled in coats and scarves, the children sipped warm juice and nibbled star biscuits, waiting for the trays of apple-candles to appear. Then they would pick out one that looked familiar and take it home to relight it at suppertime and rekindle the memories of a very special afternoon.

We have fortunately been able to repeat this experience many times since then; the theme of the celebration has remained constant but some variations delight the children. Teenagers have enjoyed taking on a rôle, perhaps dressed as Mary to carry the main candle to a seat in the heart of the spiral where she may give her light to each child; perhaps as an angel, with a simple white robe and a gold headband with a star, offering the apple candle to each child. However it is done, this simple act of receiving a candle, carrying it alone on a journey to the source of light, kindling it and placing it on the earth, is able to leave a deep impression on the hearts and minds of adults and children alike.

Evidence of this came to us out of the life of an elderly friend. Finding herself far away from her roots alone in a new town, she remembered such Advent celebrations when her child was small. So she invited the neighbours' children into her bed-sitting room, and sat them on the bed while she read a story. Then they were each given an apple-candle to light and place on a spiral path of greenery laid out on a large dining table. Tea in the kitchen rounded off the proceedings. Over the next two or three years the word spread among the children of the street and their friends until there was not an inch more space to be had on the bed on Advent Sunday!

P.S. As always, greatest care needs to be taken at such 'candle-festivals' and all adults present must be made aware of the locations in the room where buckets of water and fire-blankets are at hand.

St Barbara's Day branches

It is an old custom to cut branches on December 4th, St Barbara's Day. This saint spent a great deal of time shut up in a tower by her pagan father. Maybe this experience gave her the power to release blossoms from their winter prison, for it is said that branches cut on this day will flower at Christmas. Why not try it? Choose branches from trees such as apple, plum, almond, cherry, or from shrubs like forsythia or blackthorn. Cut the branches at a long slant and stand them in water in a cool room for two to three days. Then bring them into a warm room, slit the stems and stand them in lukewarm water. Change the water every two days. Spray the branches frequently with tepid water before the petals are visible.

The gift-bringer

St Nicholas Day opens the season of gift-giving. In different parts of the Christian world, certain of the days between December 6th and January 6th (notably December 6th, 24th and 25th, and January 6th) have become the occasion for exchanging gifts. In pre-Christian times it was common to exchange gifts in early December or at New Year.

Many folk customs all over the world recognize a super-human 'gift-bringer' and celebrate this benevolent figure in different ways. It may be of significance that different cultures choose slightly different aspects of an omniscient, creator god to embody as their gift-bringer. Is it a coincidence, for example, that the gift-bringer in Mother Russia is 'Mama Baboushka?' The archetypal 'giver' in Christian terminology is, of course, God the Father, who presented the first gift to mankind — His Creation. Two thousand years ago in Palestine, He gave the second great gift — His Son. For this reason, it seems appropriate that, on the night between Adam and Eve Day and Christmas Day, many children are visited by Father Christmas who loves and gives to all, irrespective of whether they are naughty or good.

St Nicholas embodies some of the qualities of God the Son — to whom he dedicated his life — who stands before his children as a benign judge, and works gently from within, awakening the voice of conscience, preparing for the birth of the new. In Germany St Nicholas is not the main gift-bringer but it is the 'Christ Child' who leaves quantities of presents beneath the Christmas Tree.

Santa Claus certainly derives his name from St Nicholas, and his custom of stocking-filling from Father Christmas, but his genial nature and large girth are more reminiscent of the Lord of Misrule who features in the Roman Saturnalia festivities of early December. (Saturn ranked alongside the creator gods of the Roman pantheon.) However, tradition claims that

Santa Claus comes from the north, and connections have also been made to both Odin, the Teutonic creator god who presided over the games and feasting in Valhalla, and The Norse god Thor, to whom the Yule-Log was dedicated. It is likely that the cultural melting pot of North America has evolved this jolly personage as an expression of the generous and creative social 'Spirit of Christmas.'

When all is said and done, it is not so very necessary to trace the likely origins of the gift-bringer. What is more important is that we can relate to the quality of the truth that he or she represents and find ourselves able honestly to acknowledge and foster that reality, and so become a sincere 'servant' to the gift-bringer.

These mysterious figures can loom large and god-like in the soul of a child. If we are able to approach their being with reverence and serve their truth with love, then, if questioned, we may respond without guile and say, "Yes, he is real, and I am one of his servants. Maybe you will be one of his servants, too, when you grow up!"

St Nicholas Day

For the Dutch, the Swiss and many other Europeans, St Nicholas Day is very special. In Holland it is the major 'gifts' festival of the year.

The life of this Saint has become woven with legend, but it appears that he was born in the part of the world we know as Syria in the 3rd century A.D., the long-awaited son of rich parents. He was ordained a priest while still very young, and soon afterwards was orphaned and in possession of a large fortune. He distributed his wealth to the poor, travelled to the Holy Land, and eventually settled into a humble life at the port of Myra in Asia Minor. At the death of the Bishop of Myra, one of his clerics was told by revelation that the successor should be the first man to visit the church the following morning. It was Nicholas's habit to pray in the church at dawn each day, and so it came about that he was chosen to be Bishop of Myra. Under the Emperor Diocletian he was persecuted for his faith, and spent some time in prison. He led a virtuous life serving justice, goodness and truth, and died circa 350 A.D.

Bishop Nicholas was associated with many miracles: of calming storms at sea; of restoring life and limb to three little boys who had been cut up and pickled in brine during a famine; of appearing to the Emperor Constantine in a dream and thereby securing a reprieve for three officers unjustly condemned to death. Because of such events, he has become the patron of prisoners, of children and of sailors, as well as being the Patron Saint of Russia.

He is most well known perhaps, by the story in which he saved the virtue of the three young daughters of a peasant. The peasant was too poor to keep the girls or provide them with a dowry, and they had decided to sell themselves to survive. On three consecutive evenings Nicholas passed by their hovel and cast a bag of gold through the window. These three bags are commemorated by the three golden balls of the pawnbroker's sign!

Those children who hope that St Nicholas will visit, place a clean shoe (or sometimes a sack!) on the doorstep or at the fireside, stuffed with hay and a carrot for his white horse. Among the gifts he leaves in return will always be some nuts, apples, spicy biscuits or honey cake, and perhaps a new coin or chocolate sovereign.

St Nicholas may visit a child's home or school in person. He makes an imposing figure — tall, upright, noble yet serious, and very, very old. He wears a white robe, a cloak of red or blue, a bishop's mitre, and carries the crozier in one hand and a large old book in the other. This is his 'Golden Book,' in which all the good and bad deeds of the children over the past year have been carefully recorded. Where appropriate, these entries (often in verse and recalling fairly recent events) are lovingly recited, and the Saint sees no need to praise or reprimand.

Bishop Nicholas is always accompanied by a servant, a 'Black Peter' character, half-comic, half-frightening, who traditionally does not speak, although he makes noises. He holds a switch of twigs to threaten naughty children, and also a large sack full of delicious things to reward the good deeds. Needless to say, although the threat of a lump of coal or spoonful of salt is always in the background, most children receive something nice from Black Peter's sack!

St Nicholas traditions differ widely from place to place. He may travel on a white horse, or a grey donkey; his servant (who is sometimes called Ruprecht) may be dressed smartly in Renaissance costume, or clad in furs and grunting like an animal. In whatever form they appear, they make a paradoxical pair — the one embodying all that is wise and noble in the human character, the other a crafty trickster, or coarse, hardly-human figure. Like the good and the bad in all of us, they have to be acknowledged and accepted together. St Nicholas offers us his compassionate guidance and, by his example, makes us aware of the Ruprecht who is our constant companion. In this way he can lead us deeper into the mood of Advent and the inner preparation for Christmas.

The traditions associated with St Nicholas Day all seem to engage one's awareness. How the ears prick up as names are read from the Golden Book! While the shoes are being carefully polished and the hearth or step swept clean in preparation for St Nicholas's visit, how many little minds are weighing the probability factors of the goodies or the lump of coal? In Holland, at that time, it is not unusual for a loud hammering on the front door to 'wake up' the whole household to the start of the Festival. Even the swiftest child can never reach the door in time to catch a glimpse of the Bishop or his servants, but there on the step is a large sack stuffed with gifts. A verse or a riddle (signed by Saint Nicholas, of course), accompanies each gift to indicate the recipient by identifying aspects of his character or habits. Some brain power is needed to decipher the clues, and a certain presence of mind is also required to accommodate the jokes made at one's own expense!

Wherever St Nicholas visits there will usually be a clean shoe waiting for him. We wear shoes to go out into the world, to follow our path in life, and the saintly Bishop leaves behind some sustenance for this journey. If a child is *very* lucky, St Nicholas may take a star from his blue cloak and leave it on the toe of an especially clean shoe…

Frost paintings

How about helping Jack Frost to paint a picture? You are the one who puts the colour on the paper, and Jack Frost adds the ferns! (This can only be done when there is a hard ground-frost.)

You will need:
Cartridge paper
Water colour paints and a brush
Water
Sponge

Wet the paper well on both sides by dipping it into a sink full of water. Drain, and lay it on a table or paintboard. Press out any bubbles and wrinkles with the sponge, taking care not to rub the surface of the paper. Cover the paper with areas of beautiful colours. (The paint needs to be fairly strong if it is not to disappear on the wet surface of the paper.) While the painting is still shining wet (but not dripping with pools of colour) carry it out into a shady place and lay it directly on the frozen ground. Then tiptoe away and don't peep while Jack Frost does his delicate work. When the paint has dried the picture may be brought in and admired.

Folded cut-out stars

These are very easy to make and can be used in a number of different ways. If made from gold paper, they can be hung on the Christmas tree. They make attractive Christmas cards if glued to stiff paper, especially when gold ink is used for lettering. Alternatively, back the star with coloured tissue paper and hang it at a window or in front of a lamp. Use white paper for the stars and they become more like snow flakes!

You will need:
Gold or silver paper (double-sided)
Small pointed scissors (nail scissors)

The stars can be made in any size, but let's start with a square of 7.5cm x 7.5cm. Fold square diagonally in half along dotted line.

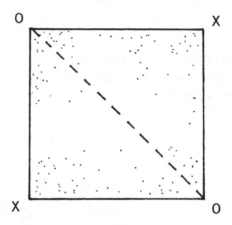

Now fold in half again.

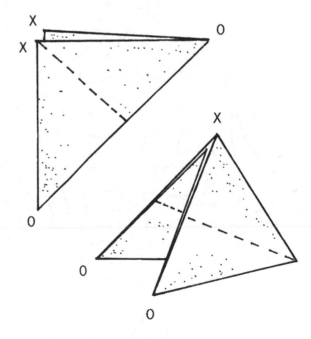

Fold this triangle again in half along dotted line.

Fold each corner O to X as shown below.

↑ = folded edges

The paper is ready to be cut. Use nail scissors and follow examples below or make your own.

Open up the folded triangle and discover your work of art! To hang the star pull a threaded needle through one corner. For a Christmas card, glue the star to a folded piece of card.

↑ = folded edges

Snowflake

Use white paper and fold as above.

To create the typical hexagonal (six-sided) impression of the snowflake, the designs must be cut in this way:

Straw stars

Straw stars make wonderful Christmas Tree decorations; the golden straw contrasts strikingly with the dark green spruce. The stars can be made with round or split straw. We shall describe some simple ones here, but there are many possibilities, ranging from basic to highly complex shapes. Once you are confident in the technique, consult one of the many books available to take you further.

If you are unable to find straw at a craft suppliers, you might have to beg a handful of wheat stalks from a farmer. Strip off the dried leaves, and divide the stalk into sections by cutting out the stem joints.

Split straw stars

You will need:
Straws from craft shop (or prepared as
    above)
Sharp knife or razor blade
Nail scissors
Iron
Thread in a 'straw' colour
Bowl of water or bath for soaking the straws

To prevent the straws from breaking, soak

in cold water for at least 2 hrs. (The time can be shortened if the water is hot.) Split stalks with a sharp knife or razor blade and iron them out flat with a hot iron.

To make a star, cut four ironed straws into equal lengths (say, 7 cm each). Group the straws in pairs, placing the bottom two to form a cross and the top two to form an X.

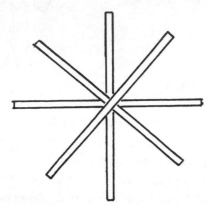

Holding the centre of the straws (at the point where they cross) firmly between thumb and forefinger of the left hand, weave thread around the straws with the right hand: start by laying the thread over the top straw, under the next and over and under succeeding straws until circle is complete. Tie off ends of thread at the back of the star, leaving enough thread for hanging. Tie firmly so that the star will not lose shape, but not so tight as to crush the straws.

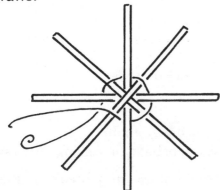

(Some people find it easier to fix the star on a wooden board by pushing a pin through the crossing point and using both hands for the weaving and tying.) Cut the points of the star with nail scissors, while the straw is still wet. Here are some suggestions:

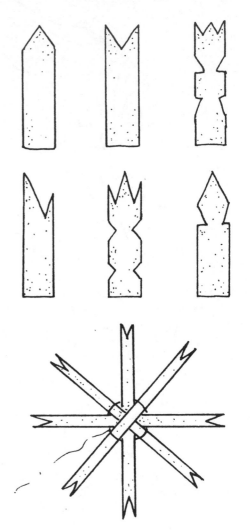

The stars can be made double (with sixteen points) by combining two simple stars. Lay two eight-pointed stars on top of each other and bind them together as described above. The two 'rings' of thread created in this way look very decorative. (In Scandinavian traditions, red thread is used for binding straw decorations.) Especially effective are the stars which are a combination of one star with narrow, long straws and the other with wide, short ones.

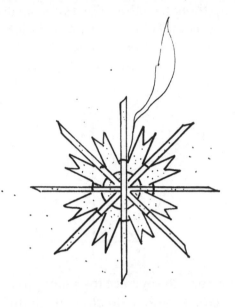

For a six-pointed star use three straws, instead of four, and proceed as described above for eight-pointed star.

To make a sturdy star, use flattened whole stalks of straw. Do not slit open, but iron flat on both sides. For an unusual Christmas decoration, group a few stars together on a mobile.

Tissue paper stars

Fix these stars to your window panes and brighten up the grey winter days! Older children can make them but great care must be taken as the folding must be exact. After making one or two basic stars, it is fun to experiment and find variations in the folding. By altering the length of the sides of the paper or by adding twice as many points to the star, you will get surprising results.

Basic star 1

You will need:
Sheet of tissue paper in any size (but we will start with a piece 30cm x 26cm)
Clear glue
White sheet of paper
Sharp, unserrated table knife

Always work on a white sheet of paper, to see more clearly when making the folds. Fold tissue paper sheet in half and cut along the fold with the knife.

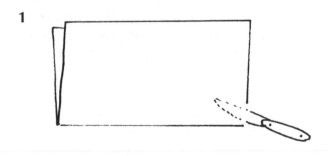

Fold and cut each of these two papers in half again, and repeat to obtain eight rectangular pieces of the same size. Each rectangle will now be folded to make one of the points of the star in the following way: Fold paper in half length-wise and unfold again.

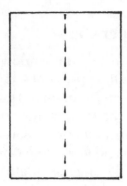

2

Fold the four corners to the middle crease.

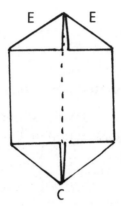

3

Call one point C (for centre) and the opposite point P (for periphery) as seen in Diagram 3. Fold edges E to the middle line.

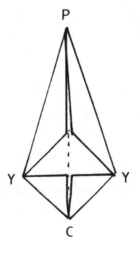

4

When all eight pieces are folded as seen in Diagram 4, arrange them in a line with points C at the bottom and points P at the top. This is to avoid making mistakes when glueing them together. Put a very small dot of glue on point C and point Y, and stick the pieces together. Centre points C meet, and points Y must lie exactly on the middle folding line.

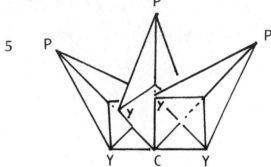

5

Continue until seven of the pieces have been fixed together. To glue the eighth point lift the first section and slide one half of the eighth point underneath.

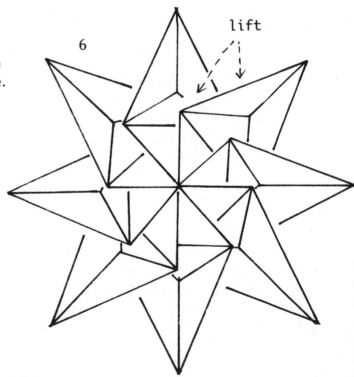

6

lift

(Use glue where the corners will not lie flat.)

Rainbow star 2

Repeat the Basic Star but use a different colour for each piece. Glue pieces together in this order: red, orange, yellow, light green, dark green, blue, purple, pink.

Star 3

This is similar to the Basic Star but has a folding variation at the end of each point. Take care not to confuse points C with points P as each is folded in a different way. Follow instructions for the Basic Star up to and including Diagram 3. Open up each corner, fold again and follow Diagrams 7, 8 and 9. Glue star together as for Basic Star. (See Diagram 5.)

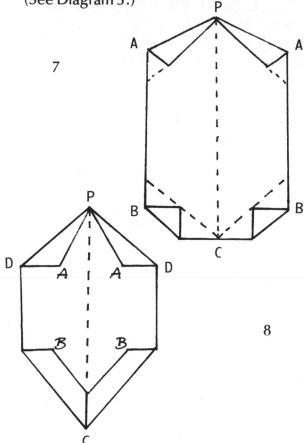

7

8

9

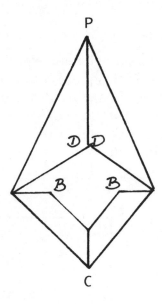

Star 4

You will need twice as much tissue paper as for the Basic Star.

This star has sixteen points, so cut out sixteen identical rectangular pieces instead of eight. Follow instructions for the Basic Star up to and including Diagram 4. Instead of glueing the pieces together at this stage, make one more fold (at C-Y) on each point. (See Diagram 10.)

10

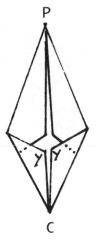

Glue the star together as for the Basic Star (see Diagram 5).

199

Star 5

For this star we need eight *squares* of tissue paper. Each square could be 8cm x 8cm. Fold the square in half and open it up again. Now fold all four corners Y to the middle crease, so that they meet in the centre (M). Open up the corners again.

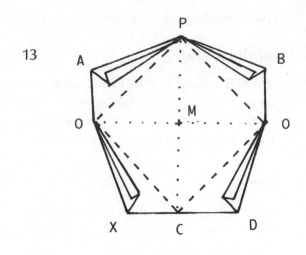

13

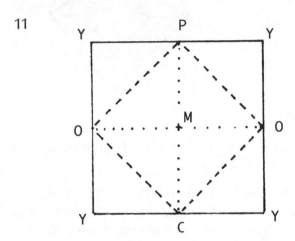

11

Fold corner Y as seen below in Diagram 12

Now fold down each corner towards M on lines P-O and O-C as seen in Diagram 14.

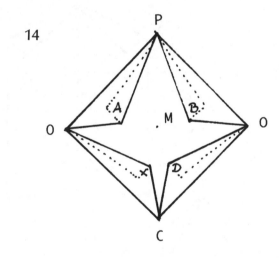

14

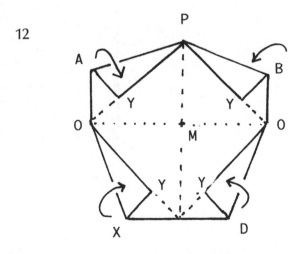

12

Fold corners Y back so that they lie on folds P-B, P-A and O-D and O-X respectively.

When all eight squares are folded as seen in Diagram 14, set them in a line with points C at the bottom and points P at the top. Put a small dot of glue on points C and O, and glue squares together. Centre points C meet and points O must lie exactly on the middle folding line C-P.

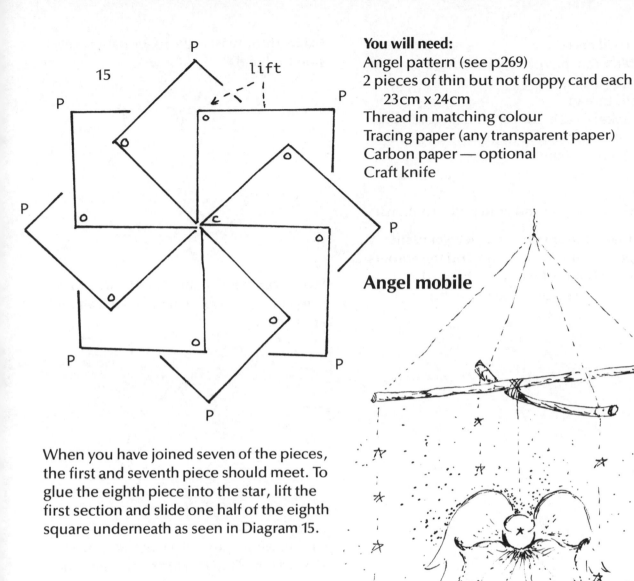

15

P

lift

P

P

P

P

P

P

P

P

You will need:
Angel pattern (see p269)
2 pieces of thin but not floppy card each
    23cm x 24cm
Thread in matching colour
Tracing paper (any transparent paper)
Carbon paper — optional
Craft knife

Angel mobile

When you have joined seven of the pieces, the first and seventh piece should meet. To glue the eighth piece into the star, lift the first section and slide one half of the eighth square underneath as seen in Diagram 15.

Angel cut-out decoration

Here is an original Christmas present which a teenager could make quite easily. It is not too time-consuming and very light for sending by post! If you are successful with this one, try your own variations…

To make this project, follow the instructions for the Palm Sunday Decoration on page 49.

This mobile also looks nice when hung from a branch instead of the cross. The branch should be hung horizontally.

You will need:

2 thin branches or very thin dowelling each
    about 20cm long
Gold thread
1 packet of self-adhesive small gold stars
Piece of white or light pink tissue paper
    30cm x 14cm
Fleece or cotton wool for angel's head
Glue
Tiny star sequin and gold pen — optional

To make the angel, cut a piece of tissue
paper 12cm x 18cm. Round off the corners
as seen below. Draw a line in gold all
around the edge of the tissue paper.

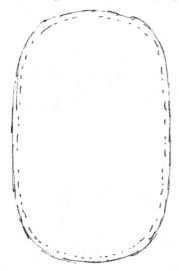

Shape fleece or cottonwool into the size of
a marble and put this into the centre of the
tissue paper. Draw the tissue paper in
around the wool and tie the head with
thread.

Make a little twist in the tissue paper at each
side for hands.

We recommend at this stage to arrange the
dress in such a way that there are two folds
at the back.

For the wings, cut a piece of tissue paper
9cm x 12cm. Fold it in the middle and cut as
shown.

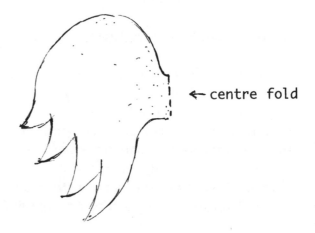

← centre fold

Open up the wings and, bunching the centre fold together slightly, tie the wings around the angel's neck with gold thread. Leave a long end of thread for hanging.

Tie gold thread around the angel's head for a crown. (Knot at the back of the head.) Stick the tiny gold star on the angel's forehead. Tie the two sticks into a cross. Hang this horizontally by tying a length of gold thread to each of the four ends of the cross. Suspend the angel from the centre of the cross.

To make 'star chains,' cut a 30cm length of gold thread and stick two golden stars together, enclosing the thread. For each chain use four or five pairs of stars, spacing them evenly on the thread. Make four chains.

Attach one star chain to each end point of the cross, surrounding the angel with stars. Alternatively, make the mobile larger with several angels and more star chains. Hang from a branch.

Christine's Christmas biscuits

Without these traditional Swiss Christmas Biscuits our Christmas wouldn't be the same. They are usually made during Advent and keep very well in a tin. The whole family joins in the baking and we have, over many years, acquired a variety of different biscuit cutters: stars, hearts, moons, animals, etc. which we use for these biscuits alone. Our three favourite recipes are:

'Brunsli'

You will need:
250g white sugar
250g grated or ground almonds
1 pinch cinnamon
2 rounded tbspns plain white flour
2 - 3 stiffly beaten egg whites
100g melted cooking chocolate (plain), or
40g cocoa powder

Mix all the dry ingredients in a bowl. Add the egg whites and melted chocolate (if you are using it). Make a firm paste and roll out on a sugared board to about 6mm thickness — cut out shapes with the biscuit cutters and arrange them, not too close together, on a greased baking sheet. Leave to dry for a few hours or overnight. Bake in a preheated moderate oven for about 10 mins.

'Mailänderli'

You will need:
250g margarine or butter
250g white sugar
2 large eggs, beaten
1 pinch salt
1 grated rind of lemon
500g plain white flour
1 egg yolk and a teaspoon milk

Cream the fat and sugar. Stir in lemon rind and eggs. Sift in the flour and knead for a short time with cool hands to make a dough. Leave dough in a cool place for an hour. Roll out to about 5mm thickness and cut into shapes with biscuit cutters. Place the biscuits on a greased baking sheet. Mix one egg yolk with a teaspoon of milk and brush over the biscuits. Bake in a preheated moderate oven for 10 - 15 mins. until golden.

'Zimtsterne'

(Traditionally only star shapes are used for this biscuit.)

You will need:
3 stiffly beaten egg whites
300g icing sugar
1 level tbsp spoon cinnamon
1 level tbsp lemon juice
350g ground almonds

Mix egg whites and icing sugar. Put aside about five tablespoons of this mixture for the icing. Mix in all remaining ingredients and knead lightly into a dough. Roll out on a sugared board to about 6mm thickness and cut out stars. Place on a greased baking sheet and paint with left-over icing mixture. Leave to dry overnight. Bake in a preheated hot oven for 3 - 5 mins.

Marije's Christmas biscuits

These are delicious little balls.

You will need:
150g butter, at room temperature
250g flour, or more if the mixture is not stiff enough
175g sugar
Pinch of salt
175g of partly ground and partly chopped nuts — almonds, pecans or walnuts
Icing sugar for coating

Stir the sugar, salt and nuts into the flour. Cut in the butter and knead the mixture well. The dough should be stiff. Roll it into small (2cm) balls and bake on a greased tray in a moderate to hot oven until slightly brown. Remove from the oven and shake them in a paper bag with the icing sugar. Leave to cool.

Christmas stollen

This is a festive Christmas loaf.

You will need:
500g flour
30g fresh yeast
200ml lukewarm milk
1 - 2 eggs
100g sugar
5g salt
100g butter
100g currants
150g raisins
50g angelica
50g blanched almonds

Warm the mixing bowl. Put in the flour. Make a hollow in the flour and pour on the milk. Crumble in the yeast and leave to rise in a warm place for 15 - 20 mins. Wash and dry the currants and raisins, cut the angelica, chop the almonds finely and melt the butter. Add these and the egg(s) to the risen flour mixture and knead well. Cover with a clean cloth and leave to rise in a warm place for at least an hour. Knead lightly and, working on a floured board, roll out to a thick oval shape, which is thinner on one long side. Brush the thicker edge with a little water and fold the thinner half over it. Transfer to a greased and floured baking tray. Cover with a slightly damp (warm) cloth and leave to rise in a warm place for about 30 mins. Brush the loaf with melted butter and bake in a hot oven for approx. 45 mins. Leave to cool slightly and brush again with butter. Finally, dredge with icing sugar.

Winter ring

Following the method described on page 136, make a ring of pine cones and seed pods. Select small cones for this.

You will need:
Ring of florist's foam
Small cones and seed pods
Medium gauge florist's wire and pliers

Cut a piece of wire 10cm long. Weave it around the scales at the base of the cone and secure, leaving an end of about 3cm.

Push the wire into the ring. (Some seed pods have stems which can be used instead of wire.) Cover the foam completely, filling any spaces with small seed pods. This ring makes a beautiful table-centre placed around a candle.

Small seed pods
Florist's wire (medium gauge) and pliers
Small pointed scissors
Mistletoe or holly — optional

Fold ribbon in half. Twist a short wire firmly around the ribbon 10cm from the fold. Open the ribbon and lay it on either side of the ball. Twist some more wire underneath the ball to hold it firmly in place.

Kissing ball

This is a variation on the mistletoe branch.

Cover the ball with wired cones and seed pods, using the scissors to make tiny cuts in the ribbon if necessary. Make sure that there are no bald patches. Some mistletoe or holly can be fixed to the bottom.

Garlands

Pine cones can be fashioned into garlands for the doorway, fireplace, window or balustrade.

You will need:
Lots of assorted wired pine cones, including large ones (see above for wiring)

You will need:
Ball of florist's foam
Red ribbon — 3cm wide and approx. 70cm long
Small wired pine cones — (see above for wiring)

Variety of seed pods
Rope (2 or 3 strands twisted) or cord —
   choose the length that you will need
Red or tartan ribbon for bows
Sprigs of holly and imitation red apples —
   optional

A centrepiece

Follow instructions as described for
Garlands above, but work only on a short
rope, about 50cm long. Start in the centre
with an abundance of quite large cones.
These should be on longer wires to allow
them to bunch together. Again, work
outwards. The cones should diminish in
size towards the ends. Complete with holly
and bows of ribbon.

At the centre of the rope, part the strands
and insert the wire from a large cone. Twist
the wire neatly around the rope.

Bird food

In some Scandinavian countries a sheaf of
wheat is traditionally put out for the birds
on Christmas Eve. Children enjoy watching
different birds visiting their garden,
balcony or window ledge — even if it means
staying really still for some time!

It is not always possible to find a
wheatsheaf, especially in a city, so we
suggest a couple of alternatives which can
be used in very frosty weather. Each recipe
will attract different kinds of birds.

Working outwards in both directions, fill in
with cones and seed pods, keeping the
garland as symmetrical as possible. Pack the
materials closely together and end with
large cones. Decorate the garland evenly as
you work, with bows, apples and holly.

You will need: (For seed eaters)
250g lard
50g sunflower seeds
75g chopped peanuts
50g budgie seeds
75g breadcrumbs
Large pine cones
String

You will need: (For insect eaters)
250g lard
50g chopped meat scraps
50g grated cheese
50g porridge oats
50g chopped bacon rind
50g sultanas
Large pine cones
String

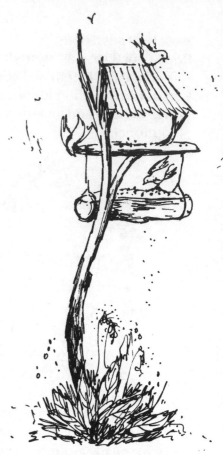

Melt the lard in a saucepan and mix with all the other ingredients. Remove from heat and let the mixture set. Leave the pine cones on top of a radiator overnight to make sure they are fully open. Tie a length of string around the top scales. Pack the bird food between the scales of the fir cones with the help of a blunt knife. Hang the fir cones somewhere well out of reach of mischievous cats and settle down quietly to watch the fun.

We have also come across a variation of the above: a split log hung horizontally with the bird food mixture spread on top.

A Yule staff

You will need:
Dowelling (18mm diam.) 50cm long
Red satin ribbon, 65cm x 2.5cm wide, for binding
90cm of the same ribbon for the bow
Red satin ribbon, 8cm x 1.5cm wide for 'headband'
5 straw stars or 5 gold cut-out stars (see pp193 and 195)
11 bushy but flattish spruce twigs approx. 22cm long
Green florist's wire, 12cm length
Hand drill bits, to drill holes approx. 1cm and 2mm in diam.
Sandpaper
Thumbtack
Adhesive

Here is an alternative to the holly wreath for your front door. Once you have the basic staff, it's quick and easy to make each year.

A

Smooth holes and ends of dowelling with sandpaper. Fix the ribbon temporarily at end A with a thumbtack, and bind the ribbon around the dowelling as shown.

When the end of the ribbon is in place, trim and secure with glue at the back of the staff. Remove thumbtack at end A, trim end of ribbon and glue into place. Glue 'headband' neatly into place and fix a loop of florist's wire as shown:

Mark dowelling as follows:

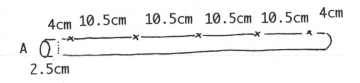

With hand drill, drill holes 1cm diam. through the dowelling at every mark. Drill a small hole, large enough for the florist's wire 2.5cm from end A. Drill a hole 0.5cm diam. and 2cm deep in end A of dowelling.

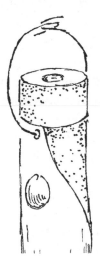

Take a pair of spruce twigs, trim the ends if necessary. Insert them from right and left, into the first hole through the dowelling. Push firmly from each side until they are securely lodged. Repeat for the other holes, reserving the most symmetrical twig for the hole in end A of the dowelling. Use the remaining length of ribbon to tie a bow at the bottom of the staff. Attach the stars of your choice between the spruce twigs as shown.

Crib figures

A set of crib figures placed beneath the Christmas tree or elsewhere in the room creates the heart of the Christmas mood. If you have made Mary's Star Path for Advent (see p174), then you will already have prepared a suitable setting for the crib figures. If you are starting from scratch, then prepare the site of the crib scene by protecting furniture or carpet with a few sheets of newspaper and then a dark plastic

sheet. Improvise a simple stable for Mary and Joseph with a few pieces of wood and bark. If necessary, cover with a dark blue or brown cloth. Build a mossy landscape around the stable and add small flowering plants, crystals or stones to enhance the scenery. A couple of nightlight candles in small glass jars set amongst the moss will light the crib with a soft, intimate glow. Check that the plastic sheet is by now well hidden.

You will need: (for each figure)
Fleece for stuffing
White stockinette 10cm x 10cm (stretchy cotton — an old T-shirt is ideal)
Skin-coloured stockinette 10cm x 10cm (a good skin colour is obtained by dyeing white stockinette in ordinary Indian tea)
Strong white thread and some sewing cotton
2 pipe cleaners

Mary

You will need: (in addition to the above)
Dark red felt for dress 11cm x 20cm
Blue cotton or silk for cloak 18cm x 21cm

To make the head:

Stuff fleece into the square of white stockinette and tie it into a round, fairly firm ball about 3cm across.

Wind a length of strong white thread twice around the middle of the ball to form the eyeline. Tie it with a knot at the back, tightly enough to make an indentation.

Cover the head with a piece (approx 6cm along the grain x 9cm wide) of skin-coloured stockinette. The fabric must stretch tightly around the head, with the grain running vertically. Overlap the fabric at the back of the head and sew together. Tie some strong thread around the neck. Gather in the edge of the fabric at the top of the head neatly with running stitches.

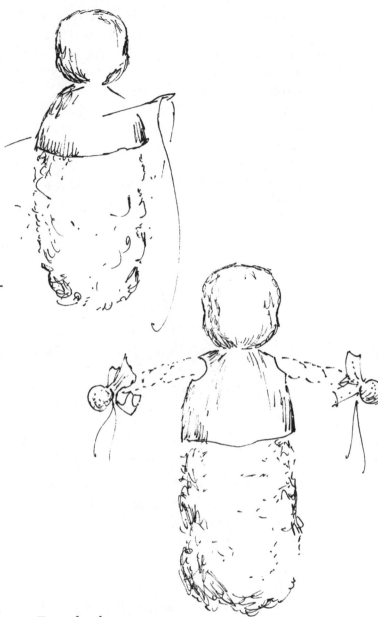

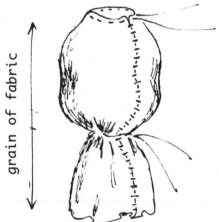

grain of fabric

To make the body:

Work some fleece into a thick roll, approx. 9cm long. Sew on the head, taking several stitches through the roll. Pull down the neck-pieces of stockinette and sew firmly into place over the roll.

To make the arms:

Twist two pipe cleaners together. Make a hole through the body with a knitting needle and insert the pipe cleaners. Make the hands by tying a tiny bit of fleece into a square of skin-coloured stockinette 4cm x 4cm. Cut the pipe cleaners to the right length and tie one hand to each end of the arms.

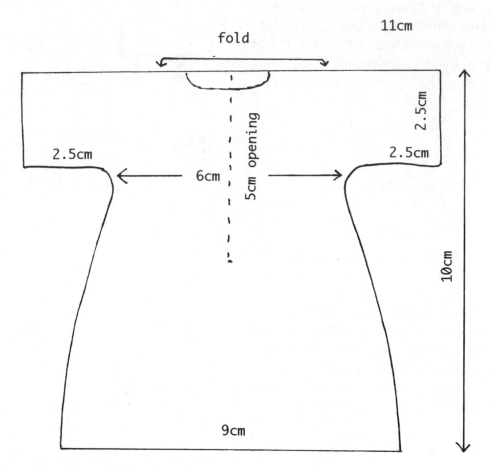

fold

11cm

2.5cm

2.5cm

2.5cm

6cm

5cm opening

10cm

9cm

Cut out a dress from the red felt using the pattern below. Sew up the side seams with small stitches very near the edge and turn the dress inside out.

not actual size

Dress Mary. (The opening in the dress is at the back.) Run a gathering thread around the sleeve and neck openings, draw the thread together tightly and secure with small stitches.

Cut out the cloak from the blue fabric. (See pattern below.) Fold 2cm of the straight edge under as indicated on the pattern, and make a 5mm hem all around the curved edge.

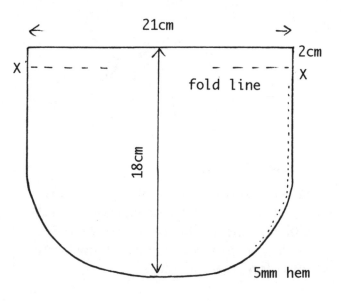

21cm

2cm

X

fold line

X

18cm

5mm hem

Fix the cloak, at the straight edge, around Mary's head with a few tiny stitches. Stitch down around the wrists at points X making a small extra fold if necessary. Hitch the cloak up just below the back of the neck, and make a little tuck there with a stitch.

Joseph

You will need:
(in addition to the basic figure)
Brown felt for dress 11 cm x 20cm
Darker brown felt, needlecord or woollen material for cloak 13cm x 16cm
Grey fleece for hair and beard (light grey mohair wool could also be used)
Small stick or twig 13 - 15cm for Joseph to hold

Follow instructions given for Mary to make the basic figure. Use brown felt for the dress. Make Joseph's cloak from dark brown felt, needlecord or woollen material, using the pattern below. If the fabric frays at the edges it will be necessary to hem it.

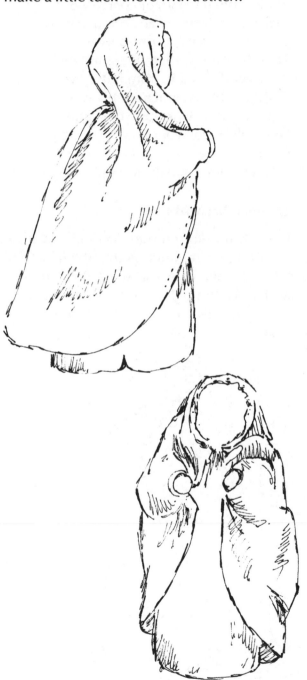

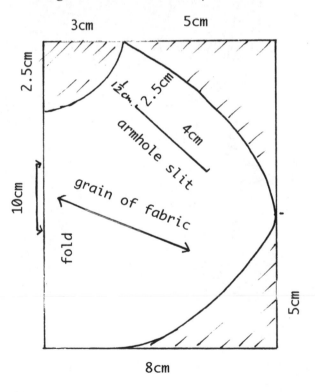

Put the cloak around Joseph with his arms through the armhole slits. Fold the front of the cloak as shown below. Hold cloak

213

together with a small stitch. Sew the stick to one of Joseph's hands and sew on grey fleece or mohair wool as hair and beard.

Shepherds

The Shepherds are made in the same way as Joseph. Instead of the cloak they wear a scrap of sheepskin. Their dress could be made from hessian, or coarse woollen material in green or any other 'earthy' colour. A piece of string serves as a belt. Their hats are knitted but could be crocheted or made from felt. (If you are a knitter, why not knit a simple waistcoat or cape as well? Hand spun or slightly 'knobbly' wool would be most suitable.) Give each shepherd a stick or use brown pipe cleaners to make a shepherd's crook.

To knit a shepherd's hat:

Use 3.75mm knitting needles and cast on 22 sts. Knit 2 rows. Knit together the first 2 and last 2 sts. of the next six rows. Break thread and pull it through the ten remaining sts. with a needle. Draw together and sew up seam.

Jesus

You will need:

Small square of skin-coloured stockinette
    5 cm x 5 cm
35 cm of narrow open-weave bandage
A length of embroidery cotton in a light
    colour

Make a tiny head by tying a bit of fleece into the stockinette square. Carefully wrap the head with the bandage leaving the face free. Create a swaddled bundle by wrapping the bandage around the free ends of stockinette, padding with extra fleece if necessary. Tie the embroidery cotton thread crosswise around the bundle for swaddling bands.

actual size

Sheep

You will need:

25 g white double-knitting wool
Small amount of dark brown double-
    knitting wool
4.5 mm knitting needles
3 pipe cleaners
Fleece or cottonwool for stuffing
Crochet hook
Scraps of dark brown felt

Cast on 16 sts. and knit 6 cm st.st. Cast off 4 sts. at the beginning of next and following row. Continue knitting another four rows in st.st. Change to brown colour and knit two rows st.st. Next row: k2 tog. repeatedly to the end of row. (4 sts. left.) Break thread and pull it through 4 sts. Sew thread in.

Working on reverse side of the knitting, and using a double thickness of white wool, cover the white part of the knitting with loops as seen below. Secure each loop with a small backstitch as illustrated.

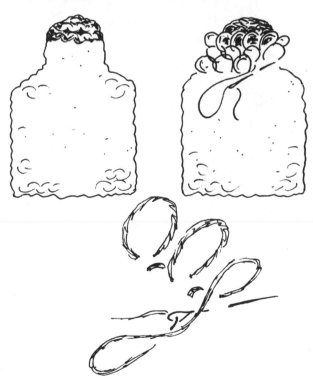

215

Make a skeleton frame for the sheep with the pipe cleaners as seen below.

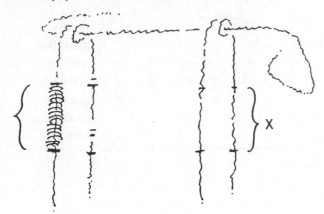

Wind some brown wool tightly around section X of a leg to conceal pipe cleaner. (See above.) Bend leg at centre of section X and carry on winding the wool around both pipe cleaners until the whole leg is covered.

Repeat for other three legs. Cover the pipe cleaner skeleton with the knitted body piece. Sew edges of the body piece together around the pipe cleaners. Starting at the nose, work along the sheep, padding head and body with fleece/cottonwool as you sew up each section.

Crochet a chain with some white wool and sew it to the sheep as a short tail. Cut ears from the felt and attach them to the head.

Christmas Eve (Adam and Eve Day)

On Christmas Eve, the final preparations for the Christmas Feast are made. The tree is now in place and the house is decorated with greenery. In Finland a sheaf of corn is placed upon the roof; in Poland, hay is spread beneath the tablecloth or sprinkled on the floor. Many Irish folk light a candle to set in the window, and English children hang a hopeful stocking by the chimney or the bed. In the days before central heating, a Yule Log would have been placed in the fireplace and kindled with the remnants of the log from the year before. The decorations in English houses always included a 'Kissing Bough' fashioned around a bunch of mistletoe, but in other parts of Europe mistletoe was hung on the outside of the house to indicate where the fairies might find shelter in the snow. Churches could be decorated with holly (the 'holy' tree) but never with mistletoe.

A multitude of customs cluster around this important Christian festival, many of them having their roots in pre-Christian rites such as the Mithraic 'Dies Natalis' on December 25th, or the Saturnalian celebrations observed around the time of the Winter Solstice throughout the Roman Empire. Other customs can be traced to Druidic rituals, or to the beliefs which accompanied the worship of the Teutonic gods Odin and Thor, or even to a much older religious inheritance from Indo-European cultures.

Most folk traditions express themselves through pictures and the Christmas customs are no exception. The erect holly tree, with its fiery berries and sharp, active glittering leaves, presents a strong contrast to the mysterious, shadowy clumps of yielding, softly-curving ivy. It is not surprising that these two plants were used in pre-Christian fertility festivals at the time of the year when the seed was, as it were, penetrating the womb of the Earth. Such symbolic picturing of the male and female principles maintained its impact into Christian times, embodied in the well-loved carol "The Holly and the Ivy." Here the male and female archetypes are celebrated in the wholly Christian images of the Redeemer and His mother.

The English custom of kissing beneath the mistletoe is not common to every country in which this strange plant features as part of the Christmas festivities. However, where it is used, it is almost always hung. Why are we not inclined to arrange it in a vase or use it in a table decoration? By hanging the bunch of mistletoe we are, consciously or not, remaining true to the 'picture' of this strange plant, which was singled out in Norse mythology as growing "neither on the earth, nor under the earth," and in which all the usual patterns of plant growth seem to have been suspended.

Such customs, and many others, have clung tenaciously to our winter festivals and indicate, perhaps, that a kind of 'picture hunger' arises in people at this time of the year, when Nature's own picture is subdued. In recent times, this hunger has been assuaged by the surfeit of greeting cards which are fed into the mailbox during the weeks before Christmas. As these cards go up on the book shelves and around the walls, more and more pictures are opening on the Advent calendar. Then the crib is arranged, the tree decorated, and we sing our way through the pictures in the traditional carols. Gradually, we surround ourselves with a multitude of images that have their life in a world a little above the everyday.

Entering into these imaginations, almost without noticing it, we are able to move closer to this world, finding joy, for example, in the starry sparkle of a tinsel-trimmed lampshade, or the gleam of a red satin bow on the stair rail, which at all other times of the year would appear merely tawdry. The richness, the glory and the light of celestial spaces beckons us nearer. For a while, we can be lifted beyond mundane existence and, like the shepherds on the hills near Bethlehem, catch a glimpse of something high above us.

If this can be so for human beings, why should not the animals also share in this elevating experience on Christmas Night and, as the legends tell, be gifted with human speech? Maybe Thomas Hardy is not alone in "hoping it may be true."

The Christmas tree

If a quiet mood of anticipation has been renewed from time to time throughout Advent, then Christmas Eve can come as a moment of inner fullness. Just as a seed will gradually swell until the point when it splits and sprouts, so we also experience an inner burgeoning, a feeling that something is about to spring into life. What better way to express this mood than with a Christmas Tree! In the depths of winter a green and living tree 'blossoms' and 'bears' its starry flowers and gifts of light.

The Christmas Tree was introduced to Britain early in the nineteenth century. It was already popular in Germany, and has subsequently appeared in every corner of Christendom. On Adam and Eve Day, if not before, it finds its place within the home. On such a day, one cannot but be reminded of the tree in the Garden of Eden, or rather, the two trees which stood there side by side: the Tree of Knowledge of Good and Evil, and the Tree of Life. The first Tree was to lead humanity away from God, and the second Tree stands at the place where God is reunited with His people — in the city of the New Jerusalem. (Revelations 22: 2.)

In some countries it is customary to leave the tree bare on Adam and Eve Day except for red apples hanging from the branches, in remembrance of the Tree of Paradise. In other places, bread decorations are also hung as a sign of redemption. German children are told that it is the Christ Child who transforms the Tree on Christmas Eve, who brings it to life and light, who crowns it with stars and strews presents beneath its branches.

If we gaze at the decorated Tree through half-closed eyes and allow our imagination to carry us away to the land of myth, we might see again the great World Tree Yggdrasil holding up the universe, its branches winding among the glittering canopy of stars, and, sheltering beneath their spread, all the marvellous gifts of creation arrayed for our delight. The topmost bough of this Tree touches the abode of the angels, and if we can see that far, then maybe we shall also hear their Christmas message of peace to men and women of good will.

It was with the light of this message flooding their hearts, that the shepherds found the way through the darkness towards their Redeemer. The long journey of Advent may often lead the adult through places of inner darkness, but the Christmas Tree stands before us like a beacon shining into the future. It reminds us that the journey goes on, but allows us to rest a while in its shadow and be restored in the light of hope.

Father Christmas and Santa Claus

On the night before Christmas, many children are shivering with excitement, awaiting a visit from Father Christmas or Santa Claus. Nowadays, commercial standards are blending the separate identities of these reticent benefactors, and it may be worthwhile to consider their differences so that, when we are called upon to be a 'helper' to one of them, we shall understand our task better.

Father Christmas is old, old, *very* old, with the wisdom to match his years. He is dignified and venerable, but modestly hooded. His rich, red, fur-trimmed gown reaches the ground, and gives the impression of kingly, radiating warmth of heart. A long white beard flows past the girdle at his waist. He enters each house from the sky, descending through the chimney to fill the stockings that are hung by the hearth. Into each stocking he puts an orange, one or two sweet things, and some small toys of strange novelty, to delight the child with their magical beauty. As in other folk traditions, a picture metaphor is used here which seems to describe the beneficent forces of creation which work unseen from above. These are the forces that give us, for example, the golden orb of the sun, whose light and warmth strengthens the very bones of the body as they grow; they give us the sweet things of the world to 'taste,' in all that enters those windows of the soul we call the five senses; lastly, they invite us to enjoy the beauty of mankind's resourcefulness and creativity of spirit.

In this part of the world, bare feet in wintertime is a sign of deprivation. All children need stockings for their feet and the clothing of love for their souls. On Christmas Eve, the Night of the Child, we can hope that every child, whatever their religion, will have the opportunity to warm their stockings near the heart of the home, in confident expectation that gifts of love will nourish, year by year, their growing body, soul and spirit.

Dutch settlers took the custom of St Nicholas, or Sinter Klaas, with them to America. There the name gradually changed to Santa Claus and his gifts became more closely connected with Christmas. Like Father Christmas, he is dressed in red, and his short tunic is trimmed with fur. His red trousers are tucked into shiny black boots, and a wide black belt is fastened around his corpulent waist. He wears a Scandinavian-style tasselled cap, a robust and cheery expression, and his thick, curly, white beard signifies not wisdom so much as health, strength and conviviality. He comes from the ice-bound north, speeding through the skies in a reindeer-drawn sleigh, to fulfil the children's secret wishes.

Pictures such as these invite comparison with the bearded Scandinavian god Thor (known to the ancestors of the Dutch as Donar), a god of the atmosphere who travelled between earth and heaven in a chariot drawn by two he-goats. He is represented in one of the poems of the "Edda" as an expansive, simple-hearted "god of the people," trying to get round the sophisticated god Odin by offering him "a share of the good things in my sack." Notoriously lacking in guile, he relied more on strength and courage to win through, aided by a magic belt which doubled the power of his limbs. He was also renowned for his drinking capacity and huge appetite.

Thor was closely connected with the family dwelling, with the earthly home of the individual, as well as with the seasonal round. He retained the affection and respect of ordinary people (many of whom named their children after him) long after Christianity had become the official religion of the northern countries.

The genial figure of Santa Claus echoes many aspects of this well-loved god who brought a hearty good nature to everything he did, who was a friend to common folk and their families, who heard their petitions, brought them seasonal blessings and cheered their difficult lives. Particularly in the long, dark winters of the north, he was brought vividly to mind as stories of his exploits were shared at the fireside.

The Romans called Thor by the name of Jupiter, or Jove, which gives us the word 'jovial.' Is there anyone more jovial than Santa Claus? His good will is infectious, bringing inner warmth and a living confidence in the future. He draws close to us at Christmas, appearing magically in the fireplace (how *does* he get that big tummy down the chimney?) to fulfil the individual, unspoken petitions of each child's heart. He confirms the child's own special value in the world through his loving recognition, and this is by far the most significant of all the gifts that he brings.

A Christmas play for the family

Have you ever thought of performing a Christmas play, just by yourselves as a family, with one or two friends or relations? There's no need for an audience, in fact it's better without one. Our families have enjoyed doing this in different ways over the years — sometimes as an opening to Christmastide, or as a way of closing it on Twelfth Night. The thought of doing 'A Play' is the most daunting part — in practice it is fun to prepare, simple to do, and can create an unforgettable mood with the good will of the players.

Costumes and 'props' may be scant for the first performance but we guarantee that once it becomes a family tradition, someone will bring home, at moments throughout the year, "just the right staff for Joseph" or "the perfect hat for the innkeeper!"

Casting is no problem: if your five-year-old son wants to be Mary, that's alright, and aunts make quite acceptable shepherds. Older members of the cast will be able to learn their lines, the younger members may need to have someone speaking with them. The Angel can be a reliable prompter!

The whole house is the stage — Shepherds sleeping at the top of the stairs, the Kings travelling from the furthest bedroom… it's all up to you, *how* it happens. Well, that's not quite true, for it's the unscripted, unexpected incidents that provide the memorable ingredients to such a family event: the time, for example, when the shepherds journeyed to Bethlehem only to find Mother Mary (a 92-year-old great-aunt, well wrapped in blue cloak and seated in a comfortable fireside chair) fast asleep and snoring loudly…

Perhaps you may also like to include the "Kings' Play" (see p241) if your performance takes place towards the end of the Holy Nights.

A final note: we include these plays, not in the hope of impressing you with their literary skill, but as examples of what can be put together, fairly quickly, to meet the need of the moment. We hope this will inspire you to pen your own version which will, of course, be far superior…

Cast:
Joseph
Mary
Innkeeper
1st Shepherd
2nd Shepherd
3rd Shepherd
Angel

Costumes and accessories:
This play can be enjoyed without any special costumes at all — but certainly a few items of clothing and accessories add to the fun and the mood of the occasion. The suggestions we make here are minimal — there's plenty of scope for elaboration!

Joseph — A dark cloak (a curtain or dyed sheet) and wooden staff (broom handle or length of young hazel branch).
Mary — A blue cloak to cover head and shoulders, a long red dress or skirt; coloured veils can also be used (see p249).
Innkeeper — An apron and a lantern or candle in a saucer.
Shepherds — Crooks (walking sticks?) or staffs, some 'rustic' dress, e.g. sheepskin jacket or waistcoat, woollen hats, sandals, etc. (their gifts can be mimed).

Enter the players — singing the first verse of Sussex Carol (No. 24 in "Oxford Book of Carols"). Everyone sits except Joseph and Mary.

Joseph: Oh Mary!
　　　　How cold we are!
　　　　Black is the night
　　　　Without a star.
　　　　Weary my feet,
　　　　We have come so far.
　　　　No house can be seen
　　　　Anywhere.

(Innkeeper stands with lantern.)

Mary: Look, Joseph,
　　　　A light is there.

Joseph: I will knock at the door —

(Joseph knocks three times.)

Innkeeper: Too many have come before —
　　　　I have no room nor food in my house;
　　　　Neither nook nor scrap enough for a mouse.

(Mary and Joseph walk on. Innkeeper sits.)

Joseph: Where can we find a friendly hearth?
　　　　 We cannot sleep on the icy earth —
　　　　 You are with child and I am old.

Mary: God will not let us die of cold.
　　　 My heart tells me that soon the birth
　　　 Of Heav'n's own child will bless the
　　　 earth.
　　　 Look, my Joseph, there's a light.

(Innkeeper stands with lantern.)

Innkeeper: Who is still about at night?
　　　　　 Alas! Alas! I am not able
　　　　　 To give you folks a bed.
　　　　　 But come with me unto my
　　　　　 stable,
　　　　　 Where ox and ass are fed.

(Mary and Joseph go to the stable — Mary
sits down. All sing "Once in Royal David's
City," verses 1 and 2, while the Star Angel
enters holding her star, at first high and
then gently lowering it towards Mary's lap.
Mary folds her arms, as if cradling a baby.
The angel goes out carrying the star aloft.)

Mary: Joseph dearest, bring some hay,
　　　 I'll line the wooden crib and lay
　　　 The child therein to make Him warm,
　　　 And pray God keeps Him safe from
　　　 harm.

(All sing "Joseph Dearest Joseph Mine,"
verses 1 and 2 — No. 77 in the Oxford Book
of Carols. On a hillside a little way off three
shepherds are preparing for sleep.)

1st Shepherd: Brothers, let us sleep,
　　　　　　 Safe are the sheep.

(Lies down.)

2nd Shepherd: Huddled together in the
　　　　　　 night,
　　　　　　 Let us sleep before the light.

(Lies down close to the other.)

3rd Shepherd: In sleep I forget my stomach
　　　　　　 grumbling.
　　　　　　 On icy ground, to Dreamland
　　　　　　 we are tumbling.

(Falls to ground by others. All sing — except
the sleeping shepherds — Alternative
refrain "Gloria in Excelsis Deo" No. 119
Oxford Book of Carols. During the singing
the Angel appears.)

1st Shepherd: Brothers, wake up!

2nd Shepherd: Aye, is it rain?

3rd Shepherd: No, not rain — an angel came
　　　　　　 To bid us go to Bethlehem,
　　　　　　 Prepare yourself, rejoice and
　　　　　　 sing
　　　　　　 To greet a child, a heavenly
　　　　　　 King.

2nd & 3rd Shepherds: What shall we bring?

1st Shepherd: I have some wool —

2nd Shepherd: I have a jug of milk, not quite
　　　　　　 full —

3rd Shepherd: I have a little lamb — high as
　　　　　　 my hem.

(Shepherds skip off singing along the way to
Bethlehem. They arrive at the stable.)

Joseph: Come in, good folks, come near...

Mary: See the little Child so dear.

(Shepherds kneel.)

1st Shepherd: Dear Child from above,
　　　　　　 I have this warm fleece,
　　　　　　 I will give you a piece.

2nd Shepherd: **Dear King of Love,**
I have no silk,
But a jug of milk — quite
nearly full.

3rd Shepherd: **Dear Child of Man,**
I bring you a lamb
As high as my hem.

(All sing "Rocking," No. 87 Oxford Book of Carols. Everyone processes off while singing first verse of Sussex Carol again — No. 24 in Oxford Book of Carols.)

Christmas singing

For a simple and pleasant alternative to a play, we have this suggestion: Sing yourselves through the Christmas Story!

Here are two possible sequences of carols which your family and friends may know. But why not make up your own programme? The carols could be sung while you sit together, or the dressing-up box could be raided and simple actions made to accompany the songs.

If singing on Christmas Eve:
From "Oxford Book of Carols."
- 1. Christmas Eve, verses 1, 3, 4.
- 3. Sunny Bank.
- 27. First Nowell, 1st verse.
- 142. Children's Song of the Nativity.
- 77. Song of the Crib.
- 87. Rocking.
- 118. Susanni, verses 1, 2, 3.
- 138. O Little Town of Bethlehem, verses 1, 2, 5.
- 195. Kings of Orient.
- 24. Sussex Carol, verses 1, 4.

Well known traditional Hymns and Carols:
While Shepherds Watched
Once in Royal David's City
Away in a Manger
Silent Night
O Little Town of Bethlehem
We Three Kings
O Come All Ye Faithful

The twelve days of Christmas

It is sometimes overlooked that Christmas is actually a festival of twelve days and thirteen 'Holy Nights.' Christmas Eve is the first of the Holy Nights, and January 5th is the Twelfth Day of Christmas. The special quality of these days has been remarked upon by many, and valued as a time for inner reflection and contemplation. Shakespeare described them as "so hallowed and so gracious" (Hamlet Act 1 Scene 1) and one may readily come to the experience that this short space is offered to us as a time 'set apart' from the routine course of the seasons. Country folklore spoke of a "year within the year," and farmers studied the weather moods of the corresponding twelve months of the year ahead. Prophecy crept into social life also, for "he who eats twelve mince pies in twelve different houses during the Twelve Days of Christmas, will have twelve happy months in the coming year." (Anon.)

Christmas is a 'night' festival, and as darkness falls on Christmas Eve the celebrations begin. The sound of a little bell may call German children to the Christmas Tree — now radiant with candlelight; elsewhere in the world larger bells ring out as churches prepare for a special service in the middle of this first Holy Night. In all corners of the globe the Christmas story is being read from the Gospel of St Luke. In Poland, the sighting of the first star is the signal for the festive family meal, and in many other countries traditional meals are shared in the evening. Now is the time when extra places are laid at the table for friends and relations from near and far, and when, in parts of Eastern Europe, a seat is reserved for Christ Himself, if He should seek hospitality in the guise of a passing stranger. Whether the meal is a simple bowl of creamy rice enjoyed on Christmas Eve in Norway, or a feast of roast turkey and plum pudding with brandy butter, served on the following day in England, it can be a high point in the family year.

A festival to celebrate the birth of Jesus was established on December 25th by the Western Church at the end of the 4th century. It had to find its place within a highly developed calendrical sequence of pagan ritual in Europe. Predictably, aspects of these rituals were too well rooted to be cast off entirely by Christian converts, and many of the customs continued to be observed, although frequently reinterpreted within the new religion. Such folk customs often became a focus for the disapproval of local Bishops, and, from time to time, attempts were made to eradicate the most suspect of them. In 1652 festival celebrations of all kinds were banned in England by a Puritan Parliament, and during the few years of their government many rural traditions, plays and songs were lost. In parts of the U.S.A. also, at that period, people were actually fined for celebrating Christmas.

Nowadays, it is the world of commerce that most effectively influences the way in which we keep Christmas, and even if we sometimes feel constrained by this, it is not always so easy to break free. More and more families are, however, finding it necessary to develop their own traditions within which they are able to enjoy family life at this time without the intrusion of the media, to delight in giving and receiving without becoming prey to consumerism, to make the space and the time and the *peace* to cultivate this festival. The shepherds listened to Christmas in awe, the Wise Men followed it in wonderment, and Mary held it to her in devotion. These are the gifts of the season — to listen, to wonder, to be content — and we have Twelve Days in which to receive and appreciate them.

One can be sympathetic towards the mother who decided to stage a murder mystery each year on Christmas morning for her children to solve, to divert them from pestering her about their presents, but, if diversions are needed, there are many possibilities to explore while remaining within the seasonal mood! Here are a few suggestions that have been tried and tested by families, and have become for them traditions of lasting pleasure and satisfaction.

For example, an absorbing occupation for the children is certainly worth planning for Christmas Day, but by far the most calming activity is some form of handicraft or simple practical project suitable for the age of the child. The necessary materials should be gathered together well in advance: gold paper for cut-out stars or simple paper chains, spruce twigs for decorating a Yule Staff (evergreens keep fresh in a paper bag outside), and biscuit dough for baking. A book on origami will interest children over eleven years, and they might like to make a string of cranes for New Year. Walnuts should be sliced in half by an adult, but children will enjoy nibbling the contents and then making little candle boats. In hard and frosty weather, materials can be at hand for Frost Paintings, or for cooking up a special Christmas treat for the birds. We've noticed that Santa Claus often chooses just the right gift to keep little fingers occupied!

A family walk becomes a special event on Christmas afternoon (or the following day) when the streets are almost deserted and bird song rings out clearly in the early dusk. Maybe a particular route could be reserved for just this time of year. The late afternoon twilight is also a good moment to gather for a while each day around the Christmas Tree, to sing carols, to read a Christmas story, to share biscuits or nuts. All age groups enjoy being read to: young and old take pleasure in traditional folk tales, and children of ten years and above will be entertained by some of the long narrative poems from the classics, delivered perhaps in serial form over several days. Adolescents may appreciate readings from a biography, or tales of exploration. Many things are possible, for the spoken word can lend a magic to passages one might normally not bother to read: try, for instance, reading aloud the Genealogy of Jesus from St Luke's Gospel...

Pantomimes do not always replace the charm of unsophisticated performance of the traditional Christmas plays and Mummers' Plays that are now mostly lost to us. It can be a surprise to discover how the simplicity of enacting one's own Christmas play leads to a rich and moving experience for everyone. (See p220.)

It is always exciting to unwrap a present, and the excitement can often be overwhelming for a child. After the feverish activity of opening a pile of gifts, many children plummet into an unexpected feeling of "is this all there is?" They may appear ungrateful and discontented simply because the experience has been too exhausting, and has left them feeling as empty as the discarded wrapping paper. Some families have developed a routine of spreading the gift-opening over a few days by 'discovering' more parcels under the Tree each morning. This allows each present more appreciation time, and how nice it is to know that there's something to look forward to tomorrow! Another way of leading a child gently down from the high pitch of the festival is to use a Twelve-Days-of-Christmas Ring (see p226). This is a simple and inexpensive way of ensuring that the joy of surprise will not disappear with Christmas Day.

The idea of the Advent Calendar could be adapted to a Twelve-Days Calendar with pictures appropriate to the twelve months of the year. Very simple ones are possible using art postcards with seasonal themes in landscape or rural activity. Older children may enjoy keeping a 'weather diary' for the Twelve Days, plotting the movement of the weather throughout the day and projecting the results into the appropriate month of the coming year: the morning giving a picture for the first half of the month, the afternoon's pattern setting the scene for the second half of the month. This could become a foolproof method for planning the summer holiday, but we are not urging you to rely upon it!

If these Twelve Days give a family the opportunity to relax together, this relaxed mood invariably includes a few squabbles! A child's squabbling is not a bad thing in itself, but sometimes it indicates boredom, and possibly a wish to socialise without quite knowing how to do it. Some good old-fashioned games may be the answer: Hunt the Thimble for those over seven years old, guessing games and quizzes for the bigger children, and charades for larger groups of teenagers or adults. Such impromptu games can live on as a source of pleasure in the family memory for years.

There are many different ways in which to use this 'time out of time' between Christmas Eve and Epiphany, and we may discover activities that become possible which are otherwise difficult to reconcile with our normal routines. I know of a hard-working single parent who takes this time to catch up with friendships, inviting a different friend or family to her home on each of the Twelve Days. Other parents may decide to read together after the children have gone to bed. Those who live on their own could take up a special project — something, perhaps, that they have been promising themselves for years. Hopefully, whatever activity we choose will ensure that the transition from the Old Year into the New will be a restoring of inner forces, a change in the scenery of the soul, as welcome as an invigorating cruise among the distant islands of a foreign sea.

The seed rests for a time in the winter earth, connecting itself with the source of strength which will enable it to unfold and blossom in the spring. Men and women also need a quiet space in the year in which to draw close to the unseen sources of their inner strength. The sequence of the Thirteen Holy Nights offers the chance of this experience to all of us.

Christine's Twelve-days-of-Christmas ring

The days following the climax of Christmas can sometimes feel empty and the children especially may experience 'coming down with a bump.' We highly recommend the Twelve-Days-of-Christmas Ring to help the Festival wind down more gently. The twelve heart-shaped baskets each contain a tiny wrapped present. These are very simple: e.g. a hairclip or ribbon, a little golden bell, a pencil sharpener, a shiny crystal or small decoration for the Christmas tree. (For a tired mother there could even be a token for an afternoon off!) Members of the family take turns in opening the baskets. We are lucky to have a friend who fills the baskets for us each year and gives the ring to us as a family Christmas present. Adults, teenagers and little ones all have had great fun and delight when their turn came, watched with interest by the rest of the family.

You will need: (for each basket)

2 strips of felt in contrasting colours 5cm x 17cm each

Strip of felt 1.5cm x 12cm in one or other of the colours

Embroidery silk in matching colour

Ruler, scissors and glue

1 wooden (or metal) macramé ring, at least 20cm diam.

2m of red ribbon, approx. 1cm wide, for hanging the ring

12 small wrapped presents

Follow the instructions on page 38 for making Heart Baskets using the four-fold weaving variation. Sew the handle strip to one side of the basket, 'thread' the basket on the ring and secure the handle on the other side of the basket with a few stitches.

Make eleven more baskets and hang them all on the ring as described above. Space the baskets evenly, securing the handles to the ring with a drop of glue. Cut the red ribbon in half and tie each end to the ring as seen below. Put a present in each basket.

St Stephen's Day

In Britain this day is known as Boxing Day. Years ago, groups of poor apprentices would carry an earthenware box with a slit in it through the streets to collect money, and this grew into the custom of presenting gifts to tradespeople. Today, however, there are few trades at work on St Stephen's Day, but we can still make up some pretty boxes to fill with star biscuits or home-made sweets for friends and neighbours.

In the Isle of Man the Christmas Box was known as the Wren Box which links it with a pagan practice of stoning the wren on this day. The reasons for this ancient ritual are obscure, although different legends still exist. In parts of Ireland, children go from door to door in disguise, chanting a verse about the wren and collecting money and sweets. St Stephen also was martyred by stoning, and a charming 15th century carol connects him with another bird — a cockerel. The song relates how Stephen served King Herod, but on his conversion he announced that he would leave the court. King Herod retorted that the beliefs of Stephen's new religion were about as true as it was that the capon served at the table could arise from the dish and crow. No sooner had he said that but "The capon crew, Christus Natus Est!"

The Feast of Stephen is, of course, the best day to sing the well favoured carol "Good King Wenceslas." This saintly king led a pious and charitable life which became unpopular with the pagan court. He sought to alleviate suffering wherever he could but, as a result, suffered death himself.

Gift boxes

These are almost a present in themselves, but the young at heart will look for the treasure inside...

Square box

You will need:
One square piece of cartridge paper
Ruler and scissors

A piece of paper measuring 20cm x 20cm will make a box 7cm square. Fold the square diagonally in half to find the centre.

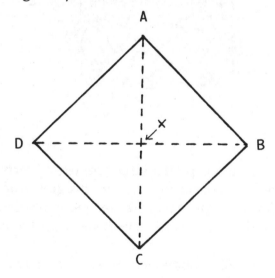

Bring corners A, B, C, D to centre point X.

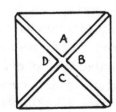

Open all the folds again.

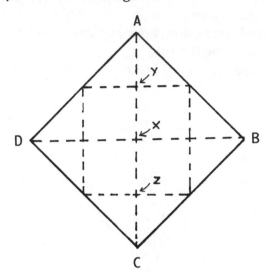

Make more folding lines by folding C to Y and after opening the square again, fold C to Z.

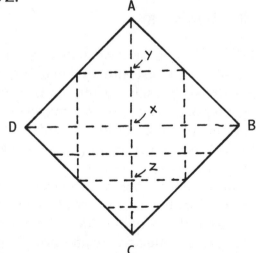

Repeat the same procedure on each side with corners A, B and D.

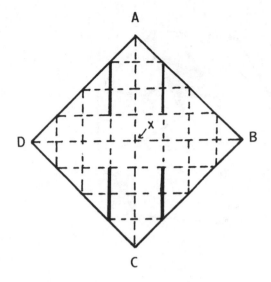

Cut along the solid lines. Fold corners D and B into the centre X and make the sides of the box as shown.

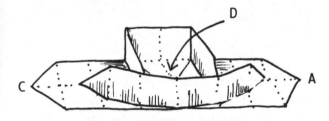

Now fold the two sides with corners A and C in such a way that they meet in the centre of the box.

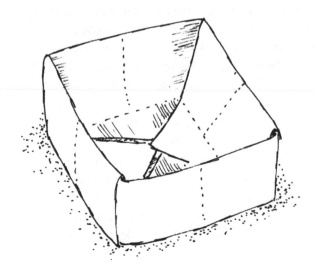

If you want to make a lid for the box, simply repeat the above instructions but start with a square which is 1 cm bigger than the base box paper. You can make the box into a basket by adding a strip for a paper handle.

Six-sided box

You will need:
Six-sided Box pattern (see p270)
Piece of thin card 20 cm x 12 cm
Ruler and scissors
Knitting needle
Glue

On the piece of card measure out and mark all the lines as shown on pattern. Cut along the solid lines and score along all the dotted (folding) lines with the knitting needle. Fold the card along all the scored lines, opening it and laying it flat again after each fold. Put some glue on the underside of flap A and stick box together with flap A on inside as shown below.

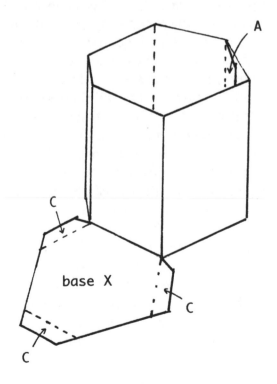

Put glue on flaps C and fold base of box into place. Stick flaps C to the corresponding sides on the inside of the box. Now glue flaps B to the underside of the base. Arrange the top of the box so that it folds down as seen below.

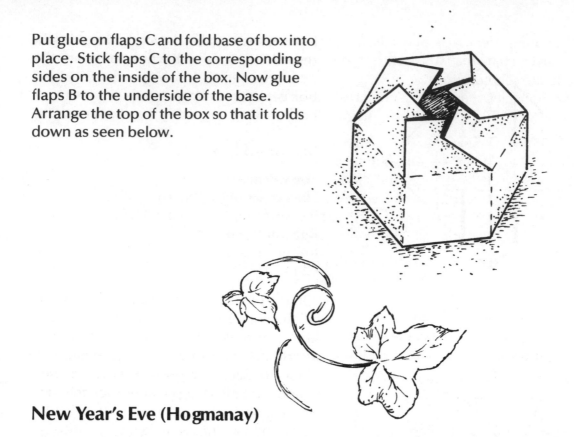

New Year's Eve (Hogmanay)

When the farmers of old followed the Twelve Days of Christmas seeking a weather chart for the coming year (see p224), they arrived on the seventh Day, December 31st, at the seventh month of July. According to astrological tradition, this month is governed by the zodiac sign of the Crab, a sign made up of two spirals. These spirals — one gathering in, one flowing out — are separated by a space, and it is always the space between the end of the Old Year and the beginning of the New that was of significance to our pre-Christian forebears. Our earthly world is governed by time, unlike the 'other world,' and it was believed that the suspension of time for even the briefest moment could dissolve boundaries and provide a crack through which unwelcome beings from the 'other world' might intrude. Therefore it was necessary to assert the human presence at this moment as strongly as possible, and today this is often done with shouts and cheers and the ringing of church bells. In Scotland, especially, the hour of midnight on Hogmanay is a signal for loud merry-making, music, dancing and general roistering. Across the North of the British Isles dramatic spectacles of ancient origin are enacted with bonfires or blazing barrels of tar, and in many houses hearths are thoroughly swept to ensure a completely new start to the New Year. Elsewhere in Europe, where the festival may be named after St Sylvester, midnight is greeted with loud fireworks, and one Swiss family we know negotiates this 'crack' in time by jumping off their chairs to the floor!

The fact that the people of bygone ages felt the proximity of the supernatural world at such times, gave rise to a multitude of prophetic practices. Some have lingered on to this day in such customs as 'first-footing,' where the first person to cross the threshold of the house in the New Year brings good luck only if he is a dark-haired male. If he also brings bread, salt, coal and a silver coin, that will ensure food, friendship, warmth and prosperity for the household in the year to come.

Weather prophecies seem to be a firm favourite all year round! Here is one for New Year's Eve:

"If New Year's Eve night wind blow South
It betokeneth warmth and growth,
If West, much milk and fish in the sea,
If North, much cold and storms there will be.
If East, the trees will bear much fruit
If North East, flee it, man and brute!" (Anon.)

For the Romans, all gates and openings came under the protection of the god Janus, and the gate into the New Year was no exception — hence the first month of the year, January, is named after him. Janus was a god with two faces, one which looked forwards and one which looked backwards. There are situations in life in which we need to embrace two opposites before we can really appreciate one of them. How can we live life fully without the knowledge of death? How can we see the brightness of light without being aware of the depth of the shadow? At the end of December, at the turning of the year, may we endeavour to look backwards in reconciliation to the past, in order that we may live in hope and new resolve for the future.

New Year cranes

Our Oriental friends have introduced us to one of their New Year traditions: they make Origami cranes and send them to each other as good luck symbols for the coming year. Bring some luck to a friend with this lovely New Year gift.

You will need:
Origami book with instructions for making
    a crane
Gold paper
Red embroidery thread, approx. 90cm
Small fir cone
Circle of red felt approx. 2cm diameter
Glue

Follow instructions for making a crane from the Origami book. Make four cranes using four squares of gold paper in diminishing sizes. Knot the thread and pass the needle and thread through the centre of the red felt circle. At 9cm from the end of the thread make another knot. Then pass the needle through the body of the smallest crane from below and thread the crane until it sits on the knot. Make the next knot 10cm from the top of the body of the crane, and thread on the next smallest crane. Continue in this way, spacing the last two cranes 11cm and 12cm apart. Complete the good luck string by tying a loop at the end of the thread for hanging, and sticking the red felt circle to the base of the fir cone. The extra weight of the cone helps the string to hang well.

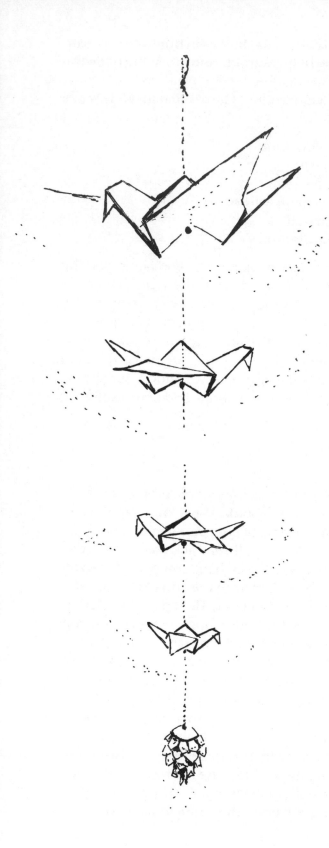

Sailing New Year boats

A festive activity for the whole family:

New Year's Eve is traditionally a time for thinking about the year that has passed and the year that lies ahead; for formulating wishes into resolutions. To dream, to wish, to imagine and to wonder — all these have a place in our lives, and on New Year's Eve you may enjoy an activity which allows plenty of room for gentle fantasy.

Ann's family uses an old zinc bath tub for this, but a plastic baby bath will do, or the largest bowl you possess. There's no real reason why your own bath should not be used, especially if you have a spacious bathroom, but we prefer the atmosphere of the sitting room, with the Christmas Tree and a log fire!

You will need:

Baby bath or large bowl

Aluminium foil (we are looking for a 'green' alternative to this!)

Your prettiest pebbles, crystals and shells

1 bunch each of: flowering plants, holly or other prickly plant, fresh herbs, white heather (if available)

4 glass vases to hold these bunches — optional

Cloth or veil (see p249) in dark blue or dark green, to drape the outside of the bath

2 red ribbon bows — optional

Some greenery — optional

Candle — medium to large

Walnut shell 'candle boat' for each person (see p28)

'Letter' for each person (see below)

'Treasure' for each person (see below)

To prepare the bath:

Place the bath or bowl on the floor or suitable tabletop (protected if necessary from water spills), and line carefully with aluminium foil, taking the foil right up over the rim. (Afterwards, the foil can be dried and stored for future years — so avoid unnecessary crumpling and tearing.) Place the pebbles, crystals and shells on the foil at the bottom of the bath, together with the four vases spaced evenly around the edge. Fill the vases, and then the bath with water to within about 6cm of the rim. Place the four bunches of flowers and greenery in their separate vases, or wedge them in place with pebbles. It doesn't matter if they become submerged, in fact it can add to their beauty and mystery, for these bunches now become islands in a magical sea. (Older children may like to add a more dramatic dimension, and call them the Isle of Joy, the Isle of Pain, the Isle of Healing and the Isle of Luck!)

Drape the veil or cloth around the sides of the bath, making it secure at the rim with pins or adhesive tape. Pin a bow of red ribbon at each end of the bath and lay a few sprigs of greenery around the base for a festive touch.

To prepare the candle boats:

Make the number of candle boats that you need from the instructions on page 28. The candles and the foil stars could be in a variety of colours to make each boat easier to identify. Prepare a tray or board with a medium large candle in a holder and a few sprigs of greenery. Settle the boats among the greenery and light the candle.

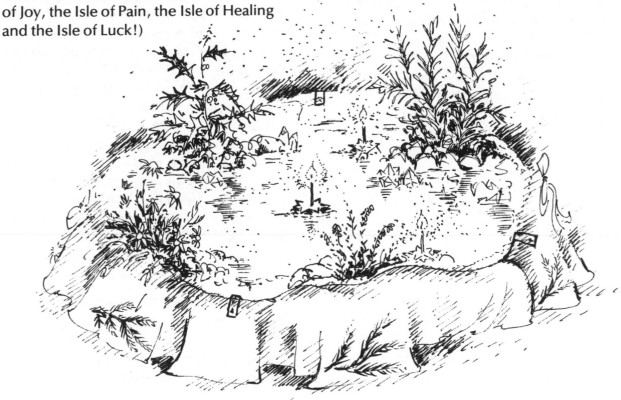

To prepare the treasure:

Gold and silver chocolate coins make very good treasure, and are easy to hide, but you may prefer to choose small wrapped presents. Of course, the treasure must be hidden before anyone else enters the room.

Setting sail:

The first person selects a candle boat and lights the mast from the larger candle. The boat is then *very carefully* set in the middle of the sea, and a Big Wish is loaded on board. A tiny dabble of the fingers at the *edge* of the bath is enough to set the boat gently moving off on its journey into the New Year. Where will it find a harbour? Let's hope that it visits the Isle of Luck! There's no hurry, all in good time the boat will come to rest, maybe lodged firmly on an island or clinging to the edge of the bath. Pushing a boat is against the rules, but there are ways of 'helping' it to skirt the Isle of Pain... However, when the boat has once touched the edge of the bath it is deemed to have landed. Then the treasure hunt begins! The letter that is nearest to the spot where the boat has landed is read out, and the owner of the boat begins a search. When the treasure has been found, the next person may light their candle boat, make their wish and set sail. If time is limited it is, of course, possible for two, or even three people, to set their boats off together.

Whatever the New Year holds for us, to spend a little time afloat in a world of magical beauty, that captures our dreams and sprinkles the light of hope over all that we see... is this not a wish come true?

To prepare the letters:

"Near to the hearth the treasure may lie
Come, will you not see it with your little eye?"

Doggerel verses such as these are fun to compose and will serve as clues to the treasure hidden around the room. Write the lines on the inside of folded slips of coloured paper. (Choose dark, rich colours of sugar paper or gold/silver paper.) Add a gold star to the outside and hang them, evenly spaced, over the edge of the bath taking care that they don't touch the water.

"Time marches on, they say,
But what does it march upon today?"

Now, where do you look to find the next piece of treasure...?

Twelfth Night — Epiphany — Three Kings' Day

The Festival of Epiphany is one of the oldest Christian festivals, older even than Christmas. The word (epiphany) comes from the Greek word 'epiphaneia' which literally means 'to shine above' or 'to shine over,' and has been translated as 'appearance' or 'manifestation' of a divine being. In early Christian thinking this was related to the description in the Gospels of the Baptism of Jesus by John: "And straightway coming up out of the water, he saw the heavens opened, and the Spirit like a dove descending upon him: And there came a voice from heaven, saying, Thou art my beloved Son, in whom I am well pleased." (Mark 1: 10, 11.)

A Feast of the Baptism was set on January 6th by the sect of Basilides at Alexandria, and later adopted by the great church. It most probably began as a Christianized form of Blessing of the waters of the Nile. Epiphanius, Bishop of Constantia in Cyprus, records (circa 360) that the water so blessed was highly prized and even exported, for it improved in storage, like wine, over three to four years.

It is interesting to note that the Miracle at Cana in Galilee, where water was changed into wine, is also remembered in some churches at Epiphany, as the moment when Christ first manifested forth His Divine glory. In a Manx prayer book of 1610 Epiphany is called "the feast of the water vessel."

There was a great deal of controversy among the early churches over the question of the *real* birth of Jesus Christ: was it to be the physical birth in Bethlehem, or the Divine Manifestation arising from the waters of the Jordan. Tertullian used the picture of the fish, the cipher of the Early Christians, when he argued: "We little fishes, after the example of our great fish, Jesus Christ, are born in the water..." Many held that the two births should be celebrated together, but this posed problems for a Bishop of Jerusalem in the 4th century. He complained to Rome that the faithful were endeavouring to celebrate the birth in the cave at Bethlehem and then scampering to the Jordan, many miles away, to hold services there, with the result that neither celebration was conducted in decorum! These difficulties were resolved in 380 AD when the Epiphany celebration became solely a commemoration of the Nativity and the festival of the Baptism was suppressed. Soon afterwards Christmas was fixed on December 25th in the Western Church and, by the 5th century, Epiphany was confined by the Roman liturgical year to the visit of the Magi, when Jesus was 'manifested' for the first time to people who were not Jews.

When Christmas began to be observed in December at the season of the winter solstice, the church of Rome was criticized for connecting itself with sun worship. However, Epiphany was likewise based on a solstice festival — January 6th being the winter solstice of the Julian calendar and of the pre-Christian Egyptian calendar. Pagan festivals gathered around this date also, for example a festival of Dionysus on January 5th. In Alexandria, the birth of Aeon from the Virgin Kore and, moreover, the re-finding or re-birth of Osiris "from out of the water," were both celebrated on January 6th.

Epiphany as a festival of the Baptism and Divine Birth, is still celebrated in some Eastern churches, but in the West it is more commonly known as Three Kings' Day, and in England the eve of January 6th is known as Twelfth Night, a name sometimes carried over into the day itself. By tradition all Christmas decorations should be removed on this Night, and the time was spent in merry-making.

'Twelve-Tyde' in Somerset was a day when the Ploughmen were given a ceremonial cake. They went into the ox-house "with the Wassall bowl, to drink to the Ox with the crumpled horn that treads out the corn..." (John Aubrey: Remaines of Gentilisme.) Then the bowl would be taken to the orchard and the fruit trees wassalled with great noise and rejoicing. Cider or ale would be poured over the trees and pieces of toast placed at the roots or in the forks of the branches. The Wassall, or Wassail Bowl was a communal cup of good cheer containing hot, spiced ale or cider. The word comes from the Anglo-Saxon 'was-hael,' meaning "be thou hale," or as we would say, "Good health." After the calendar changed, this rural custom continued to be celebrated around the middle of January. Twelfth Night (which, of course, gave its name to the play by Shakespeare), has been considered an almost magical time — a time when animals could speak and water had a strong healing power.

Celebrations in many other countries are conducted in a joyful manner. In Scandinavia, processions of 'Star Singers' move from house to house led by a large and decorative star on a stick. There may also be a 'Star Man,' a figure similar to St Nicholas, who questions the children on their catechism and gives out treats.

In Russia, children await with excitement the coming of Mama Babouschka who will fill their shoes with gifts. Other little shoes (stuffed with hay or oats for tired camels!) are placed on Spanish window sills in case the Three Kings pass by and leave them a small treasure. In France and Italy this can be a family time of fun and merry-making. French families share a Kings' Cake (see p242) and the 'King' is sometimes requested to sit on a specially prepared throne at the meal and speak only in rhyme. Italian children expect a visit from Old Befana (a corruption of the word 'Epiphania') a wise woman who loves all children and bestows her gifts accordingly. Sometimes she appears at a family gathering in witch-like costume and organises a 'lucky dip' from her hat. Some say Old Befana visits all the houses searching for the Christ Child and among her traditional gifts are a small hand-made toy animal and a piece of bread. She is rather ugly and a sad figure because, as the story goes, she wanted to go with the shepherds to bring a gift to the manger but was too late. Now she brings gifts to children everywhere, just in case one of them is the Holy Child.

Traditional Twelfth Night pastimes included exchanging riddles and a sung form of memory game. The well-known carol, "The Twelve Days of Christmas" could have been one of these, the verses added in turn by each of the company. Families can have a lot of fun with this carol, or the Scottish song on page 238.

The dismantling of the Christmas Tree is an important moment for German children, who make a little feast of the biscuit decorations stripped from the branches. In the past, small rural communities would conduct ceremonial bonfires of Trees, but nowadays the disposal of the Tree is more mundane. Over the twelve days of Christmas the Tree has become quite a friend to the family, and one way of saying goodbye less abruptly is to stand it in the garden for a while. Nuts, cooked bacon rind, bird seed and little bunches of wheat or barley heads can be tied to the branches for the birds. If the Tree disappears from the house mysteriously overnight, the place where it stood will appear less empty if a bowl of sprouting crocus or hyacinth bulbs are found there — a token of springtime yet to come.

The Christmas Crib may now have been prepared for Epiphany (see p239) when the Wise Men offer their gifts to the Child. It could be appropriate to remember this event in a quiet way, by reading the Christmas Story from the beginning of St Matthew's Gospel, singing some Epiphany carols and participating in a simple Kings' Play (see p241). In the Gospel story we hear about Wise Men guided by a star; they are never referred to as kings, nor is it said that there are three of them. An unknown but powerful tradition has transformed these sages (the 'Magoi' were Persian priests of the Zarathustrian religion) into three kings, representing them as young, middle-aged and old, and sometimes of three different races: the African, the Caucasian, and the Asiatic. They have also been given names: Caspar, Melchior and Balthazar. These three have become the patrons of all travellers, (hence, The Three Crowns or The Star are popular titles for British Inns). Each time one crosses the threshold of the house, it could be said that one is beginning or ending a journey. For this reason, a custom arose in Europe of chalking the initials of the Three Kings above the front door. This simple blessing of the threshold would be renewed each year on January 6th.

The Wise Men brought gifts of gold, frankincense and myrrh. Such offerings were symbolic, a recognition of the Child's divine sovereignty of wisdom, His high priestly mission to the world, and His dominion over the death of the body. These were the gifts that Jesus took into His earthly life: that were recognised also by the learned doctors in the Temple when He was twelve years of age (Luke 2: 46-47), by John the Baptist at the River Jordan, and by Mary Magdalen in the garden on Easter morning. In each of these encounters His true Being shone forth, eclipsing for a while His earthly personality. The light of heaven that shone only for the Wise Men, now shone for the whole world. In the words of the poet Novalis, "He is the Star, He is the Sun, He is eternal life begun."

The star that the Wise Men followed led not away into the widths of the heavenly worlds but to a house, an earthly dwelling, and an inevitable part of their journey was their encounter with evil in the person of Herod. We, too, may be following a star, seeking the abode of our highest aspirations. This is always to be found on the earth — set firmly in the ground of daily life, earthly tasks and responsibilities. On the way, we meet unforeseen difficulties, disappointments, even dangers, which may force us to change direction. But on all this the star shines: on the success and the failure, on the good and the evil, and in the clear light of its rays we are guided ever forward.

Twelfth Night memory tester:

Here is a Scottish version of a song known to the English as "Green Grow the Rushes, O!"

I'll give ye ane, boys }
I'll give ye twa, boys }
I'll give ye three, boys } green grow the ru-shes-O
I'll give ye four, boys }

{ What will be our ane, boys?
{ What will be our twa, boys?
{ What will be our three, boys?
{ What will be our four, boys?

1. My on-ly ane, she walks a-lane, And ev-er-maire has dune, boys,

2. Twa's the li-ly and the rose That shine both red and green,_ boys *(back to beginning)*

My on-ly ane, she walks a-lane. And ev-er-maire has dune, boys.

3. Three's the three thri-vers *(back to 2)*

4. Four's the gos-pel mak-ers *(back to beginning for 4 verses)* *(back to 3)*

(sing these three bars at beginning of verses 5-12)

I'll give ye five boys } Green grow the rush-es - O { What will be our five, boys
etc. { etc.

5-12
Five's the num-bers o' my bower
Six the e-choing wa - ter (to 5)
Seven's the stars of heav - ven (to 6)
Eight's the tab-le ran - gers (to 7)
Nine's the mu-ses of Par - nas-sus (to 8)
Ten's the ten Com-mand - ments (to 9)
Ele - ven mai-dens in a dance (to 10)
Twelve's the twelve A - pos - tles (to 11)

Four's the gos - pel mak - ers (to 3)

238

The Epiphany crib

On Christmas Day the shepherds gather round the Holy Family, but the Three Kings (or Wise Men), can only be seen in the distance — a far-flung corner of the sitting room. They have a long way to journey to pay homage to the Child, and their progress is noted each day as they follow a star which moves gradually closer to the crib. What an important day it is when, on January 6th, the Kings finally arrive to present their gifts to the Child!

If you study the paintings by old masters, you will notice a marked difference between the scenes depicting the adoration of the shepherds and the adoration of the kings. In the former, the Child is seen lying on the ground or in a manger, but in the latter the Child usually sits on Mary's lap. Mary often wears a crown and receives the Kings not in a stable but in a house, as described in the Gospel of St Matthew. So, in arranging the scene for Epiphany we follow the spirit of this tradition by removing the stable, crowning Mary with a string of golden stars (see p240) and placing the Child in her arms.

The three kings crib figures

You will need:
All the materials listed on page 210 for basic crib figures
Dark brown stockinette 10cm x 10cm (stockinette can be painted with water colour)
3 pieces of cotton or silk 11cm x 20cm, one each in clear red, blue and green for robes
3 pieces of velvet 18cm x 12cm, one each in red, blue and green (matching the robe colours)
Brown and white sheep's wool for hair (Mohair wool is a possible alternative)
Gold paper for crowns and gifts

Follow the instructions given on page 210 and make two basic figures. The third figure, King Caspar, is of dark skin colour, so use the brown stockinette for his head and hands. Sew some hair on each figure: Caspar and Melchior have brown hair, Balthazar's hair is white and he has a beard. Cut out and sew the three kingly robes as shown for Mary's dress (see p212). To make the cloaks: hem each of the three pieces of velvet and sew a gathering thread along one edge.

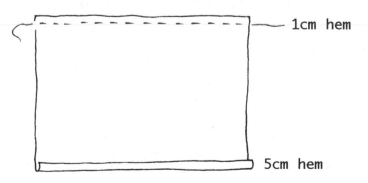

1cm hem

5cm hem

239

Gather the appropriate cloak around the neck of each King and secure with a couple of small stitches. By tradition, Caspar, the young dark king, wears green; Melchior's robe and cloak are red; and Balthazar is an old King and wears blue. Make a crown for each king from some gold paper.

For the gifts, nothing too realistic is needed (the imagination will be active in filling in the details). Simply take a small object, eg. a bead or a piece of plasticine, wrap it in gold paper and secure with a dab of glue.

Mary's crown of stars

You will need:
Gold thread approx. 20cm long
About 9 small golden star sequins, or 18 small self-adhesive golden stars

Knot each sequin on the thread at equal intervals.

Alternatively, stick the self-adhesive gold stars back-to-back in pairs, spaced evenly along the thread. Drape the star chain over Mary's head.

A short Kings' play

For the family at Epiphany:

Using the well-known carol "Kings of Orient," No. 195 in the Oxford Book of Carols.

Cast:
King Melchior, King Caspar, King Balthazar
   — wearing crowns
The Star Angel (with gold star mounted on a gold painted rod)
Joseph and Mary

(Enter the Kings led by the Angel bearing the Star on high. Singing: "Kings of Orient," Verse 1 without refrain.)

Star Angel: The star at night
   So brightly shines,
   And brightly shines by day.
   It leads Three Kings from far away
   To Mary mild
   And the Holy Child

(Indicates the First King.)

Star Angel: King Melchior looks to the star above —
   A promise of peace in the world, and love,
   With a gift of Gold
   He goes on his way
   Wandering, wandering,
   Night and day.

(Singing: Refrain "O star of wonder..." Star Angel indicates the Second King)

Star Angel: King Caspar's head is nobly crowned,
   His heart with humble prayer resounds.

With Frankincense
He makes his way
Journeying, journeying,
Night and day.

(Singing: Refrain "O star of wonder..." Star Angel indicates the Third King)

Star Angel: King Balthazar rides from desert lands,
   The healing Myrrh he bears in his hands,
   He meets two Kings who have lost their way
   Travelling, travelling
   Night and day.

(Singing: Refrain "O star of wonder...")

King Melchior: My path is not clear
   Though I follow the star;
   Come, be my companions
   It cannot be far.

King Caspar: We shall go and seek together
   God will strengthen our endeavour!
   This Child Divine we must behold,
   And give him Myrrh, Incense and Gold.

(Joseph and Mary take up their positions. Mary is cradling her arms — the Star Angel holds the Star above them.)

King Balthazar: Let us kneel at the throne
   Of the Holy King,
   And beg Him receive
   Our offering.

(Singing: Verse 2 — Melchior removes his crown and offers his gift. Then Verse 3 — Caspar removes his crown and offers his gift. Then Verse 4 while Balthazar removes his crown and offers his gift.)

Joseph: We thank you for
The gifts you bring
Of Gold, Incense and Myrrh's
Healing.
In humble state they are arrayed —
But, wisdom oft is thus displayed.

Mary: My gracious lords,
May God, our King,
Guide your path
With His blessing.

(Kings put on their crowns and exeunt led by Star Angel.)

N.B. Other sources attribute the gifts to different Kings. For example Caspar the myrrh, Melchior the gold and Balthazar the frankincense.

Epiphany cake

There is an old custom for Epiphany which children really enjoy: eating a cake, crowned with a golden crown. A dry bean or pea has been baked in the cake mixture and whoever happens to find it in their piece becomes 'King' for the rest of the day. He/she wears the crown and is allowed to reign (within limits of course!). It may be within the scope of kingly power to order a special pudding, command someone to clean another's shoes, or choose a game to play after the meal.

You will need:
250 g butter or margarine
250 g sugar
4 eggs
125 g glacé cherries, halved
100 g chopped nuts
250 g self raising flour
Grated rind of lemon
Pinch of cinnamon
1 dried pea or bean
1 tbsp of melted honey for glazing the cake

Grease and line a 30cm tin. Cream the butter and sugar together and stir in the well-beaten eggs. Sift the flour and cinnamon and gradually fold into the mixture, alternately with the cherries and nuts and lemon rind. Add the pea or bean. Pour into the prepared tin and bake at 160ºC for 1.5 - 2 hrs, until a skewer comes out clean.

Leave in the tin for 15 mins. before turning out on a wire rack. Glaze the cake with the melted honey. Make a crown from a strip of gold card (join the ends with a paper clip or adhesive tape). Crown the cake before serving.

Alternatively, if you like marzipan, try this quick traditional French recipe:

Roll out a circle of marzipan (0.5cm) to fit a large flan dish. Press a dried bean into the marzipan. Prepare two rounds of puff pastry (a packet of frozen pastry is useful here), to fit the same dish. Place one circle on the base of the dish, cover it with the circle of marzipan and add the other round of pastry. Brush with milk and bake in a fairly hot oven for 15 mins. or until golden. Serve warm.

Plough Monday

Epiphany opens up a forward-looking mood in which one naturally inclines to practical tasks. This is a time for getting to grips with life! Great satisfaction can be had in bringing the family home back to normal after Christmas. When the last crumbs of the Christmas biscuits have gone, when the last pine needle and shrivelled holly berry have been brushed off the floor, when the furniture has been restored to its usual place, then the reappearance of normality can be almost festive. Some countries allocate a special day for this. In Norway the 'clean up' day is on January 13th; in Holland, the Monday after Epiphany is set aside for a general spring clean. It is called 'Lost Monday,' presumably because one then loses all the last remnants of the Christmas season.

An English expression for taking hold of practical tasks is "to put one's hand to the plough." The Monday after Epiphany is named Plough Monday, and was the official start to the spring ploughing. Ploughs were decorated, and the horses dressed in ribbons and brasses. It was an occasion for much boisterous play by the farm boys who, before the Reformation, collected money to keep the 'Plough Light' burning in church throughout the year. (This custom has died out now, but in some rural churches the Blessing of the Plough was revived during the Second World War when Britain depended so much on agriculture.) It is unlikely that a great deal of work was achieved on these jolly Plough Mondays, but when the farmer did put his hand to the plough, he was sure to be aware that in turning the first furrow, he also turned a point in the year which would lead him again into nature's ever-renewing cycle of growth. Following the plough would become for him the first steps on a journey of sprouting, blossoming, fruitfulness and decay: a journey through life and death, all year round.

244

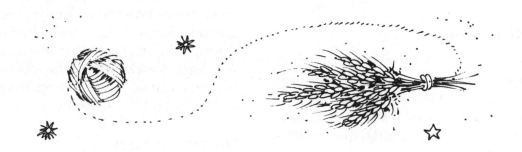

FOR ALL SEASONS

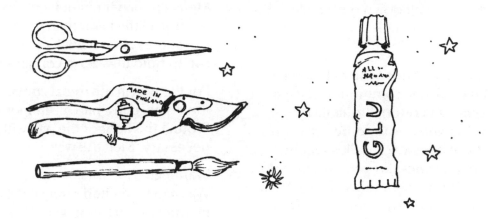

At any time of the day, at any season of the year, a candle and a pretty cloth, flowers and something good to eat, are all that are needed to transform an occasion into a Festival.

Included in this section are some of the skills and ingredients necessary for your Festival store cupboard.

Candle making

Wax:
For many centuries, beeswax has been used to make candles. However, it is expensive and often hard to obtain, although it does make beautiful candles. Today most candles are made from a mixture of paraffin-wax and stearin (usually 9:1) which ensures an evenly burning and almost smokeless candle. Such mixtures are available at craftshops as 'candlewax.' It is also worthwhile to melt down old candle stubs for re-use. (See below.)

Wick:
It is essential to choose the right kind of wick. The one most commonly used is a flat, braided wick of cotton, available in different thicknesses for different widths of candle. Pure beeswax candles require slightly thicker wicks. If you plan to make a quantity of identical candles, it is best to test one first to ensure the right size of wick. Always leave a new candle for 24 hours before burning and protect it from draughts.

Dye:
Wax soluble dyes are available in craft shops. We have found the clean stubs of our children's wax crayons to be a very good alternative. Grate them first, and add slowly to the melted wax until the required tone is achieved. Dip a white household candle into the melted wax to test the colour tone.

Re-using old candle stubs:
Melt the stubs in a non-leaking metal container set in a pan of simmering water. Protect the floor of the pan from scratches with a cloth. Stretch an old nylon stocking across another container (aluminium take-away dishes brushed with oil on the inside are ideal for this). Pour the melted wax through the stocking to clean it up and remove old wicks. When the wax has cooled it can be removed from the greased container and stored for future use.

Dipped candles

You will need:
Candlewax (and dye if required)
Wick
Source of heat (electric or gas cooker)
Metal container (an old metal pitcher or tin can, a little taller than the length of the candles to be made)
Pan to hold the above container

Put the wax in the metal container which is then placed in a pan of simmering water. Protect the floor of the pan with a cloth if necessary. Melt the wax.

Warning:
Wax can be melted safely if the above instructions are followed. However, it is inflammable and must be removed from heat source if it begins to overheat and smoke. If it should catch fire **do not use water,** but smother it quickly with the pan lid.

Holding a length of wick by one end, dip it in and out of the hot wax. Straighten the wick and allow it to cool. Continue dipping repeatedly, with a fairly swift and smooth action — in and out. (Holding the candle too long in the can of hot wax might mean that the candle grows thinner instead of fatter!)

The wax should always be at the right heat (professional candle makers use a cooking thermometer) when only a few drips of wax will fall from the candle after a dip. If the wax is too hot, the candle will grow painfully slowly; if too cool, the candle will become lumpy and the wax will not adhere properly to the previous layer. Always allow the candle to cool for a moment between each dip. It may be necessary to trim the base from time to time with a sharp knife. Top up the wax in the tin as necessary, taking care not to let it overflow during the dipping.

When the desired thickness has been reached, lay the candle on a sheet of clean white paper and trim the base back to the start of the wick.

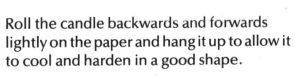

Roll the candle backwards and forwards lightly on the paper and hang it up to allow it to cool and harden in a good shape.

More fun with candlemaking can be found in the Candlemas section.

Removing candle wax from cloth

Leave wax spillages to go cold. With a blunt knife, carefully prise off any hardened wax which can be removed without damaging the cloth. Place two sheets of kitchen roll under the cloth and another on top of the wax stain, and iron. Use fresh paper as necessary until all the wax is absorbed. Wash cloth as normal. Very persistent coloured wax stains can be removed with an appropriate dry-cleaning solvent. Pouring boiling water through the cloth will remove very small drips of wax. (N.B. Do not block your drains with large quantities of wax!)

Wax stains on a carpet can often be removed with the ironing technique, but great care must be taken with synthetic materials. Use a low heat and never allow the iron to come in direct contact with the carpet. Experiment with a test area first, but when in doubt, use a dry-cleaning solvent.

A temporary candleholder

You will need:
Strong gold card (or colour of your choice)
Craft knife and ruler

For a household candle (1.8cm diam. and 12cm tall) cut the card into a 10cm square. Find the centre of the square by drawing a diagonal cross.

Remove candle once more and adjust the shape of the card if appropriate. Use the patterns below, or other design of your choice.

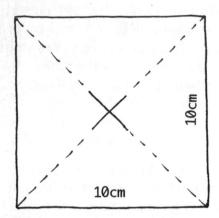

Measure the diameter of your candle and cut along the crosslines so that the opening is just large enough to allow the candle to be pushed through the card from underneath.

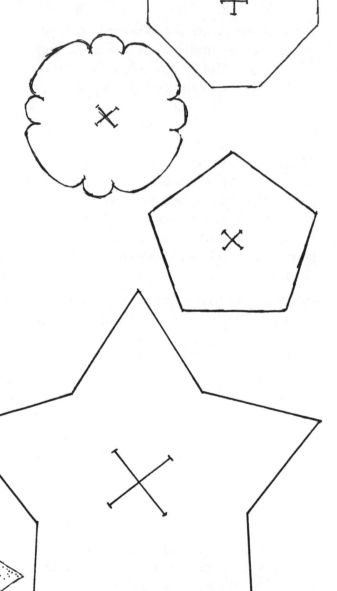

Coloured all-purpose veils

These veils have many uses and we find them an absolute 'must' in our families. They provide tablecloths and backdrops for our festival tables, and are very good at hiding unsightly vases or adding some colour to a dull corner.

The veils are also wonderful playthings! They can be bird or butterfly wings, and are excellent for building camps and dens, or becoming lakes, rivers, meadows and fields on the floor. Worn over the head with a simple flower wreath or crown, they can turn a birthday child into a prince or princess.

You will need:
Pieces of cotton gauze, buttermuslin or mull (1 square metre each is a useful size)
Red, blue and yellow, hot or cold fabric dyes

Fabric dyes can be bought in most shops which sell household goods. Dye the material according to the manufacturer's instructions, and hem the cut edges. Once you have used the basic three colours you can have great fun making more colours. To avoid 'muddy' mixtures, choose your shades carefully. For example: for a clear green, mix lemon yellow and prussian blue; for a good purple, choose ultramarine blue and crimson red; for a shining orange, mix vermilion red with golden or lemon yellow. Remember that yellow, red and blue together always make brown. Browns can vary greatly — experiment by mixing red and green, or yellow and purple, or vermilion and blue. Each combination will give you a different shade of brown, some warmer, some cooler, from which to make your choice. Generally, blue makes the shade cooler, and red will warm it.

Why not dye a number of cloths in seasonal colours? Spring: lemon yellow, pale yellow/green. Summer: golden yellow, pale pink, pale blue. Autumn: golden brown, orange, rust red. Winter: a deep rich blue is especially useful for Advent. Remember to keep some plain white muslin for winter snow!

You will never regret the effort required to make up such a stock of coloured cloths. Once you are comfortable with the dyeing process, you might try to obtain many shades of colour on one length of cloth by gradually strengthening the dye.

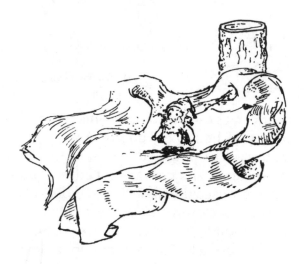

With this technique it is possible to make a rainbow-veil. Take a large piece of cloth and, working along the length, dip sections of the cloth into different colours. Batik dyes seem to work particularly well for this. In order to have one colour gradually merging into another, you need to grade the dye using, say, three red dye baths which become progressively lighter, (less concentrated), then become orange by adding a bit of yellow, etc. It sounds much more daunting than it is!

Festival bread (plait)

('Zopf' or 'Züpfe' traditional Swiss Sunday Breakfast Bread.) This makes a large size loaf — plenty for eight or nine people.

You will need:
1kg plain white flour
3 tsps salt
25g fresh yeast or 5 level tsps dried yeast
600ml lukewarm milk (blood heat)
1 tsp sugar
2 eggs, beaten
80 - 100g butter

Sift the flour and salt into a warm mixing bowl. Cream the yeast and sugar together, add a little of the warm milk and leave until frothy. Melt the butter and mix it with the milk and nearly all the beaten egg.

Make a well in the centre of the flour and pour in the yeast and milk mixture. Mix to a soft dough and knead well. Leave it to rise in a warm place until about double in size. Knead again and plait with four strands as shown below. Brush with the leftover egg and bake in a preheated oven at 200°C (400°F, gas mark 6) for approx. 45 mins. The loaf is done if, when tested with a knitting needle, the needle comes out dry.

How to plait with four strands:

Form the dough into an oblong shape and then cut it into four strands starting 5cm from one end.

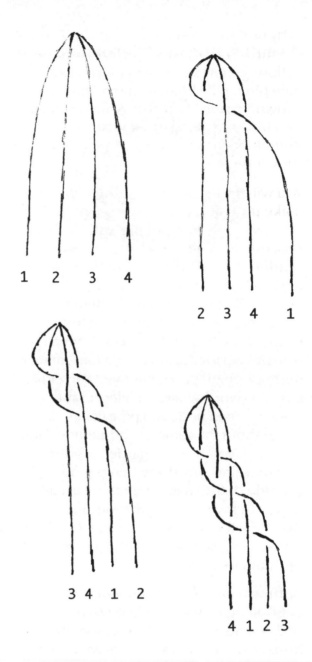

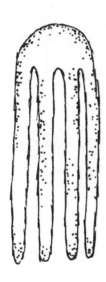

The basic method is to weave alternately over and then under another strand. (You can practise with long scarves or drying-up cloths.) Start with the left strand No.1. Weave over strand 2, under strand 3 and over 4. Now repeat this action, always starting on the left and weaving over, under and over.

Wreaths, rings and decorative balls

The wealth of summer and autumn flowers and cones can be gathered into festive rings. Use Christine's All-Year-Round Ring (see below) for seasonal variations, or make more permanent arrangements. In either case it is worthwhile to collect usable flowers, seed pods and pine cones, throughout the summer and autumn. Don't despair if you have no garden of your own, you may find surprising things growing by the side of the road! Friends are usually happy to save material for you, and don't overlook the occasional bouquet from the florist — some flowers dry well even after a few days in a vase.

Appropriate flowers for drying are: Everlasting Flowers (Helichrysum), chive, onion and leek heads, gypsophila, rose-buds, hydrangea, yarrow, lavender, statice, tansy, teasel and many others. Seed pods like those of the poppy and nigella dry well. Ordinary grasses or ornamental ones, cereals and hops are very useful, also pine cones in different sizes, acorns and nuts. Small fresh leaves from deciduous trees can be dried between paper towels in a heavy book and used for 'fill-ins.'

Pick the flowers well before they are fully opened and hang them upside down to dry in a cool, shady and well-ventilated place. For detailed instructions on the drying process see page 117. If you have a surplus or wish to store them, put them in a paper bag and keep them in a dry place — the attic, for example. Dirty cones can be washed in warm water to which some bleach has been added. Spread them out and leave to dry well.

All-year-round-ring

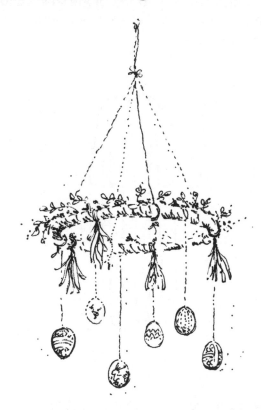

As this is a hanging decoration, it fits into the smallest apartment without taking up valuable floor or table space. This ring can be transformed with ease to suit many different occasions and festivals. The colour-mood can be changed by pinning on different ribbons and bows. On Valentine's

Day, for example, we have red satin ribbon and strings of hearts made from red card or fashioned out of felt. (See p37.)

At Easter the ribbons change to primrose yellow and pale green. (Choose the shades of colour carefully.) Decorated eggs (see p68) hang from the ring. A few butterflies pinned atop the circle finish it off nicely. (See p61 for butterflies.)

With the coming of autumn the ribbons change again, to golden yellow and fiery red. Pin on corn dollies (see p131), dried flowers and posies of dried grasses.

You will need:
Strong wire ring of about 25 - 30cm diam. — enquire at your local craft shop or cut a ring from an old lampshade of the right size
A few sheets of old tissue paper or a few handfuls of dried grasses (hay) for padding the frame
Sewing cotton
Raffia (straw coloured) to wind around the padded ring

If you are using tissue paper for padding the ring, tear it into strips and wind it round and round the wire base until the ring is padded quite thickly (about 3cm diam.) and evenly.

Secure with sewing thread. If using dried grasses, work on a 12cm section at a time, padding the ring and winding sewing cotton around it as you go.

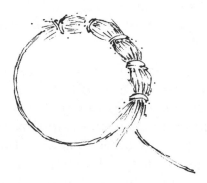

Conceal the padding by wrapping the raffia firmly and evenly all around. Sew in the end of the raffia securely with a large darning needle. Suspend the ring from three points at the height you require, using plaited raffia (at least nine strands per plait) or ribbon of your choice.

How to trace

You will need:
Tracing paper (any transparent paper)
Soft lead pencil
Coloured pencil or ball-point pen

Lay the tracing paper on top of the pattern and trace. Turn the paper over and draw, on the wrong side of the paper, along all the traced lines with the soft lead pencil. Make sure that the pencil leaves a heavy broad line. (Rest your paper on a sheet of scrap paper as you do this, as you may leave marks on the surface below.) Turn the tracing to the right side again and place it over the paper or card upon which you require the pattern. Using a coloured pencil, draw along all the traced lines once more, taking great care not to shift the positions of the papers.

You will need: (tracing with carbon paper)
Tracing paper
Carbon paper
Coloured pencil or ball-point pen
3 or 4 paper clips

Lay the tracing paper on top of the pattern and trace. Put the carbon paper, black side down, over the paper or card on which you require the pattern. Lay the traced pattern on top of the carbon paper and draw along the lines with a coloured pencil. A few paper clips will keep the papers in position.

Patterns

Five-pointed star

This pattern can be adjusted to any size of star you wish to make: Measure out and mark equal distances from the centre-point along each of the lines A, B, C, D, E. (For very large stars these lines would have to be elongated.) Then draw lines which connect the point on line A with those on C and D; B with D and E; C with E and A; D with A and B; E with B and C.

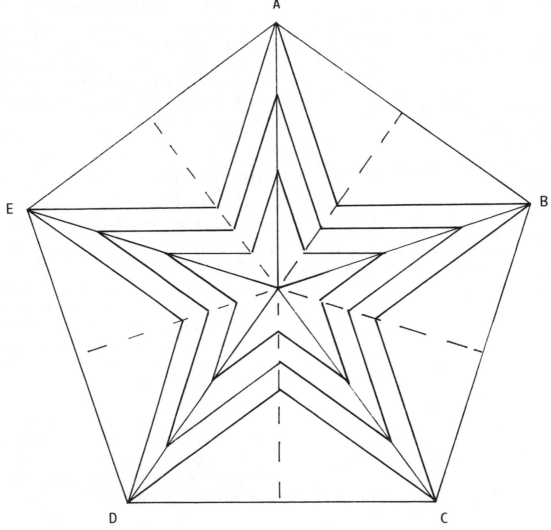

Valentine decoration

actual size

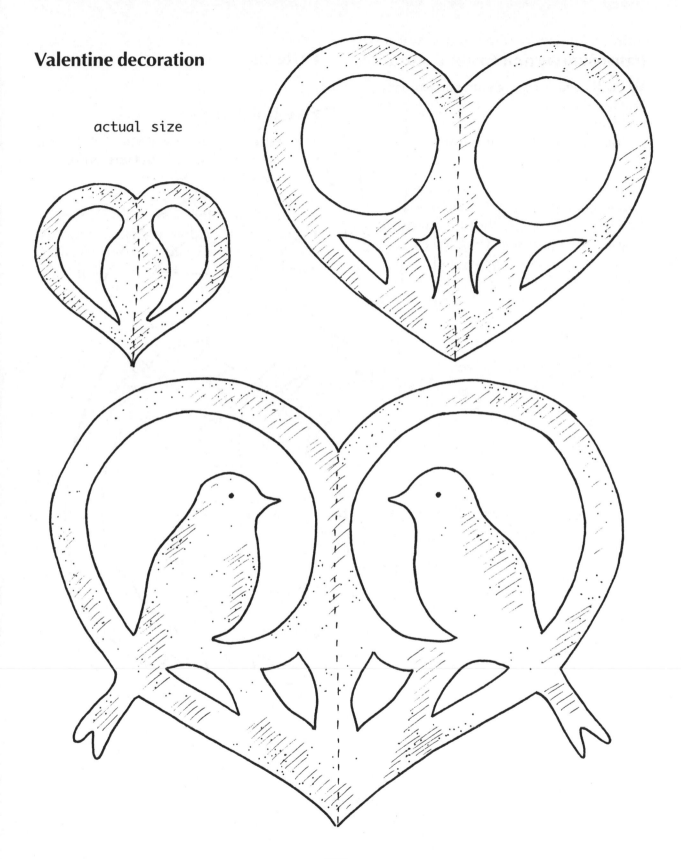

Palm Sunday and Easter decoration

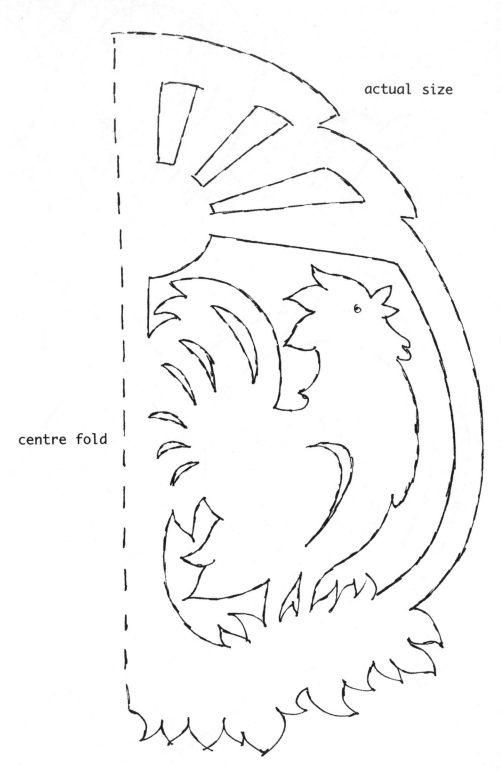

actual size

centre fold

Mayday decoration

actual size

yellow cut 4

green cut 4

GARLAND FOR HEAD

cut 8 from green paper

MAYPOLE GARLAND

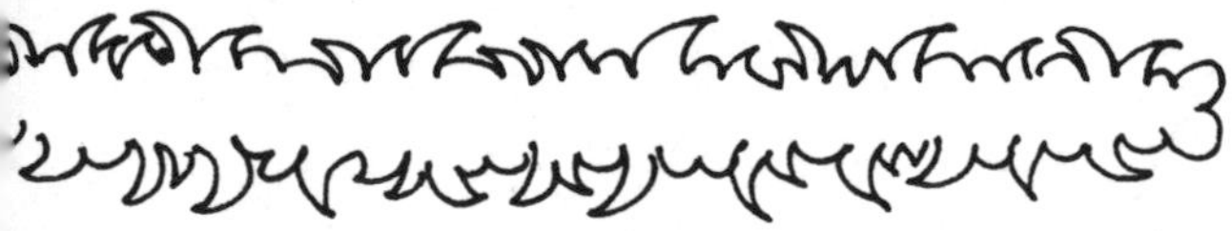

cut 1 from green paper

centre fold

Windmill 1

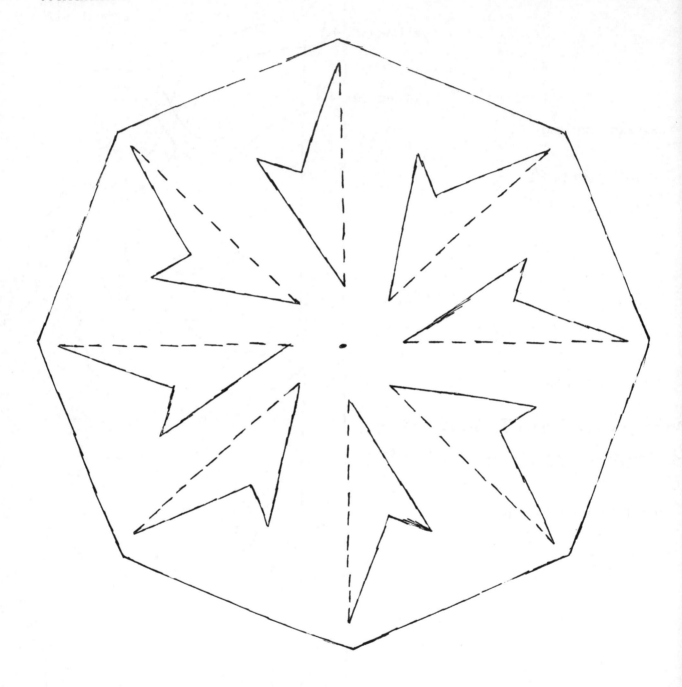

Windmill 2

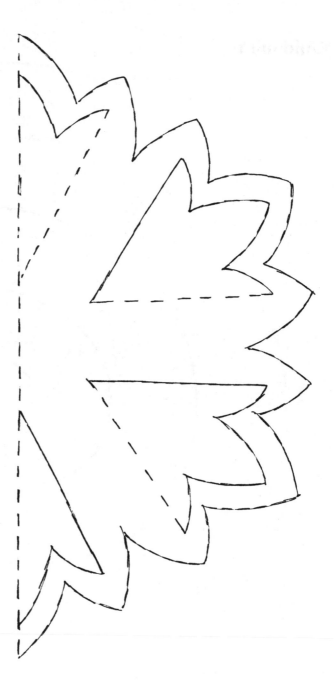

centre line – not to be cut

Gold spiral

Hallowe'en witch decoration

actual size

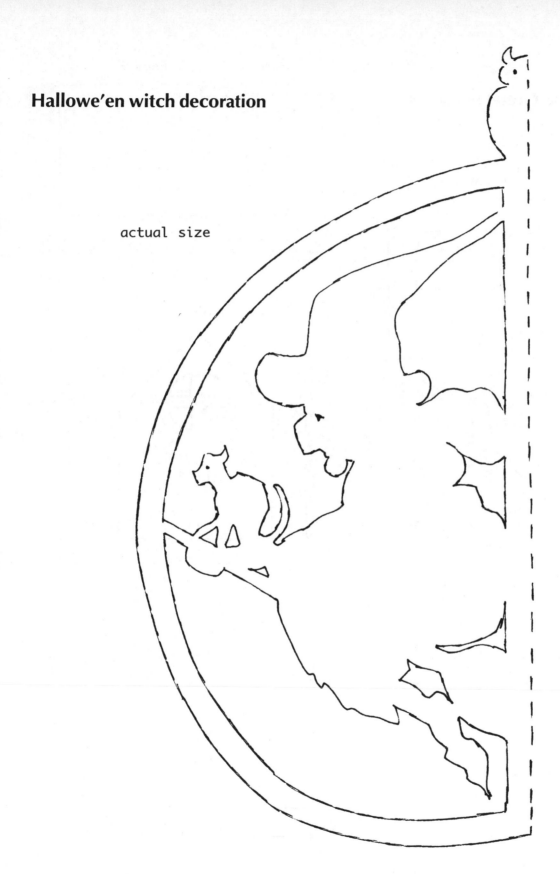

Hansel and Gretel house

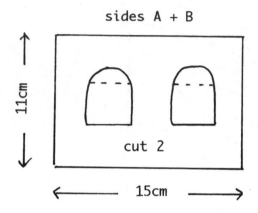

sides A + B

11cm

15cm

cut 2

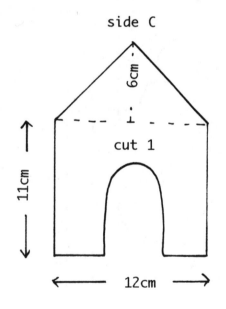

side C

6cm

11cm

12cm

cut 1

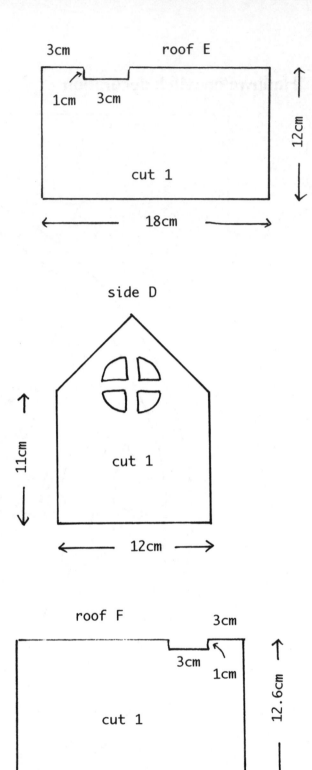

3cm   roof E

1cm   3cm

12cm

cut 1

18cm

side D

11cm

cut 1

12cm

roof F

3cm

3cm

1cm

12.6cm

cut 1

18cm

262

Lantern

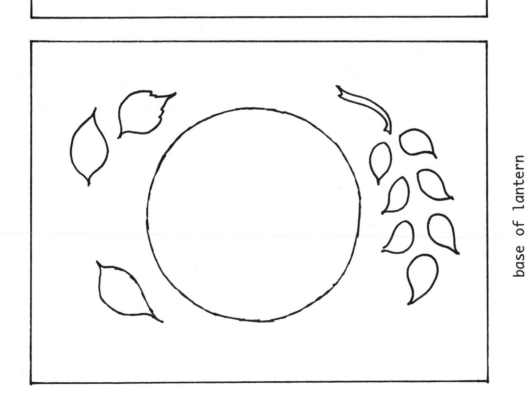

actual size

base of lantern

base of lantern

263

Advent calendar figures

1X

4X

2X

5X

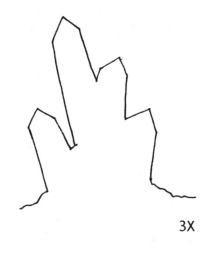

3X

6X

7X

8X

9X

10X

11X

12Y

17X

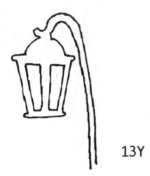

13Y

18Y

14, 15, 22 + 26 Y

19Y

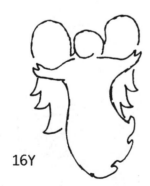

16Y

20X

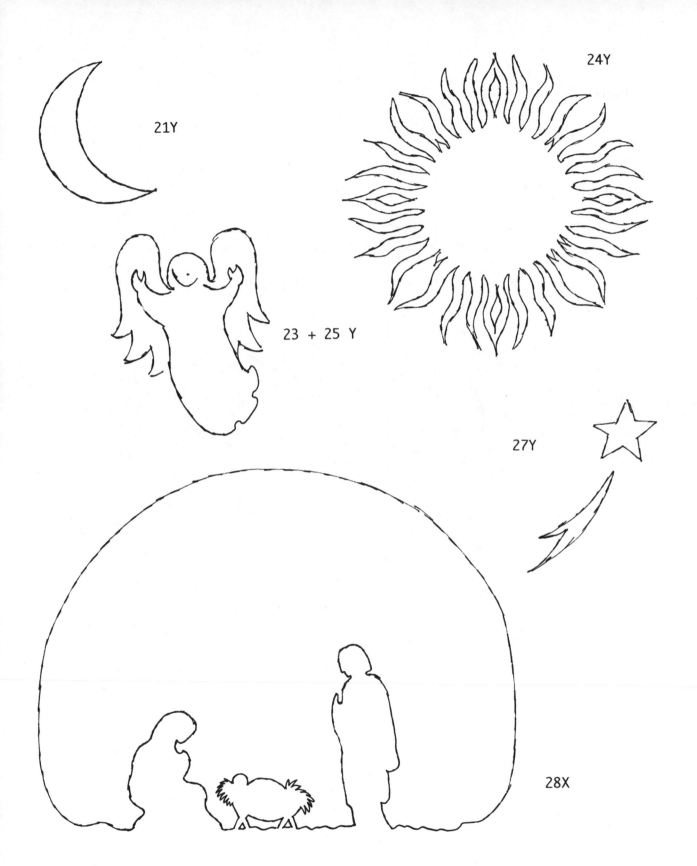

21Y

24Y

23 + 25 Y

27Y

28X

Rosette 3

Angel decoration

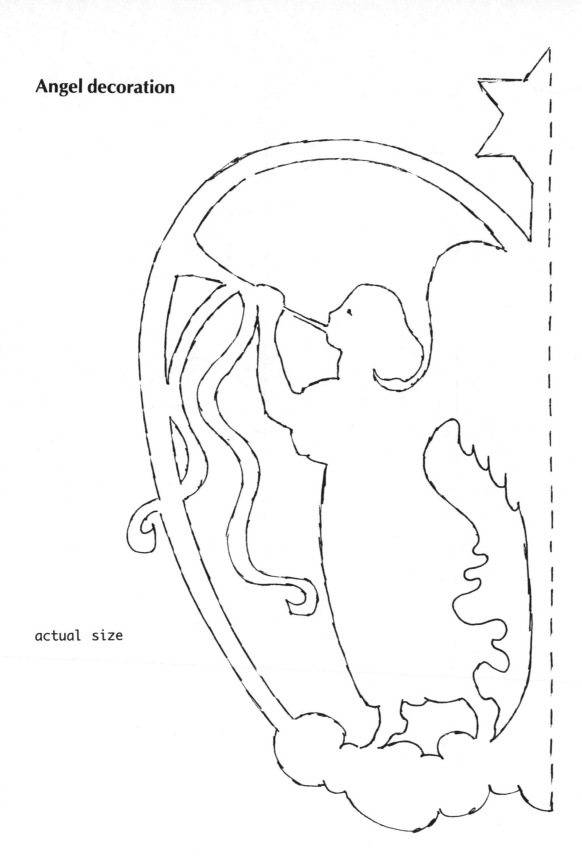

actual size

Six-sided box

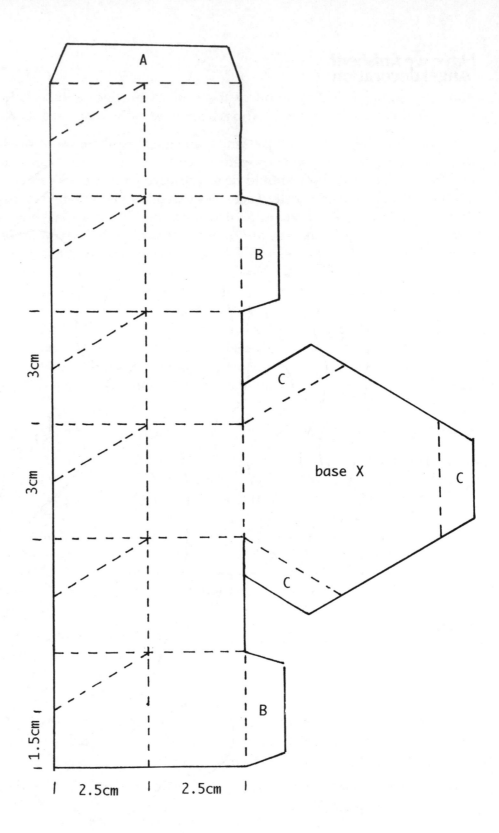

A

B

C

base X

C

C

3cm

3cm

1.5cm

B

2.5cm

2.5cm

270

Have we finished?

Ann: We are almost at the end of the book, Christine, and I wonder if you have any recommendations for someone who is becoming enthusiastic about celebrating festivals.

Christine: One thing I must say is — and I can't emphasise this too strongly — don't overdo it! Resist the temptation to go overboard on celebrating festivals, especially if you have small children. The priority here should be to preserve your strength and calmness, rather than attempt all the wonderful festival activities that other people seem to manage! Keep in mind that, by celebrating a festival in a particular way on one occasion, you have possibly begun a family tradition which will be eagerly looked forward to year after year. Festivals 'grow' family traditions the way country trees grow lichen, so at least make sure that they begin in a modest way. With hindsight, it is now clear to me that 'less means more,' and that quite simple things can sometimes build a mood more effectively than complicated arrangements or elaborate activities. A bowl of common daisies on a fresh white cloth takes little time to prepare and yet speaks clearly of Whitsun and early summer; a Christmas Tree does not have to be loaded with baubles and tinsel to look special, and a memorable Midsummer picnic can be had with bread, butter and a large watermelon! Remember, there is no one 'right way' of celebrating any festival, and it is so important that we all find the way which suits us and our individual families.

Ann: Would you ever drop a festival if life became too demanding?

Christine: I wouldn't drop it altogether. I can acknowledge a festival day with a different colour cloth or candle on the table, or a change of picture on the wall. Perhaps I should make the point again that the festivals are there to be celebrated only *if we want to*. Summer comes whether I celebrate it or not — and as a hay fever sufferer, I am not always overjoyed about it — but the festivals come alive *only* through our willing participation. There's no point in doing something because we feel we ought to, or because 'everyone else does it,' is there? If we are personally convinced of the value of living with the festivals we will want to observe them, and after a time we may notice that the festival happens *in* us, even if we are in bed with 'flu at the time.

Ann: I am sure that an inner connection and understanding of a festival, however incomplete, is especially helpful when we share these times with children. It is not enough, is it, to create amazingly inventive activities, if we cannot genuinely feel the truth of what we do?

Christine: No. Children have no time for humbug. They 'switch off,' or react by becoming argumentative and unco-operative. On the other hand, if a parent or teacher is occupied in a real way with a festival activity, it can make a lasting impression — even though the child may not outwardly appear very involved at the time.

Ann: That puts such a different complexion on the phrase 'doing it for the children,' which we hear a lot at Christmas time.

Christine: Well, of course, we do many things 'for the children,' especially at that time, and maybe if we were on our own we would do things differently. My point is, that whatever we do it can have significance not only for the children, but for ourselves as well. The festivals offer us such a treasure of meaningful images.

Ann: And these can slip through our fingers if we just play with them, if we don't enter them with heart and soul, if we adapt them to suit our own preferences...

Christine: ...or, indeed, if we try and *explain* them to a child. Great works of art need no explanation; they enrich our lives without extra words. It's the same with the festivals. If children ask "Why?" an uncomplicated answer such as "Because it's just the day for it!" is usually the best one.

Ann: Do you find that your children ask a lot of questions? Do they always want to be involved?

Christine: It varies with each child. In general, they take the festivals for granted and question very little. In fact, I can wonder at times whether they have noticed this or that detail — but if something gets forgotten, the teenagers especially can get quite indignant.

Ann: I spoke to a friend recently whose fourteen-year-old grand-daughter complained loudly on one visit, that Granny hadn't made an Easter Garden that year.

Christine: Oh yes, and I know a little girl who has already planned the festival garden her mother must make on her grave each year, if by chance she dies young!

Ann: Talking to older people about festivals they experienced as children is very inspiring to me. Their eyes light up, they become animated; one can see that, in their memory at least, they are completely engaged with that festival.

Christine: Children have many different ways of expressing their involvement. There is the child who begins planning a new design of Hallowe'en lantern in May, and the child who is content just to play and watch with half an eye while the festival is made ready. One child will help with any sort of food preparation, whereas another can't stay away when there's singing going on. But it's not necessary for children to be outwardly involved, they absorb so much from the inner attitude of the adults who are busy with a festival. Naturally, one would not exclude a child who wants to help.

Ann: As festivals come and go, year by year, I find that the preparations for them gradually get built into the family routine. In fact the predictability of it all seems to increase the children's anticipation and enjoyment of the occasion. They know what's coming and so are less likely to be disappointed. They can plan ahead, rather than fantasize about the unknown. I'm not sure that 'The Grand Surprise' is altogether successful with young children. (Of course, they *love* small surprises.) One can tell a story to a small child and set out in detail all that will happen on, say, Whitsunday — what clothes will be worn, which flowers gathered and from where, what there will be to eat — and witness the child's enjoyment grow with each telling. Mind you, it's essential that it then *does* happen like that!

Christine: I prefer to plan ahead, too, and I like to feel that I have things I need close at hand when the festival draws near. Consequently, I have become a hoarder of bits of cloth, stubs of wax crayons, metal foil 'take-away' trays, boxes, scraps of tissue paper — I never throw anything away without assessing its 'festival potential!'

Ann: I'm a similar sort of magpie myself, always on the lookout at garage sales for odd-shaped dishes, tiny vases and pretty cloths. I keep an extra large bag by me on walks for pinecones, bark, grasses, and the whole host of interesting bits and pieces one can find ... We've staggered for miles with a large rock because it was just right for an autumn gnomes' cavern. Some of our festival accessories even come from abroad: the pond in the Easter Garden, for instance, contains Norwegian pebbles, and the bridge is a locust-bean pod from Israel!

Christine: Well, let's hope this obsession we have is still healthy — I do feel a bit eccentric at times! Recently I've been prowling around scrapyards looking for the lid of a twin tub washing machine to hold the Easter Garden — I shall be triumphant when I've found it.

Ann: What about a word on the possible contents of a festival store-cupboard?

Christine: The things I have found most useful are: a range of coloured veils, candles of all kinds (excluding the 'perfumed' variety, but including some beeswax ones which look right at any festival, and really do smell wonderful), adhesive gold stars, lengths of coloured ribbon and some pretty shells, stones or crystals. With these few items — and a warm heart — a festive mood can arise in a moment.

Ann: Don't forget the store cupboard outdoors. Our garden is not large but I've managed to plant white daffodils for Easter, a Japanese snowball tree for Whitsun, Michaelmas daisies, a berried holly, of course, for Christmas, and soon I hope to include an incense rose for Midsummer. There's no room to grow pumpkins, but there is a damp and shady corner for celandines and long trails of ivy, and for my interesting rocks to quietly cultivate their moss. I'm so grateful to have access to a garden, and to look out towards woods and fields which alter with the seasons. If I lived in a city, perhaps I would make more use of art postcards and calendars with seasonal themes. Having such pictures around, maybe next to a child's bed and changing them as the months go by, could be another small way of keeping in touch with the rhythms of the year.

Christine: But time goes by *so* quickly — would I remember to change them? It's easy to forget those sorts of details. Which brings us back to 'planning ahead' — is it the key to everything?

Ann: Not at all. There are times when spontaneity is more important. A family Christmas Play, for example, can often be more successful when it's done on the spur of the moment — maybe with one person reading all the lines and the others miming it. It's good to be able to 'catch the mood' for something. Other aspects of a festival will need careful preparation, it's true, and I can think of one area that is not always given enough thought: the question of how to round off a festival day or season, especially where children are involved.

Christine: There are suggestions here and there throughout the book of ways to close a particular festival, but perhaps we should add one or two general points. It occurred to me that a play-group or kindergarten teacher will often 'round off' the morning quite literally, by making a circle with the class for a song or a poem. This has a remarkably calming effect on a bunch of exuberant children, but it doesn't seem so appropriate at home, does it?

Ann: Something different is usually needed. Sitting together with a warm drink can often settle over-excited youngsters, but one of the most helpful things is to tell them a story. A child of under five years can digest the events of a busy festival day — where perhaps, the pace has been set by older brothers and sisters — by means of a very simple story at bedtime. Such a story would recount in an undramatic way the main happenings of the day from the moment, "Emma got up and put on her red shoes" to the time when "Emma said goodnight to her dolly and went to sleep." Older children, also, are often glad of a story to help them unwind; there are many with suitable festival or seasonal themes, and these are invaluable for closing a Hallowe'en or Christmas party. We spend much time and effort in creating 'high points' in the child's experience; it doesn't seem fair just to leave them up there facing a big drop; we can help them down gently.

Christine: Some festivals link naturally into the next, and the Seasonal Table could be kept going all year. Do you think it is vital that this continuity is maintained?

Ann: I think it's much more vital that it all fits in smoothly with the household and doesn't become a nuisance. In the old system of crop rotation there were times for the fields to be fallow, and we human beings also benefit from the occasional fallow period. A clear space in a busy life, or a busy living room, can be a welcome rest.

While we are on the subject of finishing a festival, may I recommend disposing of festival objects appropriately? These things gather a special aura around them in the children's eyes, and to see them tossed away or collecting dust at the end of a shelf can actually be painful. Many parents find it best to dismantle, say, an Easter Garden or a crib scene on their own, but the tray of moss can be left outside for little fingers to fashion a garden for the butterflies, and the hay from the crib can be put on the window sill for the birds to take for their nests. Older children may enjoy ironing out the ribbons from the Advent Wreath and packing them neatly away for next year — the clearing up can become quite a ceremony in itself.

Christine: I think it's now time for our own 'clearing-up ceremony.' We stored up an awful lot of bits and pieces for this book — have we disposed of them in the proper way? Have we finished? Is there one last thought, maybe, on the purpose of the book?

Ann: For me, there were a number of reasons to write such a book, and I think I could gather them all together by saying that many, many people acknowledge the need for more balance in their lives. In past centuries, the seasonal round of festivals maintained the balance and harmony of the year, but even those festivals which are left to us cannot rely on a supportive culture — officialdom dispenses with one festival, commercialism kills the life in another. So maybe this book will contribute to a cultural life which can move to the measure of the year, carrying with it each individual, whatever their religion, wherever in the world they happen to live.

Christine: And living in Europe, or South Africa, or Australia makes a big difference to the atmosphere around a festival, doesn't it?

Ann: Certainly, the mood of a particular country or climate has a strong influence on the celebration of the festivals, and will cause them to alter their character from place to place. After all, wherever in the world I make my home, I actually *live* on something of a threshold, between what comes to me from the outside world and the inner activity of my thoughts and feelings. What I call 'Life' is lived between all the impressions around me — of the people, the air, the landscape of my country, and so on — and my inner responses to them. Here, on a threshold between two worlds, I experience my life and find it to be balanced or not so balanced.

Christine: In other words, too much outer activity, or too much inner activity are both causes of imbalance.

Ann: Yes, and the festivals are there to help us become aware of the balance that could be possible when, at different moments of the year's cycle, everything that calls out to me from Nature receives a full answer from my own soul. Out of this dialogue arise the festivals, whether in the Northern or the Southern Hemisphere, and, if one understands this, then it is plain that traditions of *how* to celebrate a particular festival cannot be transplanted from one continent to another. New forms must arise.

Christine: What advice would you give to someone trying to develop a new form for one of the Christian festivals?

Ann: I would say "Observe!" If the candles on the Advent wreath are melting in a tropical heat, that's telling you something, isn't it? Observe Nature closely, but also observe the social habits, rhythms and customs of the locality. Observe, especially, the movements of your own inner mood as it develops throughout the year — from season to season, from Lent to Easter to Whitsun… Most important of all, observe that the Christian festivals create their moment of balance *not* by echoing Nature, but by revealing a paradox: the reconciling of light and darkness, birth and death, heaven and earth and so on. In this sense, the festivals become alive when the human spirit *withstands* the claims of Nature. Then, at Whitsun in Europe, for example, as early summer disperses the pollen and calls the fledgelings to leave their nests, it is possible to celebrate community, the strength of being together, the human will to become 'of one accord.' Or, in Australia, as the spring growth rises at Michaelmas, one might begin to contemplate the Dragon's fateful fall to earth.

By means of a paradox, I find a way to unite my own spiritual striving with what is working unseen in the world. At such moments the festival is no longer a rekindling of old folk memories, but a door into a wider experience of the whole. Through it we come to realise that the festivals of the year explore a path of awareness, an ever-enhancing pattern of inner growth. They are more than an annual repetition of set forms, their cyclic celebration tells its own story — and that is the Parable of Life itself.

Christine: You've reminded me of another paradox — that every end is a new beginning. So, let's bring this conversation to an end now in the hope that it will become, for us and for our readers, the beginning of many new conversations, new celebrations, maybe even new festivals. We'll see…

STORYTIME

Stories

No children's festival is complete without a story. It may not always be possible to find a story with the appropriate festival theme, in which case a fairy tale or folk tale will usually fit the occasion for children over five years of age. Younger children will appreciate a simple story of everyday happenings with a seasonal mood.

The following stories are intended to be read aloud or, better still, told from memory. Single parents may prefer to adapt the text in some cases, to suit their own circumstances.

God's light

A Candlemas story for children of ten years and over (but still best read aloud).

The afternoon was wild and gloomy, the wind rattling the door of the fisherman's cottage, the rain falling through its chimney and hissing on the iron of the cooking pot. A young woman, her face tired and lined, spread a cloth on the table, helped by a sturdy girl of about nine years old, while beneath the table sat a little dark-haired lad solemnly playing with a piece of string.

They all looked up at a new noise at the door. A knock… and again a knock. Who could that be? Hope and fear were on the young woman's face as she turned to lift the latch. The man who stood there asked for food. He made his request in soft tones, and his face under the wet hood of his cloak was gentle and composed. The woman's expression changed; she seemed both disappointed and grateful as she nodded and opened the door wide. Her tired eyes glistened as she went to stir the pot on the fire and left the stranger to seat himself on the bench.

"Fetch a candle down, Bridget," she called to the girl. Bridget stood on the bench to reach up to a box on the shelf.

"It's the last one, Mother," she said.

"Never mind, child, bring it to the table," replied her mother twisting a spill and poking it into the fire. She turned to the stranger to explain:

"My husband is a fisherman, sir, but he has not returned from the sea these last three weeks. No boat has been found, so there is yet some hope."

She carried the burning spill to the table to light the candle. The dark-haired lad scrambled up on the bench and watched the stranger with big eyes as the flame rose and changed the shadows of the room. Then he raised a solemn look to his mother and asked,

"Why do you light a candle for Father? If he is over the ocean he'll never see it from there!"

"Hush, Tommy," whispered his mother and kissed his little fist. Then the stranger's soft voice seemed to fill the room as he spoke, "God's light reaches far," was all he said.

The meal was finished and the candle still burned as the windows of the cottage darkened. The fisherman's wife busied herself preparing the little boy for bed. Her back was to the room, but she sensed a change in the light and turned to tend the fire. With utter astonishment she saw the stranger walking out of the door carrying the candle. Indignant and dismayed she rushed to the door to call him back, but as she looked into the stormy night her cry died on her lips. Bridget had left her work with the dishes and was standing at her side. Together they watched, wondering, as the figure passed down the road and over the hill. Though the wind howled and the rain fell in silver sticks from the sky, the candle carried by the stranger still shone in his hand.

A year passed, a sad and weary time during which the fisherman's chair remained empty at the little table, and the lines deepened on the young wife's brow. The trials of the long months had almost driven the memory of the stranger from her mind, when, on another bitter stormy evening of the new year, came a knock at the door. Again a fragile hope stirred in the mother's expression, mingled with the fear of disappointment; she motioned to her daughter to unbolt the door. There stood the stranger, exactly as he had done the year before, with the rain dripping from his hood, only this time he held a lighted candle in his hand. Without saying a word he stepped inside, crossed the room and placed the candle at the window. He looked at each member of the family in turn, and they could see the light of the flame reflected in his eyes. Without a word, he opened the door again and disappeared into the gloom.

Within the hour, there was another knock on the door. The mother herself unbolted it, quite expecting to see the strange figure there again. Her startled cry brought the children both running to her hand, but it was their own father's arms they found as he embraced them, the fresh rain standing in his hair and salty rain running on his cheeks.

Later, he was able to tell the story of the events of those past months, and this is how he related it:

"It was a terrible blow to lose my boat — the craft of our own hands is always dear to us — but the storm broke it, and I lost it. I would have lost my life too if I hadn't been spotted by a sailing ship that drew near as I hung on to some of the wreckage. Oh, I thought my luck had changed right enough, and so it had — but not in the way I imagined! Brigands they were, the lot of them on that ship, and lived a desperate life. They treated me hard and made me work beyond all my powers. When my strength was gone they abandoned me, ill and without garments or food, in a harbour city of a strange land. I joined the beggars there and held on to life as best I could. Then came a day which was special — a holy day I think, for many folk were giving to the poor. I passed a house where a friendly light burned at the window; it gave me courage to beg at the door. The lady of the house must have been quite rich, for she gave me good clothes to wear and shoes for my feet, food, and a purseful of money. That made a difference to my life. Looking decent I could find work, but my strength was slow in returning and my illness was a constant trial. However, I got better than before, and made regular calls at the harbour to enquire about trading ships going west, but all the ships there worked only the local coasts and feared the brigand vessels on the open sea.

I swept a tailor's shop for my food, and it was there that I looked from the window early one morning and saw a procession making its way out of the town — a line of robed men each bearing a tall candle. Well, I always have been a curious fellow, so I joined the several hangers-on and followed. We made our way out into a wooded region and stood at last before a well, built in a hollow among lush herbage. The well was decorated with all manner of flowers and coloured bits and pieces, and there was a lot of singing before the people moved on. It was a beautiful place, and I felt rested there. As I stood to leave, the last man in the line of bearers held out to me a queer little cup on the end of a long string. He just gave it to me and walked on. I knew what it was for, so I lowered it into the well and filled it with water to drink. It's strange, but I tell you my health returned from that very moment. I was a fit and strong man again that day; but alas, my troubles were not over.

Terrible doubts began to assail my mind. I thought of the poor lives we led as fisherfolk, how hard we worked for our bread and how much better it might be if I had died and you were free to take a husband who could give you all an easier life. I even thought that something of the kind might already have come about, and that I should destroy your happiness should I return. Oh, my body was healed, but how sick was I in soul! In this despair I took to walking alone around the forsaken areas of the city. It was while pacing some open ground one night that I saw the glimmer of a flame nearby. Its promise of comfort drew me, but not much comfort did I see: a mother and her child lamenting their loss upon the fresh earth of a grave. At their side stood a youth holding the flickering light. In the shadow of his hood I could only see his eyes which gazed constantly — not at the mourners or the grave — but at me! I turned away. My mind had cleared. I was *not* dead, and my family needed me. I decided to build another boat; with a small craft I was sure I could make my way unnoticed by the pirates. Not many weeks later my boat was ready to sail.

The journey went well at first; with clear skies, navigation was easy. Only towards the end did my spirits fail. The weather had worsened and I fear I sailed in circles. My food was low; I had need to find land soon. Then, as so many times before, in the depths of my anguish it was a little light that guided me. This time it shone like a star, which I followed — for there was nothing else to follow. It grew in strength so much that it laid a track across the water: "A lighthouse," I thought, "I've reached land at last!" Soon the breakers warned me of the shore, but the light began to diminish until it was only a speck in the distance. No matter, when my feet touched the sand I anchored the boat and determined to follow that light. And it led me to these familiar cliffs, to this beloved hearth, and to the end, at last, of my long journey!"

The candle at the window was burning low. The fisherman paused, and looked around at his family:

"My dear ones, it has been a dark year for us all, and there may be more dark years to come in our lives, but one thing I have truly learned — that God's light reaches far!"

The Easter garden

An Easter story for children between four and eight years.

Once upon a time there was a little boy called Luke who had his own garden. He liked to work there when he could because he got to know all the animals and birds that visited the garden or played in the meadow on the other side of his garden fence. Rabbits and field mice lived in this meadow, and one large brown hare, who was Luke's special friend. One day in spring, Brown Hare found Luke sitting by the fence looking very unhappy.

"What's the matter, my friend?" asked Brown Hare.

"I'm unhappy because I've been working so hard to make an Easter Garden," replied Luke, "I've grown a lovely patch of daffodils but they just won't open, and it will soon be Easter!"

"Have you asked them why they don't open, my friend?" said Brown Hare.

"Yes I have, and they said it's because the breeze is so cold," replied Luke.

"And have you asked the breeze why she's so cold?" asked Brown Hare.

"Yes I have, and she said it's because there's a big grey cloud over the sun."

"And have you asked the big grey cloud to move, my friend?" asked Brown Hare.

"Yes I have," replied poor Luke, "but he's much too high up to hear me!"

"Don't be sad," said Brown Hare. "I shall tell you what to do. You must paint a picture of the sun, and put it beside your daffodils — that will warm them up."

So Luke went to find his paper and brush. First he cut the paper as round as a sun, and then he painted the best picture he could manage. He painted the sky so blue, and the sun so golden that it fairly shone off the page. Then he added a little touch of red for extra warmth, and the picture was finished. He laid the shining sun on the ground very near to the daffodil patch and went inside to have his supper.

That night the big grey cloud high up in the sky had quite a surprise. He knew the sun had gone to bed long ago, but when he looked down there was another sun shining in the darkness on the earth below him.

"Well, well," he said to himself. "What's all this about? I've never heard of a sun shining at night time before! I must get a better look." And the great grey cloud began to move closer and closer to the earth. When the morning came, the little sun picture was still shining and the great grey cloud was making the whole sky dark with his puzzlement. The early breeze danced by and the cloud asked her, "Tell me, Breeze, why is there a sun shining from the earth today?" So the breeze told him all about the daffodils and the Easter Garden and how Luke was doing his best to help the flowers to bloom.

The great cloud pondered awhile, then he said, "Well, I should like to do what I can to help. I haven't any warmth to give, but I know flowers like rain." And the cloud began to rain. Once he started to rain he enjoyed it so much that he didn't want to stop, and as he was such a very big cloud he rained and rained all day. As he rained, the colours on the sun picture loosened and floated and mingled to become a gleaming rainbow which flowed off the paper and disappeared into the ground, leaving the paper quite white. All this was not noticed by the cloud, who was not so very great and grey any more, because he had tired himself out and was rolling away over the hills to tumble into bed.

In the stillness of the night, Lady Moon walked the sky, gazing at her beautiful round face reflected in all the puddles left by the day's rain. She didn't notice that the daffodils had each opened two petals; she didn't notice a large brown hare quietly going about some secret business; and if she noticed the white piece of paper, shining now like a full moon in Luke's garden, perhaps she thought it was just another of her reflections, and she walked on.

The birds were already shaking the night air out of their feathers and calling up the dawn with their songs, when the large brown hare hopped into Luke's garden carrying a basket. He picked up the round moon of paper and tucked it under his arm, then he searched in his basket for something special and laid it down on the ground beside the daffodils. As he did so, golden sunlight spread across the earth and the morning breeze passed by, soft and warm.

The hare reached close to each flower in the garden and whispered, "Wake up! The Sun has risen!"

When Luke woke up that morning, he went to his window to look down at his Easter Garden. With joy he saw that all the daffodils were blooming! "But where is my sun painting?" he wondered, and ran downstairs in his pyjamas to look for it.

Well, of course, he didn't find his painting, but he *did* find something else, which he showed to his Mummy and Daddy at breakfast time. "An Easter Egg!" he exclaimed, turning it over and over, "and it has a picture of the sun on one side and a picture of the moon on the other!"

"A very Happy Easter, Luke!" said Mummy and Daddy.

Forgetful Sammy

A story for Ascensiontide, suitable for children between four and eight years.
Ascensiontide usually coincides with bluebell time in England, when the woods stand in magical seas of blue flowers, and picking a bunch of bluebells can become a festival in itself.

Once upon a time there was a girl called Anastasia, who lived with her mother and father in a house at the edge of a wood. One day Anastasia said to her mother, "May I go over the garden fence today, and pick bluebells?"

"Of course," said her mother, "but make sure that you're back in time for tea." She gave Anastasia a basket, and two sweet biscuits for a picnic.

283

The sun was shining and the birds were singing as Anastasia climbed the garden fence and walked over to the bluebell patch at the wood's edge. She decided to eat her biscuits before she filled her basket, so she sat down under a tree. No sooner had she done so when a strange noise began from high up in the branches:

"Boo-hoo-hoo-hoo-hoo! Boo-hoooo!" She looked up and saw a little squirrel sitting there crying bitterly.

"What's the matter, little squirrel?" called Anastasia.

"Boo-hoo, boo-hoo!" wept the squirrel. "I've just woken up from my winter sleep and I can't find my store of nuts, and I'm *so* hungry!"

"Where did you hide your store, little squirrel?" asked Anastasia.

"I hid it in a hole in a tree," replied the squirrel, "but now I can't remember *which* tree!"

"Well, come down," said Anastasia comfortingly, "and have a biscuit with me, then I shall help you to find your nuts."

The squirrel told Anastasia that his name was Sammy, and the two of them nibbled biscuits together in the sunshine and soon became friends.

Along the path hopped a rabbit.

"Excuse me, Mrs Rabbit," said Anastasia, "my friend Sammy has just woken up from his winter sleep and he can't find his store of nuts, and he's *so* hungry. Do you by any chance know of a tree with a hole in it?"

"Why, bless my soul, my dears, of course I do! You follow me and I'll show you."

Mrs Rabbit, Anastasia and Sammy ran down the path into the wood. They came eventually to a tall birch tree and Mrs Rabbit ducked into a thicket of brambles that grew around the base of the trunk. She emerged in a moment with five little rabbits behind her.

"Meet my family," she said proudly, "our burrow begins in the hole in this tree, but I don't think any of us have seen a store of nuts, have we, my darlings?"

All the baby rabbits shook their heads and quivered their whiskers.

"No," sighed Sammy Squirrel, "I'm sure this is not the right place; it's too low down."

"But thank you for letting us meet your family," added Anastasia as they turned to go.

"Good day, good day, good day!" sang a little bird sitting on the brambles.

"Oh Mr Tom Tit," said Anastasia, "maybe you can help us. My friend Sammy has just woken up from his winter sleep and he can't find his store of nuts, and he's *so* hungry. Do you by any chance know of a tree with a hole in it?"

"But not so very low down," put in Sammy.

"Why, bless my soul, my dears, of course I do! You follow me and I'll show you."

And off went Tom Tit, flitting from branch to branch just ahead of them.

Soon they came to a large chestnut tree, and Tom Tit disappeared into a small hole in the side of the trunk just above Anastasia's head. Almost in the same moment, out popped two birds and perched on a twig.

"Meet my lady wife," said Tom Tit proudly, "she is sitting on eight beautiful eggs in our cosy home. But I'm afraid neither of us have noticed a store of nuts here."

"No," sighed Sammy Squirrel, "I'm sure this is not the right place. It's still too low down."

"But thank you for introducing us to your lady wife," added Anastasia as they took their leave.

She was interrupted by a sharp noise from a neighbouring tree: Rat-a-tat-tat! Tom Tit looked up,

"Hark, that's Mr Woodpecker. Why don't you ask him to help you? He knows all about holes in trees."

"Excuse me, Mr Woodpecker," called Anastasia, "my friend Sammy has just woken up from his winter sleep and he can't find his store of nuts, and he's *so* hungry. Do you know of a tree with a hole in it?"

"But not so low down," put in Sammy.

"Why, bless my soul, my dears, of course I do! You follow me and I'll show you — but be quick!"

The woodpecker swooped away among the trees, and Anastasia and Sammy scampered after him.

They were quite breathless when they arrived at an old beech tree. High up on the trunk, Mr Woodpecker clung to the bark and poked his long beak towards a large hole. Five little open beaks appeared out of the darkness, and Mr Woodpecker fed each of them in turn.

"Meet my babies," he said proudly. "They grow more hungry every day — not that they would eat your nuts, Sammy, I'm sure, even if there were any here, which I doubt. I'm sorry I can't stop to look further for you now, I have to get the next meal ready." And off he flew again.

Anastasia and Sammy Squirrel sat down despondently, trying to think what next to do. A large bird with glossy black feathers perched on a branch above their heads. He watched them with a shrewd eye, and listened to every word they said. The two friends did not notice him until he spoke:

"You know what I should do," he said to their surprise, "I should consult Wise Owl — he knows of everything that goes on in this wood. Follow me."

"Oh, thank you Mr Raven!" cried Anastasia, as he rose heavily into the air with his legs dangling and his large wings flapping.

The raven led them to a mighty oak in the centre of the wood. The trunk was hollow and Anastasia and Sammy were able to step inside. High up in the gloom sat Wise Owl. His eyes were closed; he seemed to be fast asleep.

"Good day, Wise Owl," whispered Anastasia. "My friend Sammy has just woken up from his winter sleep and he can't find his store of nuts, and he's *so* hungry. Do you by any chance know of a tree with a hole in it?"

"Quite high up," added Sammy.

Wise Owl blinked, but said not a word. After a long time he gave a deep sigh and opened one eye:

"Foolish squirrels," he chided, "always forgetting — you're the seventh squirrel this spring."

The one eye blinked, and Sammy looked bashful. Wise Owl sighed again:

"Seek in the tallest elm at the edge of the wood."

He ruffled his feathers noisily and settled himself for sleep. As his eyes closed, he added drowsily "Many a store of good things are to be found on high."

The two friends whispered their thanks and crept away.

"Why!" said Anastasia to Sammy, "the tall elm is at the very place where we had our picnic!" and they both laughed.

They ran back to the bluebell patch and Sammy scampered into the elm tree. Up and up he went, so high that Anastasia had to tip her head backwards to see him. She watched him jumping and swinging from the branches like an acrobat. It seemed to her that one more leap would take him into the clouds that surged in the blue sky above. The thought made Anastasia quite dizzy so she lay down to rest among the bluebells. The sunshine was warm on her face and she closed her eyes for a while. When she opened them again and lazily looked about her, she saw that the sun had moved some way across the sky. She lay there, gazing at the billowing white clouds, enchanted by all the curious shapes they made as they drifted overhead.

Suddenly, she sat up. Could it be? Yes, surely that was Sammy! High up among the clouds he was playing, and enjoying himself hugely. White and fluffy with cloud mist, Cloud Sammy tumbled and rolled. His tail grew large and he wrapped it around him, peeping out from underneath. He stretched out a paw and waved at Anastasia, and the paw wandered off a little way by itself and then came back to him. Anastasia laughed merrily to see Cloud Sammy stretching and shrinking, somersaulting and skipping, until he floated lightly across the sky and out of sight.

With a start, Anastasia remembered that she had wanted to pick bluebells and be back in time for tea. Hastily she gathered some flowers and reached for her basket. To her surprise, she found it full of nuts!

"So it wasn't all a dream," she thought as she climbed the garden fence.

Nevertheless, her mother was astonished when she looked into the basket.

"What's this, Anastasia?" she said. "Nuts, in May? Wherever did you find them?"

"Oh well," said Anastasia, "that's a long story!"

The friend of the bees

A Whitsun story for children between five and ten years.

Once upon a time there was a King and a Queen who ruled a beautiful kingdom. Of all the beautiful things in it, there was nothing so beautiful as their only daughter whom they loved dearly. One day, while she was playing with a ball in the garden, a mischievous wind caught the ball and bounced it over the palace wall. Now the Princess was not allowed to leave the palace grounds, but in her great dismay she opened the garden gate and ran off to search for the ball, and no one ever saw her again. The King and Queen sent messengers to seek for the child, and when she could not be found, their sorrow was very great. Every year, on the Princess's birthday, a trumpeter was sent to the palace gate to blow his trumpet and announce that half the kingdom would be given to the person who found her.

Many years passed. The day came which would have been the sixteenth birthday of the Princess, and the trumpeter stood at the gates to make his special announcement. He was heard by a young beggar-boy who sat there patiently with his bowl. The boy was lame in one leg and could only walk with great difficulty, but when he heard about the young Princess who had been lost he was filled with an earnest desire to find her. So, he set off along the road that went into the wide world.

It was tiring for him, walking with his wooden crutches, and before long he sat down to rest at the edge of a wood. He leaned back against the trunk of a tree and gazed upward into the branches. A white streamer was tied to one twig of the tree, and fluttered bravely in the breeze.

"That looks very pretty!" he declared.

A bee alighted on his shoulder.

"I'm glad you think so," he hummed in a worried sort of tone, "you see, we bees are all very upset about it. The woodcutter is clearing some of the forest and he has tied the streamer on our tree — our tree where we have built our hive and where our baby bees will have their home — the white streamer means that this is a tree he must cut down. Oh, what shall we do!"

"Don't worry" said the young beggar-boy. "I'll save your tree." And he untied the white streamer and tied it back up in the branches of another tree nearby. "The woodcutter will cut that tree instead of yours," he said to the bees. They, of course, were delighted, and all agreed that the white streamer now looked quite pretty. They filled the boy's bowl with honey, and he went on his way refreshed.

He had not reached the far side of the wood before his attention was caught by the buzzing of a great number of bees. He followed the sound and came upon a wild bees' hive lying on the ground where it had fallen from the branches of an oak tree. The bees were in despair. "Hush, hush," said the lame boy. "I'll put your hive out of danger." And he lifted it up and housed it securely between two branches. "It won't take you long to repair it," he said. Then he caught hold of his crutches again and proceeded on his journey.

Over the hill he went and down to the river. At the river's edge he saw a cat playing with something in the grass. The cat ran off at his approach and, looking down, he saw a large and beautiful bee struggling on her back in the dirt. Carefully he placed a twig where she could catch it with her legs, and soon she had crawled the right way up again and was shaking the dust from her wings.

"I am the Queen Bee" she said, "and you are the young man who saved one hive from the woodcutter and another hive from the trampling feet of animals. Pray tell me your business in this part of the world."

So the lame beggar-boy told her he hoped to find the lost Princess, but confessed that he had no real idea of where to look for her.

"Maybe I can help you," said the Queen Bee. "One kindness deserves another. You see, the young Princess ran after her ball as it rolled into the Enchanted Forest and she was turned to stone. The goblins of the Forest built a hill over her, and there she has lain ever since. Follow me." With that, the Queen Bee spread her wings and flew to the North. The boy followed until he found himself before a hill which stood in the middle of a dark, dark wood.

"Go straight through the Forest," said the Queen Bee. "Do not look down or you will be turned to stone. Look up at the clouds and the sunlight above, until you come to the hill. There you will be safe. Pick all the flowers you find on the top of the hill and then you may begin to remove the earth that covers the Princess."

All this the boy did. The walk through the forest was long and wearisome, nevertheless, he looked steadfastly upwards and at last came to the top of the hill. He found it was covered with white flowers and he picked them, every one. Then he began the work of removing the earth. He was tired and his lame leg was hurting, but he used his crutch to dig the earth and shovelled it away with his hands. He toiled and toiled. The sun yawned and rolled into bed. The boy's hands bled, his arms and legs were aching, and he realised that his poor strength would never be enough to remove the hill that covered the lost Princess. In despair he wept bitter tears and fell deeply asleep, dreaming of the beautiful young Princess.

Now bees are everywhere, and they hear everything, so news of the beggar boy's plight reached the Queen Bee. "One kindness deserves another," she said, and straightway ordered all her subjects from every hive in the world to come to the boy's aid. All night the air was filled with a buzzing and a humming as the bees flew to the hill in the Enchanted Forest and filled the little pockets on their legs with earth and took it away. Backwards and forwards they flew as the boy slept, and by morning, the hill had gone and there lay the Princess on the bare ground surrounded by the flowers that the boy had picked. The beggar boy gazed upon her face and a deep love for her filled his heart — she was so very beautiful. But she was still enchanted in the cold hard stone.

"To break the spell," said the Queen Bee who was watching nearby, "the Princess must receive the kiss of a Prince." Again the boy despaired.

"What shall we do," he cried. "I am not a Prince. I have no crown."

"One kindness deserves another," said the Queen Bee, and she danced a queer little dance. A swarm of bees appeared, carrying something towards the lame beggar boy. "You have the heart of a Prince, so you shall have the crown of a Prince also," said the Queen Bee, and the bees placed a crown of shining, golden beeswax on the boy's head. It was so beautifully modelled with intricate carvings that it looked fit for a King's son. The boy with the crown kissed the Princess and she awoke and smiled at him.

"I shall lead you home to the King's palace," said the Queen Bee. "Take with you the white flowers, a bunch for each of you, and as you carry them through the Enchanted Forest they will break the spell of enchantment for ever."

There was great rejoicing in the land when the Princess returned. The lame beggar boy was welcomed by the King as a Prince in his own right, and given half the kingdom as a reward. In time, he asked the King for the Princess's hand in marriage and the day of their wedding was celebrated with a feast. The Queen Bee was an honoured guest, and she brought with her a very special wedding gift — a boot of shining golden beeswax. When the Prince fitted his poor lame leg into it, the leg became straight and strong again, and from that day wherever he walked in the world he was known as the Friend of the Bees.

The rusty dirk

A story for St John's Tide, for children of six years and over.
A 'dirk' is a Highland dagger, usually worn tucked into the kneesock.

Once upon a time there was a farmer — a carefree young man who sowed his fields as the spring rain fell, and made hay when the sun shone. One Midsummer's Eve, wearied by his toil at the mowing, he took off his hat and sat down to rest, all the while teasing his nostrils with the thought of his wife's potato soup. He was just imagining the raw, crisp smell of chopped spring onions, when a yellow leaf fluttered past. Idly he watched as the breeze lifted it up and held it, hovering like a meadow lark. The leaf caught the slanting ray of the sun and flashed with brilliant light as if it were the keyhole to a great ballroom hung with a thousand chandeliers. The smell of chopped onions drifted away, and in its place the perfume of wild roses settled around his shoulders as lightly as the hair of a young girl. Before the farmer's astonished eyes, from the keyhole of light streamed a troupe of little people, the like of which he had never seen before. There were fat ones, thin ones, some with long noses and large feet. Some were dressed in crimson red, some in gold or mother-of-pearl, and some in all the colours of the rainbow. There were musicians carrying their instruments, tumblers, jugglers, and dancers with glittering belts. There were cooks with trays of sweet-meats, and maids with silver jugs. On and on they came, with a jostling and a pushing, with a hurrying and a scurrying, with music and bells and flashing, flitting lights.

The young farmer chortled at their antics, his head turning this way and that to watch them. Suddenly, his ears sang with the din of brass trumpets, and the last of the entourage appeared. There were a dozen or so whimsical creatures arrayed in silver gauze, and among them, taller than them all, a stately figure of indescribable beauty clad in a tissue of gold, with jewelled slippers upon her feet and diamonds flashing from her golden crown. The farmer needed no one to tell him that this was the Queen of the Fairies, and he felt at once both afraid and entranced. He could not take his eyes from her; it was as if she was the only thing of beauty in the whole world. In an instant he had forgotten his farm, his little house and his wife, and was confessing his love for the Fairy Queen.

"I would do anything, just to follow you," he begged. She laughed at his words, and the sharp breeze of her laughter blew his hat away over the hill. She told him to throw his dirk into the ditch, and his shoes up into a tree. This he did immediately and went with her.

At sunset, the farmer's wife arrived at the mowing field with a pitcher of soup for her husband's refreshment. She was surprised to find his scythe cast down, and the field abandoned. She searched high and low, but could not find so much as a thread from his shirt. For days and weeks and months she grieved at the loss of him, and went every evening to the mowing field, calling him by name. By chance she found his dirk in the ditch, and it was black with rust from the wet. She took it home and polished it each day. After a while it gleamed a little, and after another while it shone. One day she could see her whole reflection in the blade, but the next day she saw something else. Instead of her own fair face looking at her she saw a grassy hillock. At the side of that hillock, buried up to his neck in the earth, was her

290

husband. His head was bare to the scorching sun and his eyes were dazzled by the light. His feet stuck out from the hillock into the icy waters of a rushing stream. At his side sat the beautiful Fairy Queen, smiling mockingly upon him as she fed him with a silver spoon.

"So this is fairy work" said the farmer's wife to herself, "Well, we'll see about that."

She took some sheepskin, cut it, and sewed a pair of warm slippers. She pulled some spinach from the growing patch, cooked it, mashed it, and put it in a covered bowl. Into a basket went the bowl, the slippers, a spoon and the shining dirk, and with this burden she set out.

It was the day before Midsummer, exactly a year since the young farmer had put down his scythe. The grass stood tall and flowing like green water. Her feet trod the rippling fields and squeezed the scent of thyme from the hills. She walked on, her eyes searching for the little hill she had seen reflected in the dirk. In a shaded valley she came upon her husband's hat lodged in a thorn bush. She pulled the hat into shape, dusted the cobwebs off it, and took it with her. Beyond the next horizon she found what she was looking for. There was the hillock, and there was her husband, his hair and beard grown long and tangled, his ears stopped up with thistledown, and his body trapped in the fairy mound. She called his name, but he was deaf to her voice and only squinted towards the blinding sun. She spooned the cooked spinach into his mouth and he ate hungrily. She unplugged his ears and placed the lost hat on his head. Then she sat in the grass and crooned softly to herself:

"The mower mows the field for hay
Summer's flowers fade away
Youth and strength and beauty pass
But there is goodness in the grass.
Swallows fly when summer's done
The new bud pricks when leaves are gone
Wild strawberries never last
But there is goodness in the grass."

At the sound of her voice, the farmer turned his head. The hat was shading his hot, bedazzled face, and now it was only the cool light of recognition that gained an entry to his eyes. And that recognition, like a new master who commands the place to be washed out, set the water of tears gushing over his cheeks. As his wife sang, so did this torrent become a tidal wave, soaking and softening the earth that trapped his body. When the song was finished he was able to rise from his interment and lift his feet from the icy stream. She brought him the warm slippers and he had no sooner put them on when a malignant wail came over the hill. The mob of little folk, with the outraged Queen in their midst, was bearing down upon him. The young wife reached into the basket and handed the dirk to her husband. He held it up in front of his eyes, and the polished blade, shiny as a mirror, threw the Fairy Queen's reflection back into her face. At the sight of her own image, she retreated immediately, and fled with the rest of her troupe.

The farmer and his wife returned to their house and their mowing fields, and were never troubled by the Queen of the Fairies again.

Holidays

A summertime story for the pre-school child.

Little Katie lived with her mother and father in the house next door to her best friend Charlotte. It was many days since they had played together for Charlotte was on holiday.

"Why does everybody have to go on holiday?" complained Little Katie. "The baker is on holiday, the park-keeper is on holiday, the lady with the puppies is on holiday…"

"And you'll be on holiday soon," interrupted her mother. "We go to the seaside tomorrow for the weekend. Charlotte will get back while we're away, so let's make a present to welcome her home."

Little Katie threaded some beads to make a necklace. She wrapped it in blue tissue paper and tied it with pink ribbon. She painted a picture of a house with a red door on a large sheet of paper, and when it was dry she tied it up in a roll. Then her mother took Little Katie next door and helped her to put the presents into the letterbox.

That evening, her father said "Little Katie, will you come round to Grandma Mary's house with me? I have to tidy her garden before she returns from holiday — and you can water the plants."

They worked hard making Grandma Mary's garden look pretty and neat.

"She will be surprised to see what we've done!" said Little Katie.

The next day, everyone packed suitcases and put them in the back of the car. Little Katie filled a travelling basket with sandwiches and apples, and found sun hats for Lucy and Helen, her favourite dolls. By midday all was ready, and their journey began.

Little Katie was tired when they reached the hotel, and after supper she was glad to go to bed.

"We shall go down to the sea in the morning," her mother promised, and kissed her goodnight.

The next day was sunny and bright. After breakfast, Lucy, Helen, Little Katie and her parents went down to the beach. When they got there, Little Katie looked puzzled.

"Where has the sea gone?" she asked her father, and they both gazed out across the wet sand that seemed to stretch for miles. Her parents smiled at each other.

"I expect the sea is taking a holiday" said her mother, "so let's make a present for when he comes home."

She took Little Katie's hand and walked with her along the beach. They found a piece of driftwood, a thin stick and a fragment of seaweed. Her mother fixed one end of the stick in a crack in the driftwood, and split the other end with a pair of nailscissors from her bag. Little Katie pushed the small strip of seaweed into the split stick.

"Now we've made a boat, with a mast and a flag," said her mother. "I think the sea will have fun with this!"

Little Katie ran to show her father the present for the sea. "I'll tell you another thing," said her father after he had examined the boat, "I've been looking at the sea's garden, and I must say it's got into an awful mess while he's been away. Shall we tidy it up a bit before he comes back?"

Little Katie looked around and saw the shells and stones lying higgledy-piggledy, she saw stray pieces of seaweed drying stiff and salty in the sun, she saw a squashed plastic bottle and some ice-cream wrappers half buried in the sand.

"We'll make a real surprise for the sea!" cried Little Katie.

They set to work. Her father took all the litter to a bin further up the beach. Little Katie helped dig a large hole in the damp sand, and watched in amazement as it began to fill with water. Then she put seaweed into the pool and decorated the edge with shells. She made winding pebble-paths and some fine towers with buckets of sand. Finally, her father made an extra-large tower and placed the boat on top. "I think we've managed that just in time," said her father, looking up, "the sea is on its way home!"

Little Katie lifted her head and saw the sea pushing tiny waves over the sand towards her. She stood to watch a silvery ripple as it ran with a happy, bubbly sound, and then seemed to stop and melt away, before another ripple tumbled forwards towards Little Katie's toes. Little Katie shouted with delight and hopped backwards. She held her father's hand while the sea flowed along the pebble-paths of the garden and filled the seaweed pool to the brim. The stones changed colour and gleamed under the water; the shells shifted and danced. The waters lapped over Little Katie's feet and around the towers of sand. One by one, the towers merged with the tide until only the high tower remained, with the boat sitting proudly on top. The sea tugged excitedly at the base of the high tower until the boat came down at last to bob and prance on the sparkling water.

Little Katie clapped her hands, "The sea likes his present!"

She ran to sit beside her mother on the beach, and took Lucy and Helen on her lap to show them the waves playing with the boat.

After the weekend at the seaside was over, the suitcases were packed again and everyone got back into the car to travel home. When they arrived, Little Katie found two parcels waiting by the front door. There was a small parcel with a very large label which said "Welcome home! With love from Charlotte." Inside was a tiny black and white china dog. Little Katie unwrapped the larger parcel next, and discovered a basket of ripe peaches. There was a card with the basket and she gave it to her father to read out.

"It's from Grandma Mary," he said, "and she writes 'Thank you all for tidying my garden.'"

"Now everyone has a present," laughed Little Katie. "I like holidays!"

Robert's harvest loaf

A Harvest story for children between five and eight years.
It is quite usual for wheat to grow in a cornfield, for the English word 'corn' refers not to 'maize' or 'sweetcorn,' but to grain in general.

Once upon a time there was a family of fieldmice who lived in the middle of a cornfield. Mr and Mrs Fieldmouse had made a nest for their three children — Millie, Mikey and Mo, and the days they passed there were comfortable and happy. However, Mr Fieldmouse suddenly announced that they must move house. The combine harvester had begun cutting the corn at the end of the field, and they must move out straight away.

"Where shall we go?" asked Millie.

"We can't discuss it now," replied Mr Fieldmouse. "Just follow me."

Off they went, weaving in and out of the tall yellow grain stalks, while the noise of the harvesting machine could be heard in the distance. On their way, they met many other creatures: harvest mice, rabbits, a shrew and a field vole, but everyone was hurrying and there was no time for talk. At length they came to a wall. Millie and Mikey began to climb it, but their mother called them down and showed them a crack between the stones where they could squeeze through. On the other side was a garden, and beyond the garden stood an old farmhouse. Red apples lay in the grass nearby and the three littlest mice began nibbling at them straight away, for they were hungry after their long walk. Meanwhile Mr and Mrs Fieldmouse set about finding a new house.

It was not long before they discovered the perfect place for their family. A large clay flower pot lay on its side behind a garden shed. The open end was up against the side of the shed, and the whole flower pot was almost hidden by brambles and long grass. The hole at the bottom of the pot was exactly the right size for the Fieldmouse family to clamber through.

They soon made themselves at home and enjoyed their new life in the garden. There were always apples to nibble, and scraps from the farmhouse that were thrown on the compost heap. But they did miss the golden grain from the cornfield.

"Do you remember" sighed Millie, "how we used to climb up the wheat stalks and nibble the grain when it was all soft and milky?"

"Yes, and we could have as much as we wanted," added Mikey.

"And sometimes the stalk would bend right down to the ground and you would fall on your nose," giggled Mo.

"Can't we go out to the cornfield," asked Millie, "and see if there's any grain to be found?"

Her father frowned, "Certainly not," he said firmly, "the stubble is so short — you don't want Tawny Owl to see you, do you?"

Millie shivered, "I didn't think of that," she said.

However, the next day, Mikey brought good news. He had explored one of the outhouses at the edge of the garden and found a small sack of grain there on a shelf. Nibbling through the sack was easy, and the grain was most delicious! From then on, the Fieldmouse Family went out to lunch every day at the outhouse. They considered themselves very lucky indeed.

It was also about this time that they discovered the breadcrumbs. A small pile of bread-crumbs had appeared one morning beside the hole in the flowerpot which was their front door. They didn't take long to eat them, because mice are always hungry. The next morning there was another pile in the same place, and a few crumbs of cheese as well. What a treat! After they had eaten and were washing their whiskers, they heard a voice say:

"Hello."

They looked up in surprise to see a small boy sitting very still in the grass by the corner of the shed.

"My name is Robert," he said, "I'm the farmer's son and I live over there." He pointed to the farmhouse. "I had cheese for breakfast and I thought you might like some."

"Thankyou," said Millie politely, "we all enjoyed it very much."

"I'll bring you some every day if you like," said Robert, "and cake at tea-time, if we have any."

He was as good as his word. Every day the pile of crumbs would appear by the flower pot, sometimes with a piece of carrot or a few currants. Once there was even a piece of chocolate, and Mo was allowed first bite.

On most days, Robert would stay for a chat. He had no brothers or sisters to play with, he told them, so he spent a lot of time on his own in the garden. The Fieldmouse Family looked forward to his visits and it was not long before they became firm friends with Robert and learned to take food out of his hand.

One day, Robert did not greet them with his usual cheery smile, in fact there were tears in his eyes as he told them:

"I'm very sad today, because I reaped a whole sheaf of corn at harvest time and threshed it myself. I stored it in a little sack on the shelf in the outhouse. I was going to grind it into flour and bake my own Harvest Loaf, and now I find there's a hole in the sack and nearly all the grain has fallen out and disappeared!"

Oh dear! The Fieldmouse Family were speechless. They all looked at one another. Mikey blushed and looked at the ground, and little Mo burst into tears.

"Oh, don't cry, Mo!" said Robert, "I didn't mean to upset you. There's nothing we can do… at least…" he paused, "Grandma says to put the sack outside the door and ask the fairies to fill it. I shall have to stitch up the hole, of course, but… don't you think the fairies will be too busy to bother about that?"

There was something of a gleam in Millie's eye.

"Why don't you try it?" she suggested "There's no harm done."

So Robert went to mend his sack, and Millie went to speak to her father.

"It's new moon tonight," she said, "that means it will be completely dark. Tawny Owl will never see us. Couldn't we go into the cornfield and find enough grain to fill Robert's sack? There is always some that has fallen to the ground, and they haven't done the ploughing yet."

Millie pleaded, and her father relented.

"But you all stay close to me," he commanded, "and if I say Ssh!, you stand absolutely still."

They spent a very exciting night journeying to and fro, collecting grain from the field and bringing it back to Robert's doorstep where he had placed the empty sack. He had left a small bowl of water and a tiny dish of butter there also, which was a welcome refreshment during their labours. All night they worked, and by the time the farm cock crew, the sack was fat with grain.

The next day, Robert came to tell the Fieldmouse Family about the fairy present, and, of course, Millie, Mikey and Mo kept their secret very well.

That morning they listened to the sound of the handmill turning as Robert ground his flour; they smelled the strong, heavy smell of the fresh yeast in the afternoon and, by the evening, they saw the new-baked loaf cooling by the kitchen window. Mo's mouth watered at the thought of the sweet, crusty bread, and she began to hope that Robert might bring them some fresh crumbs.

And this is where our story ends. I wonder if Robert did give some crumbs of his Harvest Loaf to the Fieldmouse Family… What do you think?

The far country

A Michaelmas/Thanksgiving story for children over five years.

Once upon a time there was a King who ruled over a happy kingdom. Throughout the kingdom the farmers worked upon the land and grew enough food for all the people. But one sad year brought a long drought when no rain fell, and the sun and the wind dried the land and shrivelled the crops. When harvest time came the earth was like dust and the farmers gazed at their fields in despair. Who would feed the people now? There would hardly be enough grain to feed the hens, certainly not enough for bread. Already a few hungry voices had been raised, asking anxiously about the harvest.

Now one of the farmers was a man called George, who had heard from an old fisherman that there was a country lying over the sea where food was plentiful and the harvest was

always good. George sometimes went down to the coast and gazed out to sea. He wished he could just take a boat and sail across to this land and find some food there for his hungry people. But no one knew exactly in which direction this country lay, and the old fisherman tut-tutted about it when he asked them and said "Our boats are too small for such a journey, and the seas too rough." George thought to himself, "Why don't I take a boat and try my luck? I am young and strong." Then he looked down at the surging sea and the sharp rocks, and fear filled his heart. He was a man of the land, born to walk the earth behind the plough — he was no sailor. So, disheartened, he went home.

An evening came when George and his family had only half a slice of bread for their supper. "And that's the end of our flour," said his wife. George looked around the table at the thin faces of his children and resolve strengthened his heart.

The very next morning he went to his old father and asked his blessing for the journey; then he made his way straight to the beach and the line of fishing boats. Without hesitating for one instant he stepped off the firm land into a rocking boat and untied the mooring rope. His hands gripped the sides tightly as the small craft was carried away from the shore and into the thick mists which gathered over the sea.

All day George sailed, tossed by the sea in a grey world of mist and spray, not knowing which direction he had taken. At night the mist vanished, but there was no moon and the darkness was heavy around him. He felt very much alone and began to doubt the wisdom of his action. With great effort he pushed his fears aside and looked up. As he did so, he saw a shooting star flying to its mark. He watched in wonder, but it did not then disappear; instead it hung in front of him guiding him, it seemed, to some far distant point. George's courage returned. He no longer felt alone, and he followed this star until it paled with the dawn. As the sun rose George found himself approaching a green and fertile country. At the water's edge stood a youth, fair and strong, who beckoned him. The boat was beached and George stepped out. "Welcome to our land," greeted the stranger. "We know why you have come and we wish to help you". He gestured towards a large sack of grain that stood among smaller sacks of apples, grapes and other fruit, vegetables and nuts. George gazed at the young man in gratitude and amazement; the morning sun dazzled his eyes and seemed to clothe the youth in fiery raiment. Together they loaded the boat. When that was done George opened his mouth to thank the stranger, but as he met the young man's gaze he could not find the right words. "My blessing go with you as you fulfil your task," said the youth and raised his hand in farewell. The boat was pushed out to sea and carried off by the strong current. George turned, again wanting to express his thanks, but the youth had gone and not even a footprint could be seen on the sandy beach.

Years and years later this story was still being told by the old farmers to their sons. Some said it must have been a good angel who had helped George in that far country. But the strangest part of the story still puzzled them, for the miller had reported that when the sack of grain was brought to him to grind, no matter how many scoops he took out of it to pour on the mill-stone, there was always plenty of grain still left in the sack.

The rowan berries

A story for children of eight years and over.
The rowan, or mountain ash tree, grows widely in Europe. Local folklore considers its wood and its bright red berries to be a protection against fairy enchantment of all kinds.

Once upon a time, within the stone walls of the city, there lived and worked a clockmaker's apprentice. He was a clever young man, hard-working and devoted to his master. Each year, at the end of October, he begged leave to visit his grandmother who lived beyond the city. This year he had a currant cake to give her, and a pot of honey. His master consented, and so, at the end of the day's work, the apprentice packed the gifts in a knapsack, swept the floor, wiped the tools, and locked the door of the workshop behind him.

The night was frosty bright, and the apprentice pulled down the brim of his hat and lifted his collar against the cold. He hurried, for his grandmother's cottage lay a long way off. The moon cast a shadow under his feet as he walked the familiar path around the city walls towards the eastern gate, where the winds of the wild country pushed through the gap in the stone. He was still a fair distance from the gate when he noticed a narrow door set in the thick walls at his left hand. The door was not quite closed, and the young man was mighty curious to see where it led, for he had no recollection of ever having seen such a door there before.

"It might be a useful short cut for me," he thought, as he pushed the door open and stepped through. As he did so, the city clock struck eight.

Beyond the narrow door he was met by wind and rain, and the crackle and smoke of a small fire. Seated by the fire was an old crone, so old that the hair was growing long out of her ears, and the skin on her face was as brown and wrinkled as a fresh-ploughed field.

"God bless you, mother," said the apprentice, "may I ask where this path leads?"

"Ask away!" cackled the old crone. "The path leads everywhere and nowhere. But tell me, my son, do I look fair?"

The young man was taken aback, and for a moment had no reply for the ugly woman. Then he smiled and said, "Why, mother, you look as fair as a new furrow to the farmer!"

This made her laugh all the more, and she clicked her tongue against her toothless gums.

"Now tell me, my son," she said at last, "what are you looking for on this side of my door?"

"I thought to find a way to visit my grandmother who lives beyond. I'm taking her a currant cake and a pot of honey."

"I'll give you some advice, my son," wheezed the old crone, "use some of the honey to stick your hat to your head."

The apprentice thought this strange advice, but to humour the old creature he smeared honey inside his hat and pulled it firmly on to his head.

"Can you show me the way to go, mother?" asked the apprentice, who was now smelling strongly of honey.

"How can I see a way for you when my fire burns so low?" she whined, pulling her cloak over her head.

The young man felt sorry to see such old bones sitting out there in the cold and the wet, so he searched around for firewood, and gathered together a fine pile of sticks.

"That will see you through the night, mother," he said, and made ready to go.

"Don't leave before your pockets are filled with the fruit of the rowan tree!" croaked the old woman, her little eyes gleaming in the firelight.

Again, the young man did as she bade him, plucking handfuls of the scarlet berries and stuffing them in his jacket pockets.

"I'd give you a drink for your journey," said the old crone slyly, "only my jug is almost dry."

The apprentice was anxious to be on his way, but nevertheless he took the empty jug and climbed down a bank to fill it from the nearby river. The old crone received the brimming jug without comment, and waved the young apprentice off, pointing across the river to the darkness beyond.

"Only follow what comes to meet you," she said, yawning her empty mouth and chafing her withered hands at the fire.

With hasty steps, the young man made his way over the river and into woods that lay on the other side. The trees blotted out the moonlight and the undergrowth confused his path. The wind squeezed through the trees and caught him first from one side and then from another, until he had completely lost sense of direction. Once, he heard the sound of voices, and he moved towards it, expecting to find other travellers on the same path. He groped through the bushes but found no one. The voices came again to his ears, this time coming from an altogether different part of the wood. Hopefully, he plunged across in the new direction, but when he stopped to listen again he heard only a dry rattle of laughter — or was it the wind scraping the parched oak leaves?

He sat down to consider his plight. Suddenly, something dropped to the ground beside him. He felt for it and picked it up. It was a crab apple. Immediately, a second apple hit him on the back, and then another, and another. Soon, crab apples were thudding on his head, and in fright the young apprentice ran from the place. He dodged to and fro beneath the branches, but the apples continued to bombard his head, each one coming with such force that his hat would have been knocked clean away, had it not been stuck on with the honey. Now he could hear the laughter clearly, echoing from tree to tree, tittering on the wind. His fear turned to anger, and he stopped in his flight.

"Two can play at that game!" he shouted, taking a fistful of rowan berries from his pocket. He flung the berries with all his strength, and the peals of malicious laughter became shrieks of pain. He emptied his pockets towards his unseen tormentors, and their broken wails drifted into the blackness and were gone.

The silence and peace that remained were barely disturbed by a faint new sound that caught the ear of the young apprentice. It was the crooning babble of running water.

"A stream!" he thought. "The old mother told me to follow only what comes towards me. Well, I shall walk upstream from now on."

So he followed the water against its flow, and in no time at all was at the door of his grandmother's cottage.

"God bless you, Grandmother," he greeted her, giving her the currant cake and the pot of honey.

"And peace be with you, Grandson," she replied, sniffing the sweet aroma of honey as he held his hat politely in his hand.

They passed a pleasant hour together before the young man took his leave. He had no difficulty in finding his way back to the city wall. The fire was burning brightly near the narrow door, but the old crone was no longer there. Instead, a young child, hardly more than a babe, with pretty cheeks and dimpled hands, was gathering acorns into her apron. Her feet and head were bare, but she showed no sign of discomfort in the chill night.

"God bless you, child," said the apprentice, "Where has the old mother gone?"

The child looked at him gravely.

"Nowhere and everywhere," she replied. "But tell me, sir, do I look at all wise?"

The young man looked down at the babe, and chuckled.

"You look to me as wise as a wheat seed, that chooses a cold, damp bed for its comfort."

The child nodded approvingly, and returned to her gathering. The apprentice stepped through the narrow door, closed it behind him, and started down the road. Somewhere ahead, the city clock chimed eight times. He looked back again to the door, but he could see nothing except the solid stone of the city wall.

The apprentice hurried home through familiar streets, and the moon cast a shadow beneath his feet.

The little lamb

An Advent story for children between four and ten years.

Long, long ago, winter was coming to a small village. Among the flocks of sheep that grazed on the hillside nearby, some new lambs had been born, and each evening two or three shepherds would gather to spend the night around a fire, chatting and dozing, but always on the look out for the green light of a wolf's eye near the lambs' fold.

On this particular evening, a young shepherd, whose name was Gregory, stood beside the fold counting his flock. One mother sheep was quite distressed, and before he had done all his sums properly he realised that her lamb was missing. There was nothing for it, he would have to go and find the poor creature. Night was drawing in, the wolves would soon be out hunting, and on that steep hillside a lamb might easily fall and injure itself. He called to his companions to watch the fire, and set off on the search.

In the twilight Gregory could see that the lower pastures were empty, so he decided to head for the rough land above. The moon rose behind the hill, darkening it with shadow. But Gregory stumbled on, climbing ever higher, panting with the effort, stopping every now and then to listen for the bleat of the lost lamb. He heard — nothing. He reached the bank of a narrow mountain stream, and there Gregory's tired feet fell over one another, and he found himself lying on the ground. He closed his eyes. He wasn't hurt by the fall, but the walk had exhausted him and it was a temptation just to lie there and have a nap. Maybe he did have a nap, we don't know, but he told his friends afterwards that a very strange thing happened then.

From far off in the distance came the delicate bleat of a lamb. The tired shepherd opened his eyes and looked about him. The moon was hidden, and so it puzzled him to see a soft glimmer not too far away. Peering carefully across the stream, Gregory saw a flight of steps leading up the hillside. With a leap he was over the stream, and it was then that he saw that these steps were made of shimmering gold! He began to walk up them, his weary legs glad of the easy progress, and soon he found that with each step he trod he grew fresher and less

sleepy. Up, up he went, his boots tapping lightly on the shining stair, until he felt as high as a cloud in the sky — but the stairs did not come to an end. Soon he was sure he could reach out and touch the stars, for their sparkles were glittering on his hair and his clothes. There, among the stars, the stair ended, and Gregory stood before a golden gate.

At first, everything was quiet, and then from behind the gate came, once again, the bleating of a lamb. But it was not a lost-sounding bleat, it was definitely a happy bleat. Shyly, Gregory lifted the latch of the gate and stepped over the threshold. He entered a pleasant courtyard lit by twelve great lamps (or were they stars? Gregory couldn't tell...) and one mighty lamp hung in the centre. Beneath the golden rays of this lamp sat the figure of a lady, ("the Mistress of the House" thought Gregory). Her cape was of deep blue and her gown was red. At her feet was a still pool, shining silver in the light from above, and by the pool stood the lamb. The Mistress of the House was combing his fleece and taking the softest of the soft wool to spin a fine yarn, and the lamb nuzzled her hands contentedly, every now and then giving a little 'maa' of pleasure.

Gregory felt like an intruder there; he took his hat off and fumbled with it. How could he take his lamb away from this wonderful place? But the Mistress of the House looked up, and her face was so welcoming and kind that Gregory approached and patted his lamb.

"I shall soon be finished, Gregory," said the Lady gently.

"She knows my name," thought Gregory, amazed, and his heart was filled with wonder at it all.

"You see, Gregory," she went on, "I am making a little nightshirt for my child, and it is the most beautiful nightshirt in the whole world." She smiled as she held it up. The garment shimmered with light; silver and gold threads were worked in intricate patterns, and the collar was edged with stars.

"But it must also keep out the cold," the gentle Lady continued, "and this dear little lamb came to offer his wool — it is so white and soft that when I weave it in, my child is sure to stay warm."

"Your child must be the most beautiful child in the whole world," Gregory murmured, gazing at the wonderful shirt and at the lovely face of the Lady.

"Yes, Gregory," said the Lady softly, then smiled again as she finished her work and put her spindle away. "Now you must take your lamb home. His mother will be pleased to see him back."

The young shepherd gathered up the lamb into his arms — he was loath to leave. "May I... may I see this child, the most beautiful child in the world?" he asked.

"Soon I shall be taking Him to Bethlehem," she replied. "You may come and see Him there."

Gregory's face fell. "Bethlehem is so far," he said. "Winter is approaching and the world is dark. I fear I shall not find my way."

"Do not lose heart," said the gracious Lady, rising to light a candle from the great golden lamp that hung above her. "Take this light that I offer, Gregory. It will never fail you. Go, tell your friends to journey also to Bethlehem to see this most beautiful Child. Your steps will be guided by my little light — just as, in future times, men will be guided by this Child whom they will call *The Light of the World*."

Gregory took the candle in his right hand, and the lamb under his left arm, and departed from the courtyard. The gate closed behind him as he descended the golden stairs. On reaching the bottom step his foot slipped slightly, and the lamb leapt from his grasp. Gregory saw him bound across the stream and off into the dark night, so he, too, jumped the stream to follow. At this moment he realised that he was no longer carrying the candle, but, strange to say, the light was still with him! Gregory wondered at this as he followed its guiding ray which brought him, eventually, back among his friends by the fire.

"Where have you been, Gregory?" they demanded. "Your lamb found his own way back a long time ago!"

So Gregory told his story. He had forgotten some of the details because it was all beginning to feel so much like a dream, but he did tell his shepherd friends about the most beautiful Child in the world, and his light did guide them safely to Bethlehem — yes, all three shepherds went, and the little lamb went too.

The four creatures and the child

A Christmas story for children between four and ten years.

Once upon a time, long ago, there was an ass with silky ears and dainty feet. One day, Mary her mistress said:

"We are going on a journey, you and I, to Bethlehem; Master Joseph will accompany us with the ox, and there in Bethlehem, God-willing, I shall become the mother of the most special Child in the whole world. You are a noble and sure-footed creature. I give to you the task of seeing that we get there safely."

Mary's news filled the ass with excitement as they prepared for the journey. The most special Child in the whole world was soon to be born! And her mistress had said "You are a noble creature…" Noble! What a beautiful word! So on each day of the journey she tried to look more noble than the day before, and each day she took more pride in choosing just the right spot to place her feet so that Mary would have a smooth ride.

Behind the ass walked Master Joseph leading the ox. The old ox had shared a stable with the ass for many years and they were good friends. He was slow but strong; he was kindly and patient. He listened with delight to Mary's singing, as she rode and he plodded after. He pondered upon the birth of Mary's Child and his thoughts strayed among distant memories. Had his Grandfather told him stories of a little child who was to be the true Friend of all creatures? He was filled with expectation for the event that was to come.

Even so, on this day he was feeling rather lonely. When the journey had begun, the ass had often walked beside him and chatted about this and that — and, of course, about the important task she had undertaken.

"I feel very proud that I was chosen to do something for this Child," she had confided. "It's not an opportunity that's given to *every* animal, you know."

"No," thought the ox rather sadly as he walked now on his own, "not every animal is clever enough to help at an important time like this. I'm certainly not very clever."

He gazed ahead at the little hooves of the ass as she stepped so daintily along the steep and rocky path. Yesterday she had told him, "I'm afraid I can't walk with you any more, for talking to you distracts me, and I need all my concentration to do my task well." So the last days of their journey were very solitary ones for the old ox, who missed his friend and found the long hours on the road rather dispiriting.

At last the travelling ended and the animals were resting on clean straw in a stable well out of the wind. Master Joseph and Mary were also preparing to sleep there for the night. However, they were not the only occupants of the stable — a cockerel roosted on the handle of a cart in the corner, and, high in the rafters, a little robin slept.

When the newcomers had first entered the stable, the birds had each opened one eye and drowsily watched the preparations for the night. But when the ox and ass had settled themselves and began exchanging stories about the journey and the Child, the two birds opened both eyes and were listening hard. Soon the two of them flew down to ask all the questions they could think of, and it was not long before the cockerel began to crow with excitement.

"Hush!" said the ass firmly, "Mary needs quiet for her rest."

The robin hopped upon the ox's back, also saying "Hush!" as she cocked her little head to one side and listened. They hushed, and into the silence rose the sound of singing, at once as soft and as bright as if all the stars in heaven were giving voice to joy. At the same moment a light began to grow in the stable, at once as soft and bright as if all the stars in heaven were crowding within its walls. The animals listened and stared, realizing that the moment they had long awaited had at last come. As they blinked in the radiant light, all the weariness and ache of the long journey fell away and they knew that the Child had been born into the world.

For a long time the ox and the ass did not speak; each was lost in their own thoughts. The ass looked over at the heavy shoulders of the ox and felt rather sorry that he had not been chosen to help the Child. The ox gazed back at the fine head of the ass and realized that she was sad because her task was over and she would not be needed any more. Each resolved to cheer up the other.

The music grew softer but the light still glowed around the manger in which the Child slept. Strangers had entered the stable: three shepherds in rough clothing with a little lamb at their side. They were bringing gifts to the Child and kneeling before Him on the straw. The cockerel settled on the side of the manger, but remembered not to crow, and the robin hopped after him and shook her wings. Then they both flew down to the ox's flank and lamented, "The shepherds have given what they have, but we creatures have nothing to give. How can we ever show the Child that we wish to serve Him?"

The ox sighed deeply and shook his heavy old head.

"Not all of us are given that chance," he said, and he blew through his large nose.

The shepherds departed followed by the lamb; Mary and Joseph rested. The four dejected creatures did not notice that the Child's eyes had opened and he was looking out at them, but as the music of the heavens grew fainter, a new music could be heard quite close at hand. The animals looked up, suddenly aware that the Child was actually speaking to them. When He stretched out His hands and said, "All creatures will find a way into my service," they were astonished, for they knew that He had listened to them, and *never* had their conversations been understood by the human world before. When they had got over their surprise they all clamoured, "What can we do? What can we do?"

The Child gazed first at the ass and said, "You, dear ass, with your nimble feet, be as patient as the ox, for there are still important journeys that we must take together."

The cockerel could not restrain himself at this moment — he flew into the rafters and crowed at the top of his voice!

"And you, dear cockerel," continued the Child, "must go out into the world each morning and wake everyone with your fine voice to tell them that a new day has dawned for the whole of creation."

The Child then turned to the old ox.

"The night is cold, dear ox," He said. "Please warm me with your sweet breath."

The ox moved his great head to the side of the manger and breathed warmth into the lowly bed. The Child's hand rested on the gentle creature's cheek like a benediction, and the ox's mighty heart heaved with joy and contentment.

"Your service to me this night, dear ox," said the Child, "will never be forgotten. I, too, hope to serve the world with patience, love and wisdom."

All was peaceful within the stable; only the robin hopped anxiously about. She peeped forlornly now and then until at last the Child spoke:

"Little bird, I have not forgotten you. Come, sit by me and listen well to the song of the angels."

So the robin nestled in the manger while the heavenly music could still be heard. In a while the Child spoke again:

"The music you have heard resounds still in the heavens, but it is lost to human ears, and men and women will ever yearn to hear it again. Will you, dear robin, take on the task of learning the angels' song and bringing it as a gift to all humankind?"

"Oh, very gladly will I do that!" cried the robin.

She puffed up her red breast and began to pour out all the music she had so faithfully remembered. She never forgot the beauty of that song, and even today, wherever she goes, people say that the little robin sings like an angel.

The gift

An Epiphany story for children of ten years and over.
The name Jabez comes from the First Book of Chronicles in the Old Testament and is pronounced Yah-bets.

Jabez never knew why his mother had given him that name. Certainly, he knew no other living soul who was called by it, and when he learned that Jabez meant 'causing pain and sorrow', it gave him a lot to think about. However, he did not think about it for too long at a time, for Jabez was an active boy with a lively interest in everything around him — and beyond. He often dreamed about life in far distant places, and was scolded by his mother for not paying attention. His father, a well-to-do merchant, expected him to take on responsibilities in the business as his two older brothers had done, but Jabez found it difficult to think of money all day. He preferred to help the village children mend their fishing lines, and to listen to the old men as they sat in the shade and told him stories of their youth. His father called him lazy, his mother wept and said he was thoughtless.

Then a day came which threw the whole village into commotion. What a day that was! A royal caravan was passing through — a long train of camels and horses and mules, of rich personages in costly robes, servants, musicians, merchants and other camp-followers. Three large tents were set up and carpets were unrolled. The word spread that these were for no less than three Kings, from lands whose names echoed and re-echoed in Jabez's ear like the language of fairy tale. Jabez knew what he must do. He presented himself to his parents, and begged them to let him join the caravan. Never had he expressed himself so decidedly, never had he seemed so much in earnest. At last his parents reluctantly agreed, gave him their blessing and allowed him to go.

And that, Jabez thought, was how he came to be here, sitting on a luxurious carpet by the tent door. For in the same hour that he had asked for work with the caravan, a strange chance had smitten one of the royal pages with a serious illness. The sick boy was left in the care of village women when the caravan moved on the following day. Jabez, being a quick-witted and presentable youth, had been given the job of page to King Melchior. Each night, dressed in a long white shirt and richly woven sash, he watched over the old King as he slept.

They had been travelling for about a week, and were camped near the city of Jerusalem within sight of its high yellowing walls. Today they had visited a King's palace and Jabez was agog with excitement. His master had been unusually restless after the visit and tonight he wasn't sleeping well at all. "I feel our journey is near its end," he had said. But when Jabez had plucked up courage to ask where they were going, he had only murmured thoughtfully, "I do not know." That was the answer Jabez had always received from the camel drivers and other servants of the caravan. "A funny sort of journey," he thought, "when you don't know where you are going!" They were following that special star, of course, the like of which Jabez had never seen before. Its light was so bright that even the sun could not hide it completely, and now — although rain was falling — starlight still gleamed at the door of the tent.

The light fell upon the brow of the old King, upon the books that lay in their leather bags just by his outstretched hand, and upon the King's own crown that sat on a plush cushion an arm's length from Jabez. The gold and jewels of the crown glinted in the gloom of the tent and Jabez watched the colours shift and change through half-closed eyes. He imagined himself in fine robes with a crown upon his head and a ring upon his finger. "The crown would be heavy, I expect," he thought to himself. "I wonder just how heavy?" And before he quite realised what they were doing, his hands reached out towards the plush cushion.

King Melchior lay on his fur rug. His eyelids were shut. He breathed deeply, but he was not asleep. The starlight troubled his drowsy eyes and they opened a little. With astonishment he watched as his page placed the crown over his curly black hair. He opened his eyes wider, and Jabez froze. The youth grew pale with fright, but the King became white with fury. His anger broke and the words beat at Jabez's head like blows, bringing him to his senses: "The crown is sacred! No hand may touch it, save that of a King or High Priest. Impious wretch!" There and then, Jabez had his fine sash removed and was banished to the rear of the caravan to take on the work of water-carrier.

And so it was that, before daybreak, Jabez was journeying back and forth to the gully where the hill rain ran in torrents, filling the heavy water bags. The urchins with their goats laughed at him, for water-carrying was women's work. Indeed, as the sun rose in a rain-washed sky, the women of the district were busy fetching the day's water, children running at their heels. All of a sudden, their happy chatter was broken by a scream from further up the gully. Jabez turned and saw at once what had happened. A mother was filling water jars from the river, and her baby had loosed itself from the cloths on her back and fallen into the rushing water. Jabez dropped his burden and leaped into the river in time to seize the child as it was swept downstream. Gripping the wet bundle on his shoulder he fought with the current, the cries of the baby increasing his energy and determination. At last he pulled himself from the clutch of the river and lay exhausted on the bank. The dripping infant was lifted up and the cries of mother and child mingled with the screams of the river birds.

Jabez got to his feet and walked back to his water bags. He had returned with them to the camp, when the mother with her baby pursued him calling all the time, "Amos! Amos! Amos!" Her cries attracted a number of others who entered the camp shouting and cheering. A flock of pigeons, foraging among the fires where the morning meal was being prepared, was disturbed by the noise and rose up in a cloud of clapping wings. Jabez moved quickly away, eager to avoid any fuss. Just at that moment, King Melchior stepped out of his tent, seeking the cause of the hubbub. Jabez saw the stern look of his admonisher and halted.

What King Melchior himself saw is not easy to describe, for words cannot serve a picture well when it is the picture itself that speaks. King Melchior saw in the light of the rising sun, not a curly-headed youth but a man in his prime, water glistening on his skin and dripping from his hair. The sun's rays translated his human form into an exalted figure of gold. As the King watched, a single bird detached itself from the wheeling flock of pigeons and alighted for an instant on Jabez's head, its wings shining brilliant and translucent, each spread feather tipped with rosy gold and flashing like a jewelled crown, set in the corona of the sun.

If the crowd of onlookers had been asked what they saw, they would have described an old man at the door of his tent who fell suddenly to his knees and covered his noble face with his hands. They would have reported the woman's cries of "Amos! Amos!" the baby's screams, and the general tumult of laughing and weeping. They would have told how Jabez kneeled at the old King's feet and asked "Master, are you ill?"

At last, King Melchior stood. He listened solemnly as the whole story of the baby's salvation was recounted. Then, resting his eyes with wonder on Jabez, he spoke:

"Pain and sorrow have accompanied you in the past, Jabez, but today is a new day, and you shall have a new name. This woman has called you Amos — The Courageous One — and by this henceforth you shall be known. I, too, shall call you Amos, but I shall remember that it also means 'Bearer.' For I, who deemed you unworthy to bear my crown in your hands, have today seen God's crown upon your head."

No more was said. Amos was restored to his former position as page to King Melchior. By the end of the day the star had led them to a house in the town of Bethlehem, and their journey ended at the feet of a young child, seated on his mother's knee. The three wise Kings removed their crowns and Amos knelt to bear his master's precious diadem on its cushion, proud to be the servant of so humble a King. There, among the gifts of gold, frankincense, and myrrh, Amos felt blessing stream from the presence of the Child, as light had streamed from the star. He thought to himself: "As the sun rose today, I received the gift of a new name, but now, as the sun is setting, I know that from this Child I shall receive the greatest gift of all, the gift of new life!"

Index